Praise for the "Kids Love" Guidebook travel series

On-Air Personality Comments (Television Interviews)

"The great thing about these books is that your whole family actually lives these adventures" – **(WKRC-TV**, Cincinnati)

"Very helpful to lots of families when the kids say, I'm bored...and I don't want to go to same places again!" – **(WISH-TV**, Indianapolis)

"Dividing the state into many sections, the book has something for everyone...everywhere." – **(WLVT-TV**, Pennsylvania)

"These authors know first-hand that it's important to find hands-on activities that engage your children..." **(WBNS-TV**, Columbus)

"You spent more than 1000 hours doing this research for us, that's really great – we just have to pick up the book and it's done..."
(WTVR-TV, Richmond)

"A family that's a great source for travel ideas..."
(WBRA-TV, Roanoke)

"What a great idea...this book needed to be done a long time ago!"
(WKYT-TV, Lexington)

"A fabulous idea...places to travel that your kids will enjoy"
(WOOD-TV, Grand Rapids)

"The Zavatskys call it a dream come true, running their own business while keeping the family together. Their goal, encourage other parents to create special family travel memories." - **(WLVT-TV**, Pennsylvania)

"It's a wonderful book, and as someone who has been to a lot of these places...you hit it right on the money!" – **(WKRC-TV**, Cincinnati)

Praise for the "Kids Love" Guidebook travel series
Customer Comments (actual letters on file)

"I wanted to tell you how helpful all your books have been to my family of 6. I rarely find books that cater to families with kids. I have your Indiana, Ohio, Kentucky, Michigan, and Pennsylvania books. I don't want to miss any of the new books that come out. Keep up the great ideas. The books are fantastic. I have shown them to tons of my friends. They love them, too." – H.M.

"I bought the Ohio and Indiana books yesterday and what a blessing these are for us!!! We love taking our grandsons on Grammie & Papaw trips thru the year and these books are making it soooo much easier to plan. The info is complete and full of ideas. Even the layout of the book is easy to follow...I just wanted to thank you for all your work in developing these books for us..." – G.K

"I have purchased your book. My grandchildren and I have gone to many of the places listed in your book. They mark them off as we visit them. We are looking forward to seeing many more. It is their favorite thing to look at book when they come over and find new places to explore. Thank you for publishing this book!" - B.A.

"At a retail price of under $15.00, any of the books would be well worth buying even for a one-time only vacation trip. Until now, when the opportunity arose for a day or weekend trip with the kids I was often at a loss to pick a destination that I could be sure was convenient, educational, child-friendly, and above all, fun. Now I have a new problem: How in the world will we ever be able to see and do all the great ideas listed in this book? I'd better get started planning our next trip right away. At least I won't have to worry about where we're going or what to do when we get there!" – VA Homeschool Newsletter

"My family and I used this book this summer to explore Ohio! We lived here nearly our entire life and yet over half the book we never knew existed. These people really know what kids love! Highly recommended for all parents, grandparents, etc." – Barnes and Noble website reviewer

KIDS ♥ LOVE ILLINOIS

A Family Travel Guide to
Exploring "Kid-Tested" Places
in Illinois...Year Round!

George & Michele Zavatsky

Dedicated to the Families
of Illinois

For the latest major updates corresponding to the pages in this book visit our website:

www.KidsLoveTravel.com

- ❑ **REMEMBER:** *Museum exhibits change frequently. Check the site's website before you visit to note any changes. Also, HOURS and ADMISSIONS are subject to change at the owner's discretion. If you are tight on time or money, check the attraction's website or call before you visit.*

- ❑ **INTERNET PRECAUTION:** *All websites mentioned in KIDS LOVE ILLINOIS have been checked for appropriate content. However, due to the fast-changing nature of the Internet, we strongly urge parents to preview any recommended sites and to always supervise their children when on-line.*

ISBN-13: 978-0-9774434-0-6
ISBN-10: 0-9774434-0-X

KIDS ❤ ILLINOIS ™ Kids Love Publications

TABLE OF CONTENTS

State Map

(With Major Routes and Cities Marked)

Chapter Area Map

CITY INDEX (Listed by City & Area)

CITY INDEX (Listed by City & Area)

> Cities appearing in *italics* occur only in the Seasonal Chapter

Acknowledgements

We are most thankful to be blessed with our parents, Barbara (Darrall) Callahan & George and Catherine Zavatsky who help us every way they can – researching, proofing and babysitting. More importantly, they are great sounding boards and offer unconditional support. So many places around Illinois remind us of family vacations years ago…

We also want to express our thanks to the many Convention & Visitor Bureaus' staff for providing the attention to detail that helps to complete a project. We felt very welcome during our travels in Illinois and would be proud to call it home!

Our own kids, Jenny and Daniel, were delightful and fun children during our trips across the state. What a joy it is to be their parents…we couldn't do it without them as our "kid-testers"!

We both sincerely thank each other – our partnership has created an even greater business/personal "marriage" with lots of exciting moments, laughs, and new adventures in life woven throughout. Above all, we praise the Lord for His so many blessings through the last few years.

We think Illinois is a wonderful, friendly area of the country with more activities than you could imagine. Our sincere wish is that this book will help everyone "fall in love" with Illinois.

In a Hundred Years…

It will not matter, The size of my bank account…

The kind of house that I lived in, the kind of car that I drove…

But what will matter is…

That the world may be different

Because I was important in the life of a child.

- author unknown

HOW TO USE THIS BOOK

If you are excited about discovering Illinois, this is the book for you and your family! We've spent over a thousand hours doing all the scouting, collecting and compiling (*and most often visiting!*) so that you could spend less time searching and more time having fun.

Here are a few hints to make your adventures run smoothly:

❑ Consider the **child's age** before deciding to take a visit.

❑ Know **directions** and parking. Call ahead (or visit the company's website) if you have questions *and* bring this book. Also, don't forget your camera! *(please honor rules regarding use).*

❑ **Estimate the duration** of the trip. Bring small surprises (favorite juice boxes) travel books, and toys.

❑ Call ahead for **reservations** or details, if necessary.

❑ Most listings are **closed major holidays** unless noted.

❑ Make a **family "treasure chest"**. Decorate a big box or use an old popcorn tin. Store memorabilia from a fun outing, journals, pictures, brochures and souvenirs. Once a year, look through the "treasure chest" and reminisce. "Kids Love Travel Memories!" is an excellent travel journal & scrapbook that your family can create. *(See the order form in back of this book).*

❑ Plan **picnics** along the way. Many state history sites and state parks are scattered throughout Illinois. Allow time for a rural /scenic route to take advantage of these free picnic facilities.

❑ Some activities, especially tours, require **groups** of 10 or more. To participate, you may either ask to be part of another tour group or get a group together yourself (neighbors, friends, organizations). If you arrange a group outing, most places offer discounts.

❑ For the latest **updates** corresponding to the pages in this book, visit our website: **www.KidsLoveTravel.com.**

❑ Each chapter represents an area of the state. Each listing is further identified by city, zip code, and place/event name. Our popular **Activity Index** in the back of the book **lists places by Activity Heading** (i.e. State History, Tours, Outdoors, Museums, etc.).

MISSION STATEMENT

At first glance, you may think that this is a book that just lists hundreds of places to travel. While it is true that we've invested thousands of hours of exhaustive research (*and drove over 4000 miles in Illinois*) to prepare this travel resource…just listing places to travel is <u>not</u> the mission statement of these projects.

As children, Michele and I were able to travel extensively throughout the United States. We consider these family times some of the greatest memories we cherish today. We, quite frankly, felt that most children had this opportunity to travel with their family as we did. However, as we became adults and started our own family, we found that this wasn't necessarily the case. We continually heard friends express several concerns when deciding how to spend "quality" and "quantity" family time. 1) What to do? 2) Where to do it? 3) How much will it cost? 4) How do I know that my kids will enjoy it?

Interestingly enough, as we compare our experiences with our families when we were kids, many of our fondest memories were not made at an expensive attraction, but rather when it was least expected.

It is our belief and mission statement that if you as a family will study and <u>use</u> the contained information <u>to create family memories,</u> these memories will grow a stronger, tighter family. Our ultimate mission statement is, that your children will develop a love and a passion for quality family experiences that they can pass to another generation of family travelers.

We thank you for purchasing this book, and we hope to see you on the road (*and hear your travel stories!*) God bless your journeys and happy exploring!

George, Michele, Jenny and Daniel

General State Agency & Recreation Information

Call *(or visit the websites)* for the services of interest. Request to be added to their mailing lists.

- ❑ Looking For Lincoln - historic sites and participating communities - (217) 782-6817 or **www.lookingforlincoln.com**.
- ❑ Illinois Tourist Information - 800-2CONNECT
- ❑ Illinois Historic Preservation Agency - (217) 782-4836 or **www.state.il.us/hpa**
- ❑ Illinois Department of Agriculture - County Fairs - **www.agr.state.il.us/fair/countyfairssched.php**
- ❑ Illinois Department of Natural Resources - (217) 782-6302 or **www.dnr.state.il.us**
- ❑ Northwestern University Big Ten Athletics - (847) 491-3741 or **www.nusports.com** (Evanston, Ryan Field/Welsh Ryan Arena)
- ❑ University of Illinois General Information & Sports - Champaign. (217) 333-1000 or **www.uiuc.edu**. Sports: (866) Illini-1 or **www.fightingillini.com**. Campus resources include the world's largest public university library, the National Center for Supercomputing Applications and Memorial Stadium (home of the Fighting Illini football team).
- ❑ **C** - Springfield Area CVB - **www.visit-springfieldillinois.com** or (800) 545-7300
- ❑ **CL** - Aurora Area CVB - **www.enjoyaurora.com** or (800) 477-4369
- ❑ **CL** - City Of Chicago Tourism - (877) CHICAGO or **www.877chicago.com**

- **CL** - Greater Woodfield CVB - **www.chicagonorthwest.com** or (800) VISIT GW
- **CL** - Heritage Corridor CVB - **www.heritagecorridorcvb.com** (Starved Rock, Rte 66, Joliet areas)
- **CL** - Lake County (North Chicago) CVB - (800) 525-3669 or **www.lakecounty.org**
- **EC** - Champaign County - **www.visitchampaigncounty.org** or (800) 369-6151
- **EC** – Illinois Amish Country – (800) 722-6474 or **www.illinoisamishcountry.com**
- **N** - Galena/Jo Daviess County CVB - **www.galena.org** or (877) GO GALENA
- **N** - Rockford Area CVB - **www.gorockford.com** or (800) 691-7035
- **SW** - Southwestern Illinois Tourism - **www.thetourismbureau.org**
- **W** - Peoria Area CVB - **www.peoria.org** or (800) 747-0302
- **W** - Quad Cities - **www.visitquadcities.com** or (800) 747-7800

Check out these businesses / services in your area for tour ideas:

AIRPORTS

All children love to visit the airport! Why not take a tour and understand all the jobs it takes to run an airport? Tour the terminal, baggage claim, gates and security / currency exchange. Maybe you'll even get to board a plane.

ANIMAL SHELTERS

Great for the would-be pet owner. Not only will you see many cats and dogs available for adoption, but a guide will show you the clinic and explain the needs of a pet. Be prepared to have the children "fall in love" with one of the animals while they are there!

BANKS

Take a "behind the scenes" look at automated teller machines, bank vaults and drive-thru window chutes. You may want to take this tour and then open a savings account for your child.

CITY HALLS

Halls of Fame, City Council Chambers & Meeting Room, Mayor's Office and famous statues.

ELECTRIC COMPANY / POWER PLANTS

Modern science has created many ways to generate electricity today, but what really goes on with the "flip of a switch". Because coal can be dirty, wear old, comfortable clothes. Coal furnaces heat water, which produces steam, that propels turbines, that drives generators, that make electricity.

FIRE STATIONS

Many Open Houses in October, Fire Prevention Month. Take a look into the life of the firefighters servicing your area and try on their gear. See where they hang out, sleep and eat. Hop aboard a real-life fire engine truck and learn fire safety too.

HOSPITALS

Some Children's Hospitals offer pre-surgery and general tours.

NEWSPAPERS

You'll be amazed at all the new technology. See monster printers and robotics. See samples in the layout department and maybe try to put together your own page. After seeing a newspaper made, most companies give you a free copy (dated that day) as your souvenir. National Newspaper Week is in October.

RESTAURANTS

PIZZA HUT & PAPA JOHN'S

☐   Participating locations

Telephone the store manager. Best days are Monday, Tuesday and Wednesday mid-afternoon. Minimum of 10 people. Small charge per person. All children love pizza – especially when they can create their own! As the children tour the kitchen, they learn how to make a pizza, bake it, and then eat it. The admission charge generally includes lots of creatively made pizzas, beverage and coloring book.

KRISPY KREME DONUTS

☐   Participating locations

Get an "inside look" and learn the techniques that make these donuts some of our favorites! Watch the dough being made in "giant" mixers, being formed into donuts and taking a "trip" through the fryer. Seeing them being iced and topped with colorful sprinkles is always a favorite with the kids. Contact your local store manager. They prefer Monday or Tuesday. Free.

SUPERMARKETS

Kids are fascinated to go behind the scenes of the same store where Mom and Dad shop. Usually you will see them grind meat, walk into large freezer rooms, watch cakes and bread bake and receive free samples along the way. Maybe you'll even get to pet a live lobster!

TV / RADIO STATIONS

Studios, newsrooms, Fox kids clubs. Why do weathermen never wear blue clothes on TV? What makes a "DJ's" voice sound so deep and smooth?

WATER TREATMENT PLANTS

A giant science experiment! You can watch seven stages of water treatment. The favorite is usually the wall of bright buttons flashing as workers monitor the different processes.

U.S. MAIN POST OFFICES

Did you know Ben Franklin was the first Postmaster General (over 200 years ago)? Most interesting is the high-speed automated mail processing equipment. Learn how to address envelopes so they will be sent quicker (there are secrets). To make your tour more interesting, have your children write a letter to themselves and address it with colorful markers. Mail it earlier that day and they will stay interested trying to locate their letter in all the high-speed machinery.

Chapter 1
Central Area (C)

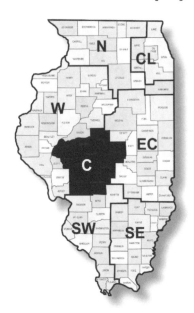

Our Favorites...

* Macon County Historical Museum - Decatur

* Lincoln's New Salem - Petersburg

* Abraham Lincoln Presidential Museum - Springfield

* Lincoln Home - Springfield

* Knight's Action Park - Springfield

A Visit With the Lincolns

LINCOLN LONG NINE MUSEUM

Athens - *200 South Main Street, 62613. Phone: (217) 636-8755,* **Web:** *www.a-lincoln-long-nine.com. Hours: Tuesday-Saturday 1:00-5:00pm (June-August). Admission.* Located on the way to Lincoln's New Salem Site, Lincoln visited it many times. It now houses audio-dioramas about Lincoln's connection to this town. In 1837, Abraham Lincoln and his dedicated cadre of eight other Illinois legislators had won the General Assembly's approval to move the state capital from Vandalia to Springfield. The nine men were called the "long nine" because they averaged over 6 feet in height, uncommon in that day and age. In August, 1837, the "long nine" members were honored at a banquet. This banquet was held upstairs in this same building.

CHILDREN'S MUSEUM OF ILLINOIS

55 South Country Club Road (Scovill Park, US 36 east across Lake Decatur. Turn right at first light),

Decatur 62521

❑ Phone: (217) 423-KIDS, **Web: www.cmofil.com**

❑ Hours: Tuesday-Friday 9:30am-4:30pm; Saturday 10:00am-5:00pm; and Sunday 1:00-5:00pm. The museum is closed on Mondays (except June 6-August 15th and also major holidays. The museum is open on most Decatur school district holidays.

❑ Admission: $3.50 (age 2+).

Explore two floors of hands-on exhibits focusing on people and cultures, the arts, physics, humanities, the ecosystem, and even health. Children mail pretend letters, make money withdrawals, and shop in the Johnston Supermarket/Bank/Post Office exhibit. Making giant bubbles, painting on Plexiglas, and maneuvering toys through a water maze are favorites. Upstairs play stations include following the energy trail from coal mine to household appliances, piloting an airplane, and building with giant blocks. The museum's centerpiece: "Luckey's Climber," where children climb a two-story spiral of platforms, encased in safety net. Is it art or is it science? Climb in and decide.

MACON COUNTY HISTORICAL SOCIETY MUSEUM COMPLEX

5580 N. Fork Road (US 36 west to right on Airport Road to right on N. Fork), **Decatur** 62521

- ❑ Phone: (217) 422-4919
- ❑ Hours: Tuesday-Saturday 1:00-4:00pm & every 4th Sunday afternoon.
- ❑ Admission: FREE, donations accepted.

The prairie years and the Victorian era come to life in various exhibits and buildings set up in a village. Indoor exhibits cover the Lincoln connection and video "Looking for Lincoln"; Victorian years and the Prairie. Located behind the museum, the two-story Lincoln Log Courthouse structure was new when Thomas Lincoln's family trudged into Decatur in 1830. A tall man like Lincoln would have had to be careful not to bump his head on the second floor supports when he later tried three cases there. The Prairie Village also features a one-room schoolhouse, log cabin, replica of Mueller's (the famous inventor) gun shop, a train depot, a blacksmith shop, and a print shop. During busy days, you'll find costumed interpreters. The new site director is very focused on keeping the exhibits fresh and interesting to kids. For instance, in the print house, you can observe & take home a fresh old-fashioned print.

MUELLER MUSEUM, HIERONYMUS

*Decatur - 420 West Eldorado, 62521. Phone: (217) 423-6161, **Web:** www.cityofdecatur.com/mueller.htm. Hours: Thursday-Sunday Noon-5:00pm (April-September); Friday-Sunday 1:00-4:00pm (October-March). Closed major holidays. Admission: $0.50-$1.00.* Experience the life of Decatur's unsung genius, the man whose inventions revolutionized our everyday lives. Exhibits reflect the story of Hieronymus Mueller's immigration to this country in the mid-nineteenth century, through his brilliant mechanical inventions, the growth of his family and company. Mueller began his business as a gunsmith and repairman of various mechanical devices. In 1872 he patented his first major invention, the Mueller Water Tapper, one still used today. It is difficult to turn on a faucet, roller skate, use a water fountain, or watch firemen use a fire hydrant without using a product made at Mr. Mueller's waterworks factory. Beyond waterworks, Mueller indulged in autoworks. A replica of the original Mueller-Benz, winner of the first unofficial car race in the U.S. in 1895 is on display.

ROCK SPRINGS CENTER FOR ENVIRONMENTAL DISCOVERY

Decatur - *3939 Nearing Lane (US 48 south from downtown to west on Rock Springs Rd), 62521. Phone: (217) 423-7708.* **Web:** *www.maconcountyconservation.org. Hours: Trails: Daily 7:00am-dusk. Visitors Center: Weekdays 8:00am-5:00pm, Weekends 10:00am-4:00pm. Homestead Prairie Farm open Weekends 1:00-4:00pm (June-October). Closed New Years Day, Easter, Thanksgiving and Christmas. Admission: Donations accepted, with fees for some events.* The 1,343-acre center is devoted to getting to know our environment first hand. including 8.5 miles of hiking trails, 2.2 miles of the Rock Springs/Fairview Park Bicycle trail, two picnic pavilions, and the Homestead Prairie Farm historic site. The Rock Springs Visitor's Center features historic and environmental displays. Living History programs are offered in the Homestead Prairie Farm, a restored 19th-Century farmstead. Today the house is furnished to reflect the lifestyle of the Trobaughs, their boarders, and neighbors in 1860, whose lives were being affected by the important changes sweeping the nation in the last years before the Civil War. A good combination of history and nature. Try to visit during their numerous special events and programs for the best experience.

SCOVILL ZOO

Decatur - *71 South Country Club Road (Scovill Park, US 36 east across Lake Decatur. Turn right at first light), 62521. Phone: (217) 421-7435,* **Web:** *www.decatur-parks.org/zoo/index.php. Hours: (April-October) Spring Hours: Monday-Friday 10:00 a.m.-4:00pm; Saturday & Sunday 10:00am-6:30pm. Summer Hours: Open Daily 10:00am-7:00pm; Fall Hours: Monday-Friday 10:00am-4:00pm, Saturday & Sunday 10:00am-6:30pm. Admission: $2.25-$3.75 (age 3+).* The zoo covers 10 acres and is home to more than 500 animals. Visitors can enjoy a train ride through the zoo and catch a glimpse of timber wolves, spider monkeys or kangaroos. Children may also enjoy the zoo's petting area or a trip to the herpaquarium with reptiles, amphibians, invertebrates and fish. Be sure to meet the newest additions, cheetahs Runako and Jafari. Be sure to allow time to ride the new "Endangered Species" carousel. Howl with the wolves in a Wolf Howl, feed pygmy goats or have lunch in the Zoopermarket.

UNDER THE PRAIRIE FRONTIER ARCHAEOLOGICAL MUSEUM

Elkhart - *109 Governor Oglesby Street (I-55 exit 115), 62634. Phone: (217) 947-2522,* **Web: www.undertheprairie.com**. *Hours: Wednesday-Sunday 10:00am-4:00pm. Closed: New Year's Day, Easter Sunday, Thanksgiving Day, Christmas Day. Admission: $3.00 (age 6+). Miscellaneous: Bluestem Bake Shop with baked goods, soups and sandwiches.* Located in central Illinois at the base of Elkhart Hill, a stop along a 300-year-old overland trail, the Under the Prairie Frontier Archaeological Museum features one of the largest single collections of pre-Civil War archaeological artifacts in the Midwest. On display are a wide range of authentic frontier-era relics from the late 1700s and early 1800s, excavated at sites across Illinois and the Midwest. The center is also home to a working archeology lab.

MT. PULASKI COURTHOUSE STATE HISTORIC SITE

P.O. Box 355 (SR 54 exit SR 121. Turn left at Dekalb St., left on Vine, left on Jefferson, turn right and travel two blocks to the City Square), **Lincoln** 62656

❑   Phone: (217) 792-3919

   Web: www.illinoishistory.gov/hs/Pulaski.htm

❑   Hours: Tuesday-Saturday Noon-5:00pm (March-October); Noon-4:00pm (November-February). Closed winter holidays.

❑   Admission: Donations accepted.

Mt. Pulaski Courthouse State Historic Site on the city square in Mt. Pulaski is one of only two surviving Eighth Judicial Circuit courthouses in Illinois where Abraham Lincoln practiced law. When Lincoln first came to Mt. Pulaski Courthouse in 1848 he was senior partner to associate William Herndon in their Springfield law firm. Lincoln's growing ability and reputation helped fuel his political career. After one term (1847-1849) in Congress, Lincoln returned to his law practice with renewed vigor.

POSTVILLE COURTHOUSE STATE HISTORIC SITE

Lincoln - *(I-55, take Lincoln Exit 126 (State Route 10). At the first stoplight turn south. At the next stoplight (Fifth Street) turn east), 62656. Web: www.illinoishistory.gov/hs/Postville.htm. Phone: (217) 732-8930. Hours: Tuesday-Saturday Noon-4:00pm. Open until 5:00pm, summer. Admission: Suggested donation: $2.00 adult, $1.00 child.* Visit the historic downtown Lincoln, where you'll see the 1905 Logan County Courthouse. The present Postville Courthouse, a reproduction of the original 1840 Courthouse, was visited by Lincoln while he traveled the 8th Judicial Circuit. Abraham Lincoln, like most lawyers of his day, traveled the circuit to make a living. Most communities were too small to support resident lawyers. Lincoln and his contemporaries handled simple, low-paying cases. A statue of Abraham Lincoln is nearby. Watermelon Christening Site: As the first lots were sold in the town of Lincoln, residents asked Abraham Lincoln to come from Springfield to christen the first town to be named for him. He did so using the juice of a watermelon. The Lincoln College and Museum (300 Keokuk Street - 217-732-3333) houses a major collection of Lincoln artifacts as well as the Hall of Presidents Museum, honoring the nation's Chief Executives from George Washington through the present.

DIXIE TRAVEL PLAZA (RTE 66 TRUCKERS' HOME)

McLean - *(junction I-55 and US 136), 61754. Phone: (309) 874-2323.* Heading north from Springfield to the Windy City you can travel all but 11 miles of the original Route 66. Travelers will want to be sure and stop at the famous Dixie Truck Stop, where you'll find homemade biscuits and gravy, and a big slice of apple pie. The Dixie also boasts an extensive Route 66 Hall of Fame collection from its heyday as America's crossroads. Many people say Route 66 is the most famous highway in the world. Most would also agree it was an important passageway that helped shape our country's history and culture. Today, Route 66 still offers an exciting experience, a chance for people around the world to discover America.

LINCOLN'S NEW SALEM STATE HISTORIC SITE

15588 History Lane, Illinois Route 97 (2 miles south of Petersburg, 20 miles NW of Springfield), **Petersburg** 62675

❑ Phone: (217) 632-4000, **Web: www.lincolnsnewsalem.com**

❑ Hours: Daily 9:00am-5:00pm (mid-April - Labor Day); closed Monday & Tuesday (rest of year)

❑ Admission: FREE, suggested $1.00-$2.00 donation.

❑ Miscellaneous: In 1995 archaeologists discovered the remains of two previously unknown house sites and a road that once crossed the hilltop. On-site displays describe the remains found there, and a remnant of the early road can be seen at the end of the trail. Deli & Pizzeria on site except winters. They serve up some good sandwiches with lots of extras. Bike/hike trails, boat launch, picnic areas and campgrounds are here, too.

This site is a reconstruction of the village where Abraham Lincoln spent his early adulthood. The six years Lincoln spent in New Salem formed a turning point in his career. What changed him? His victories, his failures, his friendships? The stories you hear - are they fact or gossip? Did you know his favorite hobbies were reading and wrestling? Although he never owned a home here, Lincoln was engaged in a variety of activities while he was at New Salem. He clerked in a store, split rails, enlisted in the Black Hawk War, served as postmaster and deputy surveyor, failed in business, and was elected to the Illinois General Assembly. In 12 log houses costumed interpreters re-create pioneer life. The Rutledge Tavern, ten workshops, stores, mills and a school where church services were held have been reproduced and furnished as they might have been in the 1830s. Rent a "bed and breakfast" for 37¢. Chat about the weather or politics with a storekeeper or go to "blab" school. From June through August (generally Friday-Sunday) make plans to come back for an evening of entertainment at New Salem's outdoor theater — Theatre in the Park. This park should be proud of its work to keep the village lively and the characters interesting. Bravo for the State Park to administer such a great site yet only take donations from the public.

BEAVER DAM STATE PARK

Plainview - *14548 Beaver Dam Lane (Travel on 108 west through Carlinville, three miles north of Plainview), 62685. Phone: (217) 854-8020. www.dnr.state.il.us/Lands/Landmgt/PARKS/R4/beaver.htm* Fishing, picnicking, hiking, winter sports and tent and trailer camping are among the most popular activities. Although the beaver is virtually gone from this area, the park is named for a beaver dam that created its lake. Approximately 8 miles of hiking trails are found in the park. These trails encircle the lake, lead past the marsh, and extend through various wooded areas in the park. An archery range is located across from the concession and may be used free of charge. Archers must bring their own bow and arrows (age 16 and under, must be with adult).

RAMSEY LAKE STATE PARK

Ramsey - *Route 51/State Park Road, 62080. Phone: (618) 423-2215. www.dnr.state.il.us/lands/landmgt/parks/r5/ramsey.htm.* Rolling hills, timbered shoreline and beautiful Ramsey Lake make this park a popular recreation spot. People who want to relax or energetic outdoor people who want to hike, fish or camp can visit. A one-mile trail winds through the park. Visitors also often use the unmarked fire lanes which make good paths for easy walking. A 13-mile horse trail is located in the north end of the area along with a small campground for horses. This area is one mile north of the park entrance. Ice fishing, snowmobiling, cross-country skiing, sledding and ice skating are among recreational activities for the cold weather sports enthusiast. The 13-mile designated snowmobile trail provides a winter wonderland view of the park when snow cover and weather permits.

SANGCHRIS LAKE STATE PARK

Rochester - *9898 Cascade Road (I 55 North to Exit 82 (Route 104). Route 104 east 6.1 miles through Pawnee and turn left, north, at Sangchris Lake sign), 62563. www.dnr.state.il.us/lands/landmgt/parks/r4/sangch.htm. Phone: (217) 498-9208 Admission to Illinois State Parks is free. Camping fees range from $6.00-11.00 per night, depending on amenities; a $5.00 fee is charged for camping reservations.* Nestled in native forests and brimming with a record bass population, the three-fingered lake extends into both Sangamon and Christian counties, earning it the name "Sangchris". Enjoy camping, fishing, and power boating on the lake. Wildflowers and song birds abound along 3 miles of scenic nature trails, and there are several unique albino deer living in the area. For the equestrian, there is a 5-mile horse trail, and for those preferring greater horsepower, there is an 11-mile snowmobile trail for winter use.

AIR COMBAT MUSEUM

Springfield - *835 South Airport Dr., Capital Airport, 62670. Phone: (217) 698-3990. Hours: Monday-Friday 8:00am-5:00pm. Call to arrange tours. Closed New Year's Day, Easter Sunday, Thanksgiving Day, Christmas Day. Admission: Donations suggested.* The Air Combat Museum was established to recognize, remember and pay tribute to both men and women veterans who operated, maintained and otherwise directly supported America's military aircraft, through the display of a dozen or so military aircraft. The ACM owns and operates two aircraft, one each from WWII and one from the Vietnam conflict. Notable examples include a Beechcraft AT-11 used to train bombardiers in WWII, a P-51 Mustang, a B-25 Mitchell, and a Soko G-21 Galeb, the first Yugoslavian jet.

ABRAHAM LINCOLN PRESIDENTIAL MUSEUM & LIBRARY

212 North 6th Street, **Springfield** 62701

- ❏   Phone: (217) 558-8844, **Web: www.alplm.org**
- ❏   Hours: Daily 9:00am-5:00pm. Open until 8:30pm on Wednesdays. Last ticket sold one hour before closing. Closed: New Year's Day, Thanksgiving Day, Christmas Day.
- ❏   Admission: $7.50 adult (age 16+), $3.50 child (5-15), $5.50 senior (62+), student & military (ID required).
- ❏   Miscellaneous: While the museum exhibits are designed for children grades 4th and up, some small children may be frightened by the myriad of sights and sounds inside the special effects theaters (cannons fire, seats rumble). We nicknamed these theaters the Lincoln Disneyworld experience! A Café and Museum Store are on site, too.

Curious about who Lincoln really was? The museum has taken what could be boring artifacts, and magically turned them into historical entertainment. The site uses several galleries to bring Honest Abe to life using the high-tech interactive methods of ghostly images, live actors and high action. A trip through The Whispering Gallery in this museum might change people's perspective about old politics. The Treasures Gallery showcases personal effects, such as the original handwritten Gettysburg Address. Other "Exhibit Journeys" lead guests through dioramas of key events in Lincoln's life, including a reproduction of the Old State Capitol where Lincoln practiced law and where he lay in state after his April 1865 assassination. The multi-screen, multi-stage special effects theater presentation, "Lincoln's Eyes" tells Lincoln's story through the eyes of an artist painting Lincoln's portrait (do you know what color his eyes were? This video has some loud noises and seat rumblings for effect). The Holavision® Theatre's "Ghosts of the Library" presentation aims to answer the question: "Why save all that stuff?" This theatre takes the idea of "boring history" and brings historical figures back to help us understand (a teacher's dream)! Is the narrator real or a holo-ghost? In Mrs. Lincoln's Attic, kids can play with a model of the Lincoln Home, try on period clothing, perform chores from the 1800s, and play with reproduction historic toys. They can also have their photos take with life-size models of Abraham Lincoln as a boy and an adult, as well as with Mary Todd and the Lincoln children (excellent photo ops). Daniel's favorite area: Ask Mr. Lincoln - this unique interactive theater is a chance to ask our 16th President a question and receive the answer in his own words. Our daughter Jenny's overall reaction, as she silently wept, "I feel like I knew him..." This place is that well done to solicit such a response from youth!

EXECUTIVE MANSION

Springfield - *410 E. Jackson (5th and Jackson Streets), 62701. Phone: (217) 782-6450, **Web:** www.state.il.us/gov/mansion2/. Hours: Tuesday & Thursday 9:30am-11:00am & 2:00-3:30pm; Saturday 9:30-11:00am. Closed government holidays and during state functions. Admission: FREE.* Home of the Illinois governor, and seven U.S. Presidents, including Abraham Lincoln, have been received here. Three levels are open to the public including four formal parlors; a state dining room; ballroom; four bedrooms, including the Lincoln bedroom; and a library handcrafted from native American Black Walnut. The bed and dresser in the Victorian President Lincoln bedroom were given to Lincoln as a gift from Springfield friends before he traveled to Washington, D.C. The furniture has been placed in storage, waiting for Lincoln's return. Best for late elementary or older students.

ILLINOIS STATE MILITARY MUSEUM

Springfield - *1301 N. MacArthur Blvd. (Camp Lincoln), 62701. Phone: (217) 761-3910. Hours: Tuesday-Saturday 1:00-4:30pm or by appointment. Closed government holidays. Admission: Donations accepted.* On the grounds of the headquarters of the Illinois National Guard, the museum is committed to collecting, preserving, interpreting, and exhibiting the military artifacts associated with the citizen-soldier of Illinois. The exhibit includes rare items such as the artificial leg of Mexican General Santa Anna, a target board shot at by President Lincoln, as well as vehicles, weapons, uniforms, equipment and photographs. The Citizen-Soldier exhibit features the military experiences of famous Illinois soldiers such as Carl Sandburg, Robert McMormick, John A. Logan and Abraham Lincoln. All displayed in a WWII-era Civilian Conservation Corps barracks.

LAKE SPRINGFIELD

Springfield - *(I-55 exit 88), 62701. Phone: (217) 757-8660 or (217) 483-DOCK marina. Web: www.lakespringfieldmarina.com. Hours: Daily 9:00am-5:00pm or 7:00pm (seasonally).* Swimming - Lake Springfield Public Beach, Open Memorial Day through August 8. Small Admission. Boating - Boats allowed on Lake Springfield include canoes, motorboats, pontoons, rowboats and sailboats. Public boat launch facilities: Bridgeview Park/I-55, Lindsay Bridge, Marine point (windsurfers and canoes only). North Park and Spaulding Dam. Fishing - About 15 sport fish species can be caught in Lake Springfield, including Channel Catfish, White Crappie, Bluegill, Largemouth Bass, Flathead Catfish, Carp, Striped Bass and Tiger Muskie. Public fishing spots are located throughout the lake area. Fishing licenses are required. Marine Point and the bridge spanning East and West Forest Parks are accessible fishing areas for people with disabilities.

LINCOLN DEPOT

Springfield - *10th and Monroe, 62701. Phone: (217) 544-8695 or (217) 788-1356. Hours: Daily 10:00am-4:00pm (April-August). Admission: FREE.* "No one, not in my situation, can appreciate my feelings of sadness at this parting." Bittersweet words spoken by President-elect Abraham Lincoln as he departed his beloved Springfield to lead the country and change the course of history. The Depot contains restored waiting rooms (one for ladies and one for the luggage and tobacco-spitting men), exhibits of people and places dear to Lincoln, and a state-of-the-art video presentation recreating farewell address and the 12-day journey to his inauguration.

LINCOLN HOME NATIONAL HISTORIC SITE

413 South Eighth (8th and Jackson, I-55 exit 92A @ Sixth Street (Bus I-55) heading 4 miles to downtown. Right on Capitol, right on Seventh), **Springfield** 62701

- ❏ Phone: (217) 492-4241, **Web: www.nps.gov/liho/**
- ❏ Hours: Daily 8:30am-5:00pm. Closed: New Year's Day, Thanksgiving Day, Christmas Day.
- ❏ Admission: Free tickets are required and may only be obtained at the Lincoln Home Visitor Center.
- ❏ Miscellaneous: Nearby (321 South Seventh Street) you can view Lincoln's Family Pew at the First Presbyterian Church.

A great starting point for your tour of Springfield. Upon entering, check in and get your timed tickets for the house tour. While waiting, visit the theatre showing short videos about different aspects of this neighborhood. The Quaker-brown residence where the Abraham Lincoln family lived for seventeen years (1844-1861) is a national treasure. It's located in the midst of a four-block historic neighborhood. Your 15-minute guided tour of the only home the Lincoln's ever owned will be conducted by friendly, entertaining National Park Service rangers. Stand in the room where Lincoln accepted the nomination for President. Did you know Mary Todd was a party girl? - her favorite - Strawberry Parties. And, the closest you'll ever come to shaking Lincoln's hand? Wrap your hand around the same handrail Lincoln used every day. We really liked this place - especially stories about the Lincoln boys and the family life.

DEAN HOUSE & ARNOLD HOUSE -Visit permanent exhibits located in two restored historic houses in the Lincoln Home neighborhood. Both exhibits are located across from the Lincoln Home, admission is free, and can be toured on a self-guided basis. Dean House: "What a Pleasant Home Abe Lincoln Has," explores the history of the Lincoln Home and Family. Arnold House: "If These Walls Could Talk: Saving an Old House" explains the preservation and restoration process of a historic house and tells the story of the residents that occupied the house.

LINCOLN TOMB STATE HISTORIC SITE

1500 Monument Avenue (Oak Ridge Cemetery, 1 mile west of 9th Street (old Rte 66, BL55), **Springfield** 62701

- ❏ Phone: (217) 782-2717
- ❏ Hours: Daily 9:00am-4:00pm. Closed New Year's Day, Martin Luther King, Jr. Birthday, Presidents' Day, General Election Day, Veterans' Day, Thanksgiving Day, Christmas Day.
- ❏ Admission: FREE
- ❏ Miscellaneous: Oak Ridge is the largest cemetery in the state of Illinois and the second-most visited cemetery in the U.S. This 365-acre cemetery is also the final resting place of seventy other notable historic figures including labor leader John L. Lewis, the famous poet Vachel Lindsay, four Illinois governors, and Lincoln's law partner, William Herndon. An audio tour, entitled Stories in Stone, provides a guided tour of unique monuments from the 1800s. The cemetery office is located at the Monument Avenue entrance to the cemetery.

Visit president Lincoln, his wife and three of their sons last resting place. Be sure to see the statuary inside the tomb that shows Lincoln at different periods of his public career. Abraham Lincoln was buried in Springfield's Oak Ridge Cemetery at the request of Mrs. Lincoln after his assassination in 1865. The original receiving vault in which Abraham Lincoln was buried can be seen on a tour of the cemetery. (Ask about the special Civil War Retreat Ceremony held at the Tomb each Tuesday evening during the summer.) In the tomb, they request silence or quiet conversation - not a problem - the mood will sober you.

LINCOLN-HERNDON LAW OFFICES STATE HISTORIC SITE

1 Old State Capitol Plaza (Sixth and Adams Streets, one-half block east of the Old State Capitol), **Springfield** 62701

❑   Phone: (217) 785-7289

    Web: www.state.il.us/hpa/hs/Herndon.htm

❑   Hours: Daily 9:00am-5:00pm (mid-April to Labor Day week); Tuesday-Saturday 9:00am-4:00pm (rest of year). Closes: Daily Noon-1:00pm. Closed New Year's Day, Martin Luther King, Jr. Birthday, Presidents' Day, General Election Day, Veterans' Day, Thanksgiving Day, Christmas Day.

❑   Admission: Donation suggested.

❑   Miscellaneous: Next door is Del's Popcorn. Freshly popped and flavored popcorn, ice cream cones and candies are yummy and the atmosphere is playful. The place to go with the younger set as the Law Office tour may be boring for youth.

Abraham Lincoln practiced law in the offices above Tinsley's store. The Law Offices have been restored to appear as it may have looked from 1843 until about 1852, when Abraham Lincoln practiced law on the building's third floor. It was an ideal location for a rising young law firm — near the Capitol and Springfield's finest hotel of the day and just above the local post office and Federal Courtroom. Stephen Logan (1843-44) and William Herndon (1844-52) were his partners during this time. This is the only surviving structure in which Lincoln maintained working law offices. Today, the first floor features an orientation center where visitors may view exhibits and a video describing the site's history. Guided tours are the only way to go upstairs. Hear the story of the trap door and how Lincoln used it.

OLD STATE CAPITOL STATE HISTORIC SITE

Old State Capitol Area (I-55 exit SR 29 north to Sixth Street/ 5th
and Adams Streets), **Springfield** 62701

❑   Phone: (217) 785-7960

   Web: www.state.il.us/hpa/hs/Capitol.htm

❑   Hours: Tuesday-Saturday 9:00am-4:00pm or 5:00pm. Daily
      9:00am-5:00pm (mid-April to Labor Day week).

❑   Admission: FREE guided tours.

"A HOUSE DIVIDED against itself cannot stand." These immortal
words were spoken by Abraham Lincoln in the historic Old State
Capitol Hall of Representatives in the turbulent days preceding the
Civil War. He tried several hundred cases in the Supreme Court,
borrowed books from the state library, and read and swapped
stories with other lawyers and politicians in the law library.
Around historic downtown, you'll notice "HERE I HAVE LIVED"
EXHIBITS - View over 30 outdoor interpretive exhibits placed
throughout the downtown area to experience Springfield as
Abraham Lincoln knew it. Each exhibit is intended to capture a
moment in time for Lincoln and how he was affected by the
people, places and events he encountered in his hometown. Each
story is accompanied by graphics or photographs and a medallion
that is symbolic of that particular story. Visitors are encouraged to
collect rubbings of each medallion.

SPRINGFIELD TROLLEY - An old-fashioned, open-air trolley
(closed and heated in the winter) with regular stops at the major
historic attractions. Tickets sold at several downtown locations
($5.00 Circle tour, $5.00-$10.00 for all day reboarding tour). For a
list of stops, ticketing locations and days of operation, call (217)
528-4100.

SHEA'S GAS STATION MUSEUM

2075 Peoria Road [north side of town, Business Loop 55 south (Peoria Rd.), ignore the recent elignment of IL-4 that continues straight)], **Springfield** 62701

❑   Phone: (217) 522-0475

❑   Hours: Hours: Tuesday-Friday 7:00am-4:00pm; Saturday 7:00am-Noon; Closed during Illinois State Fair.

❑   Admission: $1.00-$2.00 donation for museum.

Over on the north side of town you'll find Shea's Truck Covers with owner Bill Shea, a Route 66 Hall of Fame Member, dishing up a few good stories. He'll be sitting on that old bench next to the door if the weather's warm. An original Texaco station owner, Bill has one of the most complete Route 66 museums of more than half a century of gas station memorabilia. The Gas Station Museum is the result of not throwing much away over the last 60+ years. The collection consists of thousands of oil cans, fuel pumps, even an antique Sears and Roebuck auto air conditioner designed to be mounted on the car's window sill. These days, Bill spends his time selling a truck cover or two and sharing his infinite knowledge about the old highway with people from far away lands and locals (he stopped selling gasoline in 1982). 'Wanna start an easy conversation? Just ask about the weather.

SPRINGFIELD THEATRE CENTRE

Springfield - *420 S. Sixth Street (Hoagland Center for the Arts), 62701.* **Web:** *www.springfieldtheater.com.* *Phone: (217) 523-2787.* The Springfield Theatre Centre, originally called The Springfield Theatre Guild, is a not-for-profit organization incorporated in 1947 to provide Central Illinois with quality theatre, educational opportunities, and a creative outlet for live theatrical arts. Their White Rabbit Series includes titles like Alice in Wonderland, Aladdin and Santa Claus.

DANA-THOMAS HOUSE

Springfield - *301 E. Lawrence (I-55 take Clear Lake Ave exit, head west. Turn left (south) onto 9th Street. Turn right onto Cook), 62703.* **Web:** *www.illinoishistory.gov/hs/Thomas.htm.* *Phone: (217) 782-6776. Hours: Wednesday-Sunday 9:00am-4:00pm. Last tour begins just before 4:00pm. Closed New Year's Day, Martin Luther King, Jr. Birthday, Presidents'*

Day, General Election Day, Veterans' Day, Thanksgiving Day, Christmas Day. Admission: Suggested donation $3.00 adult, $1.00 children (under 17). It was 1902 in Victorian Springfield when local socialite and activist, Susan Lawrence Dana, hired a rising young architect from Chicago to remodel her family home. What resulted and remains today is one of Frank Lloyd Wright's finest prairie-style homes, complete with original furniture, art glass doors, windows and light fixtures. Frank Lloyd Wright (1867-1959) was thirty-five in 1902, the year he began work on the Dana House. Already well known for his innovative design, Wright was revolutionizing American domestic architecture in the Midwest.

ILLINOIS STATE CAPITOL

Springfield - *Capitol Avenue and Second Street, 62703. Phone: (217) 782-2099. Hours: Monday-Friday 8:00am-4:00pm, Saturday-Sunday 9:00am-3:30pm. Closed from Noon-1:00pm and on all major holidays. Admission: FREE. Tours: Tours are given every half-hour, except on weekends when they are conducted on the hour.* Designed in the shape of a Latin Cross and capped by a 361-foot-high dome, the building stands 74 feet taller than the U.S. Capitol dome. In addition to watching Illinois politicians from the balcony-level seating area, visitors can view the awe-inspiring artwork, statues, and paintings of the limestone Italian Renaissance Revival building. Murals, a variety of different marbles, and a unique architectural design add to the elegance.

ILLINOIS SYMPHONY ORCHESTRA

Springfield - *524 1/2 E. Capitol Avenue (performs at Sangamon Auditorium), 62703. Web: www.ilsymphony.org. Phone: (217) 206-6160.* A traditional orchestra with series for families: Sneakers and Jeans and the Pops series.

THOMAS REES MEMORIAL CARILLON

Springfield - *Washington Park, 2500 S. 11th Street (one block south of Lawrence Street and Chatham Road), 62703. Phone: (217) 753-6219 or (217) 544-1751. Web: www.carillon-rees.org. Hours: Tuesday-Sunday Noon-8:00pm (June-August); Weekends only (Spring & Fall). Closed: December-March, Easter Day, Columbus Day, Veterans' Day, Thanksgiving Day. Admission. Miscellaneous: Regularly scheduled concerts are given each Sunday afternoon throughout the year, with the addition of a Wednesday evening concert during the summer months. Tours of the tower are given on a daily basis, when open.* Surrounded by gardens and a reflecting pool, the magnificent bell tower in Washington Park is the third largest in the world and one of the few open to the public.

View the bells and playing mechanism, during a tour with a video presentation. A spectacular view of the city awaits those with stamina enough to make it up the final circular staircase to the top. Or, you can take an elevator to one of the most beautiful views in Springfield. (Don't miss the International Carillon Festival held one week in the middle of June).

ILLINOIS STATE MUSEUM

502 S. Spring Street (corner of Spring & Edwards Streets, south side of State Capitol complex), **Springfield** 62706

❑   Phone: (217) 782-7386, **Web: www.museum.state.il.us**
❑   Hours: Monday-Saturday 8:30am-5:00pm, Sunday Noon-5:00pm.
     Closed New Year's Day, Thanksgiving Day, Christmas Day.
❑   Admission: FREE.

Permanent and changing exhibits tell the story of Illinois' land, life, people, and art. The attendant will give each guest an ID badge that can be used to reveal answers and activate sound stations within the 1st floor exhibit halls. A completely new natural history hall, Changes: Dynamic Illinois Environments, reveals the exciting changes in Illinois environments over time. Interactive elements, audio and video effects, life-sized dioramas and thousands of authentic fossils and specimens illustrate the processes that shaped and continue to transform Illinois' diverse environments. In Changes, you can walk through a Fluorite (used in welding and to get fluoride for toothpaste) Mine; travel through an Ice Age tunnel and limestone cave - all within a few feet of each other. Explore French Illinois and meet the people who lived here. From woolly mammoths to the Prairie to modern subdivisions, children can see, hear, and touch in A Place for Discovery.

HENSON ROBINSON ZOO

1100 E. Lake Drive, **Springfield** 62707

❑   Phone: (217) 753-6217, **Web: www.hensonrobinsonzoo.org**
❑   Hours: Monday-Friday 10:00am-5:00pm, Saturday-Sunday
     10:00am-6:00pm (March-October); Summer Wednesdays until
     8:00pm; Daily 10:00am-4:00pm (November-February). Closed
     winter holidays.
❑   Admission: $1.50-$3.25 (age 3+).

Henson Robinson Zoo (*cont.*)

❑   Miscellaneous: Special events are held throughout the year and provide many hands-on experiences for children and adults alike. Also, take a Zooper Edventure with the zoo's education programs for children ages 5-17. Gift shop, concessions & a petting area.

The Zoo is home to more than 300 animals native to Australia, Africa, Asia and North and South America. Over 90 species of native animals are housed here among naturalistic exhibits. Enjoy the relaxing atmosphere of the lagoons and watch mischievous spider monkeys at play on monkey island. Delight at the river otters. Marvel at the grace of the cheetahs and the deceivingly cuddly appearance of the Asiatic black bear. Then take a walk on the wild side with cougars, gibbons, lemurs, and more.

KNIGHT'S ACTION PARK / CARIBBEAN WATER ADVENTURE/ ROUTE 66 DRIVE IN

1000 Recreation Drive (I-55 Sixth Street Exit, follow signs to Chatham Road & Recreation Dr.), **Springfield** 62707

❑   Phone: (217) 546-8881, **Web: www.knightsactionpark.com**

❑   Hours: Action Park: Opens Daily 9:00am-10:00 or 11:00pm (March-October). Water Park: Opens Daily 10:00am-7:00pm (mid-May – late-August) & Labor Day Weekend.

❑   Admission: Action Park: Pay as you Go ($1.00-$5.00 per activity). Water Park: $16.95-$22.95 pass, $3.00 infants (2 & under w/swim diapers). $4.00 discount on pass after 3:30pm. Landlubbers $10.00. This price includes all the water attractions in the water area except the games, such as water wars. There is no additional charge for tubes or parking. Lockers are only 50c.

In this 60-acre family fun park, you can splash down a giant waterslide or sprayground, test your mini-golf putts, or catch a flick. With two parks at one location, the water park offers its newest attraction - "The Devil Ray" (thrill ride, G forces giant halfpipe) along with a wave pool (one of our favorites), waterslides, and action river ride (an awesome lazy river with gentle geysers and waves), pedal boats, activity pools and children's water-theme area (Seal Bay). The dry attractions include a golf practice range, miniature golf courses, batting cages, go karts, and their newest attraction, "The Big Wheel" (ferris wheel). What a clean, compact, fun day to be had! Next door...Load up the car and throw in the lawn chairs. It's time to head back in time to the Route 66 Drive In. Newly restored, located on an original alignment of Route 66 in Springfield, it shows double features (G, PG or PG13 only) nightly (beginning around 9:00pm) from Memorial Day weekend through Labor Day and on weekends through October. Concession stand featuring all your drive-in favorites. **www.route66-drivein.com**.

LINCOLN MEMORIAL GARDEN

Springfield - *2301 East Lake Shore Drive, 62707. Phone: (217) 529-1111,* **Web:** *www.lmgnc.com. Hours: Daily sunrise-sunset. Nature Center: Tuesday-Saturday 10:00am-4:00pm, Sunday 1:00-4:00pm. Closed several major holidays. Admission: FREE.* A nature center with five miles of wooded trails lead you on a journey through the Illinois landscape Lincoln walked. Depending on the season you visit, you could discover springtime dogwoods in full bloom, colorful wildflowers of summer, burnished autumn leaves, or snow-covered maple trees bursting with sap. All the plants found at the Garden are native to the three states Lincoln lived in - Kentucky, Indiana and Illinois. The oaks, maples and hickories, as well as the prairie grasses and forbs, would have been known by Lincoln, and reflect the landscape of his time. Located on the shores of Lake Springfield, it was designed as a "living memorial" to Abraham Lincoln.

PRAIRIE'S EDGE FARM

Springfield (Rochester) - *(20 minutes from Downtown Springfield), 62563. Phone: (217) 498-8251. Hours: By reservation only.* Join in the farm activities! From collecting eggs to feeding the livestock, this family owned and operated farm is the perfect hands-on experience for the family.

SILO ROCK CLIMBING GYM

Springfield (Rochester) - *130 S. John Street (east of Springfield), 62563. Phone: (217) 498-9922, Web: www.daretoclimb.com. Hours: Wednesday and Friday 5:00-9:30pm, Saturday and Sunday Noon-6:00pm. Admission.* This rock-climbing facility offers four stations, including two indoor 100-foot routes, considered to be among the tallest in the country. Climb inside a recycled silo.

SUGGESTED LODGING AND DINING

COMFORT SUITES, 2620 South Dirksen Parkway, **Springfield**. (217) 753-4000. Indoor Pool, micro/frig in each room and big complimentary continental breakfast. Within 10 minutes of all Springfield/Lincoln attractions.

WEINER DOG, 113 N. 6th Street (downtown near Old Capitol), **Springfield**. (217) 744-3644. I know what you're thinking, we're recommending a hot dog place? Because they're so unique (they only serve hot dogs), we couldn't resist. Try a Chicago Dog (even has a pickle spear on it), a New Yorker (with kraut), Chilidogs, Burnt Wienie, etc. or Brats, Polish or Italian sausage. Only serving lunch (Monday-Saturday), the guys here only charge around $5.00 for combo meals, $3.50 for kids meals.

COZY DOG DRIVE IN, 2935 South Sixth Street, **Springfield**. (217) 525-1992, **www.cozydogdrivein.com**. Hours: Monday-Saturday 8:00am-8:00pm. Closed New Year's Days, Memorial Days, July 4th, Labor Day, Thanksgiving Day, and Christmas through New Year's Day. Miscellaneous: In the morning they have fresh cake donuts and other breakfast items such as eggs, pancakes, and french toast. For Illini, the nostalgia, charm and spirit of Route 66 can still be found in the secret corners of this Midwestern community. Take the Cozy Drive In for instance. A familiar Springfield landmark on old Route 66 since 1949, the original owners, the Waldmire family, are still serving up the same friendly atmosphere. Their specialty: a home-cooked recipe of Cozy Dogs (hot dogs deep fried in a secret bread batter- corn dogs) that travelers from around the world have come to love. For lunch or dinner they serve world famous Cozy Dogs along with fresh cut french fries, hamburgers, homemade chili and homemade bean soup, pork tenderloins and other delicious food items. Inside the diner, you'll find an amusing array of Route 66 memorabilia and souvenirs. Most everything is under $2.00.

Chapter 2
Chicago & Chicagoland (CL)

Our Favorites...

* Blackberry Farm - Aurora
* SciTech Hands-On Museum - Aurora
* Brookfield Zoo - Brookfield
* Long Grove Confectionary - Buffalo Grove
* Chicago Transportation Tours (Trolley, Boat, Fire Truck)
* Eli's Cheesecake World - Chicago
* Hancock Observatory - Chicago
* Navy Pier - Chicago
* Shedd Aquarium - Chicago
* Joliet Area Historical - Joliet
* Spring Valley Nature Center & Farm - Schaumberg
* Illinois Beach State Park - Zion

Window Washing Fun! - Hancock Building

ARLINGTON HEIGHTS HISTORICAL MUSEUM

110 West Fremont Street, **Arlington Heights** 60004

❑ Phone: (847) 255-1225, **Web: www.ahmuseum.org**
❑ Hours: Friday-Sunday 1:30-4:30pm.
❑ Admission: FREE, donations accepted. Tours cost $2.00-$4.00.
❑ Tours: Saturday and Sunday 2:00 and 3:00pm.

The Museum Complex includes late 1800s and early 1900s buildings. Here's some of the areas you'll see:

BOEGER CARPENTRY SHOP- a recreated circa 1874 carpentry shop with authentic woodworking machinery.

BLACKSMITH SHOP- a recreated setting of the town smithy, one of the most important businesses to the early growth of the village of Arlington Heights.

ARLINGTON HEIGHTS DIORAMAS- dioramas of the local area before European settlement, the first school, the train coming to town, the growth of the village, ice harvesting, and the first library.

LOG CABIN- a replica 1830s log cabin representing the homes of early settlers in the groves of Northeastern Illinois. Family activity centered around the hearth in this one room home.

MÜLLER HOUSE- a Victorian period house circa 1890s. The home features a restored parlor, office, kitchen, dining room, and bedrooms. Müller was a German immigrant and operated a soda pop factory in Arlington Heights.

BANTA HOUSE- an Arts and Crafts house.

DOLL COLLECTION- Collection of over 1000 dolls ranging from modern to antique, cloth to porcelain, miniature to 36".

DOLLHOUSE COLLECTION- Collection of three dollhouses and miniatures.

PHILLIPS PARK & ZOO

828 Montgomery Road (accessible from Smith Boulevard, Parker Avenue, or Howell Place off of Montgomery Road. Zoo is 901 Ray Moses Drive), **Aurora** 60505

- ❑ Phone: (630) 898-7228 park or (630) 978-4700 zoo
- ❑ Hours: Daily 9:00am-5:00pm (zoo). Open until 8:00pm summers. Mastodon Island & Visitors Center open same hours, weekdays only.
- ❑ Tours: Tours of the Zoo are offered during the hours of 9:00am and 2:00pm, Monday through Friday. All tours must be scheduled at least 2 weeks in advance.

Zoo exhibits include: Bald Eagles "Kenai" and "Denali"; the Gray Wolves "Dakota" and "Cheyenne"; "Fly" the fox; "Graycie" the Artic Fox; "Snowflake" the Platinum Red Fox; North American River Otters "Teeter" & "Totter"; Llamas "Dahlai" & "Socks"; "Hank" the Elk Bull and his herd; Goats; a Pot-bellied Pig; Reptiles; Swans; Ducks; Turkeys; Peacocks and more.

- ❑ <u>MASTODON ISLAND</u>: The Mastodon Peninsula site features a tusk maze and a mastodon slide. The site is easily accessible from the pedestrian bridge on the east side of the lake, along Wyeth Drive. The mastodon bones that were unearthed in the park during a 1934 Civil Works Administration Project. The skull being the largest of the artifacts, weighs 188 pounds, and greets visitors at the entrance. The bones, estimated to be between 10,000 to 20,000 years old, include a 92-pound lower jaw, a 6-foot-long tusk, ribs and vertebrae.
- ❑ <u>WEST RECREATION AREA</u>: located southwest of the lake, features a playground for youngsters, sand volleyball courts, horseshoe pits and a pavilion. On-site parking is available off of Parker Avenue. In addition, you'll find three fishing piers located around the lake.

WALTER PAYTON'S ROUNDHOUSE

205 N. Broadway (Route 25), **Aurora** 60505

❏ Phone: (630) 892-0034, **Web: www.auroraroundhouse.com**
❏ Admission: FREE to Museum, cover charge for some events, dining offers a menu around $8.00-$10.00 average. Kids menu is around $5.00 each.

MUSEUM: The Walter Payton Museum was created in 1996 to honor the accomplishments of Walter's life and careers. It features his High School, College and Professional Football Careers, but, also his Auto Racing, Musical, and Roundhouse Development Careers. Walter's Football Helmets, Race Car Helmets, and Hard Hat are all there to tell a story. Just as are his Super Bowl XX Ring, Hall of Fame Bust and numerous NFL Awards. Scrapbooks are available allowing visitors to review hundreds of articles.

RESTAURANT: Inside a renovated 1856 (America's 1st railroad roundhouse) is a stylish entertainment and fine dining complex. The Aurora Roundhouse is the oldest existing limestone roundhouse in the nation. Giant, man-sized steaks, pork and burgers are the "meat" of the menu for lunch or dinner. Their sides are unique like gourmet mashed potatoes or onion straws. Like steak and salad? - try the yummy mandarin orange steak and greens salad - what a fun presentation, too! Portions are large and we recommend their own beer - Root Beer, that is. Try some fresh from the vats. At times, you can even watch this process in the brewing room.

BLACKBERRY FARM'S PIONEER VILLAGE

100 South Barnes Road (I-88 Orchard Road exit, head south. West on Galena Blvd, left on Barnes),

Aurora 60506

❏ Phone: (630) 892-1550
    www.foxvalleyparkdistrict.org/facilities/bbf/bbf-intro.html
❏ Hours: Monday-Friday 9:30am-3:30pm, Weekends/Holidays 11:00am-5:00pm (May-Labor Day). Friday-Sunday only (after Labor Day-Columbus Day).
❏ Admission: $4.25-$7.00 adult, $3.75-$6.00 senior/child

Blackberry Farm's Pioneer Village *(cont.)*

❑   Miscellaneous: Food service is available at the outdoor pavilion,
       the Summer Kitchen, overlooking one of the ponds with a spraying
       fountain. Visitors may also bring a picnic lunch to enjoy along the
       lake shore. The paths are very stroller/wheelchair friendly.

Part amusement park and part museum, this Village is a great place
for kids to have fun and learn a little American history along the
way. Take a train ride or wagon ride through this 54-acre pioneer
village and see an 1840s farm, an authentic depot, a carriage
collection, a carousel and a petting zoo. Ever seen a Snow Roller
used to compact the snow for sleighs? Recite a lesson from your
McGuffey Reader with the Schoolmarm or try to figure out how to
use the "contraptions" displayed around the Farm Museum (look
like something from Chitty, Chitty, Bang, Bang). Little ones have
their own play area called Discovery Farm where kids can ride
pedal tractors, load corn or pick apples. Kids especially enjoy the
general store and the toy store. Many period craft demonstrations
bring the Village to life. They are blacksmithing, spinning,
weaving, sewing & pottery, as well as a one room schoolhouse, an
Aurora home from the 1840s and a farm cabin. With a lake, ponds
and a meandering stream, the Park allows families to wander, at
leisure, through local history.

SCITECH HANDS ON MUSEUM

18 West Benton Street (Take I-88 to Aurora, exit at 31 South.
Proceed south on 31 until you reach Benton St. (one block after 31
becomes one way.) Turn East (left), **Aurora** 60506

❑   Phone: (630) 859-3434, **Web: www.scitech.mus.il.us**
❑   Hours: Monday-Saturday 10:00am-5:00pm, Sunday Noon-
       5:00pm. Reduced afternoon hours during school year.
❑   Admission: $6.00-$7.00 (age 2+).
❑   Miscellaneous: Discovery Zone has "experiments" for little tikes.
       Across the street is the Swimming Stones kinetic water sculpture.
       Does it look like magic or an earthquake?

Colors are Chemistry: Try mixing two colors is one thing, but have
you ever UN-mixed them? In the Chromatography exhibit you can

separate black ink into different colors - pretty cool. They have bubble science areas (did you know there were physics involved in making bubbles?), exploring light and magnetism, or motion and chemistry. Who's older, jellyfish or dinosaurs? Find out or just play with prehistoric and modern toy animals on the Era Staircase. See tiny live animals wiggling and swimming and find out the different ways they do it in Microscopic Movement. Investigate the inside of a tornado and anchor the weather today. The Outdoor Science Park has giant experiments like the Human Yo-Yo, Bike on a Tightrope, or Hoist the Large Lever (kids, can you lift your parents?) There must be hundreds of experiments inside and outside this building!

SPLASH COUNTRY WATER PARK

195 S. Barnes Rd. (across from Blackberry Farm), **Aurora** 60506

❑   Phone: (630) 906-7981
     www.foxvalleyparkdistrict.org/facilities/splash/splash-intro.html

❑   Hours: Sunday-Friday Noon-7:00pm, Saturday 10:00am-5:00pm.

❑   Admission: $4.00-$6.00 per person (age 2+). Add $1.00 if non-resident or weekend/holidays. Subtract $1.00 after 5:00pm.

❑   Miscellaneous: Full concession stand with umbrella tables, Sand play area with seating and shade, Lap lane swimming available at designated times. Both the facility and the staff have won state and national awards for safety, operations and facility design.

Splash Country Water Park features: Six lane zero depth pool with children's play features, the 2nd largest lazy river in Illinois (with 1,100 feet winding through dumping buckets, sprayers, jets and a bubbling rapids), and one winding (enclosed tube/flume) slide & one winding (open tube/flume) slide. An enclosed kid-friendly area with spray guns, waterfall, and other interactive features for kids under 48 inches tall. 2 regulation sand volleyball courts.

AURORA REGIONAL FIRE MUSEUM

Aurora - *53 North Broadway (downtown, near Paytons Roundhouse), 60507. **Web:** www.auroraregionalfiremuseum.org. Phone: (630) 892-1572. Hours: Thursday, Friday, Saturday 1:00-4:00pm. Admission: $2.00-$3.50 per person.* This museum is housed in the old Central Fire

Station. What would a fire museum be without fire trucks? The Aurora Regional Fire Museum has nine pieces of fire apparatus in the collection dating from an 1850s hand pumper to a 1960s aerial ladder truck. Different exhibits focus on topics such as equipment and uniforms.

FERMILAB SCIENCE CENTER

(Exit I-88 at the Farnsworth exit, north. Farnsworth becomes Kirk Road. Follow Kirk Road to Pine Street), **Aurora (Batavia)** 60510

❑   Phone: (630) 840-3351 or (630) 840-5588, **Web: www.fnal.gov**

❑   Hours: The Lederman Science Center is open Monday-Friday from 8:30am-4:30pm and on Saturday from 9:00am-3:00 p.m. Pedestrians, bicyclists and motorists may enter the lab every day of the week from 8:00am-6:00pm (mid-October to mid-April) and from 8:00am-8:00pm when daylight hours are longer.

❑   Tours: Self-guided: The Center can accommodate groups of five or less on a walk-in basis. Walk-in visitors can use the Visitor's Guide to explore more than 30 experiments.

❑   Miscellaneous: Fermilab visitors are allowed to go into the Lederman Science Center and the first and ground floor of Wilson Hall. Ask-a-Scientist program on selected Sunday afternoons. Behind the scenes tour and crazy questions answered. Exhibits are geared towards 5th-12th graders but younger ones will have fun playing with balls (although they won't get the science behind it).

This physics research center has the highest energy accelerator in the world! Visitors are welcome to visit the "Quarks to Quasars" exhibits to gain hands-on experience as they experiment with exhibits that demonstrate how Fermilab physicists understand nature's secrets. Start at the Intro Videos to orient. Then, follow cartoons as they introduce each exhibit. Now, play (actually, experiment). Learn how accelerators "kick" energy in linear, circular and bending modes. Race cars, balls and yourself - scientists show you how. Now, kick it up a notch. Next, discover how to detect Invisible Particles (like uranium in stoneware or plastic). What material shields you from harmful radiation? Catch cosmic rays. Even play pool ball or pinball and see exactly where the energy from the cue ball goes. Patterns are the secret. Play nature's piano (can you hit the right keys?). The Margaret Pearson Interpretive Trail is a quarter mile self-guiding nature trail through a portion of Fermilab's restored prairie. See insects, fungi and geese that live in the prairie. Visitors are welcome to view Fermilab's herd of about sixty buffalo, too. Awesome science and nature here - for the older kids.

RED OAK NATURE CENTER

Aurora (Batavia) - *(Route 25, 1/2 mile north of Rte. 56), 60510. www.foxvalleyparkdistrict.org/facilities/redoak/redoak-intro.html. Phone: (630) 897-1808. Hours: Monday-Friday 9:00am-4:30pm, Saturday/Sunday 10:00am-3:00pm. Admission: FREE.* Nestled on the east bank of the Fox River is a museum surrounded by forty acres of woods called Red Oak Nature Center. Choose between several trails with side signage to learn about the sights you see. One trail takes you to "Devils Cave" which is rich in folklore. Done hiking? Stop a while on the new observation deck overlooking the Fox River or explore the nature center. Displays invite "hands-on" participation and lead you to a better understanding of the natural world.

HEALTH WORLD CHILDREN'S MUSEUM

Barrington - *1301 South Grove Avenue (I-90 to Rte 59N exit. East on Rte. 68, then left on South Grove), 60010. Phone: (847) 842-9100, Web: www.healthworldmuseum.org. Hours: Tuesday-Saturday 10:00am-3:00pm. Admission: $7.00 per person (age 2+).* Walk inside a giant heart, test your reflexes, take a video ride in a racing ambulance, escape the house of hazards and more. This large facility was the first hands-on health museum for kids in the nation.

PLUM CREEK NATURE CENTER

Beecher - *27064 Dutton Road (1.25 miles east of IL 1 and I-394 on Goodenow Road, south of Crete), 60401. Phone: (708) 946-2216, Web: www.fpdwc.org/plumcreek.cfm. Hours: Tuesday-Saturday 10:00am-4:00pm, Sunday Noon-4:00pm. Admission: FREE.* Nestled among forests, fields, cattail marshes, and a small pond, the Nature Center is the perfect place for discovering the outdoors. It offers something for little children who like to touch feathers and rocks, school children who marvel at the structure of animal skulls, adults who wonder how to attract butterflies in their gardens, and seniors who enjoy watching winter birds at the feeders. A large window provides an observation area for the bird feeding station.

Surrounding the bird feeders is a butterfly garden which demonstrates plants that attract a variety of wildlife. Picnicking, hiking, and camping await those looking for summer fun. In winter, enjoy cross-country skiing and ice-skating. Stop by the nature center to rent an inner tube ($1.00/all day with a valid ID) or bring your own sled (no snowboards or sleds with runners) and try sledding on our 30-foot hill. Afterwards, warm up in the Nature Center by the crackling fire. Enjoy a warm cup of coffee while viewing birds at our bird feeding area.

BROOKFIELD ZOO

3300 S. Golf Rd (I-290 exit 20, follow signs from 1st Ave),

Brookfield 60513

- ❑ Phone: (708) 485-3509, **Web: www.brookfieldzoo.org**
- ❑ Hours: Open 365 days a year. Daily 10:00am-5:00pm. Extended hours in summer and on weekends.
- ❑ Admission: $10.00 adult, $6.00 child (3-11) and senior (65+). Parking $8.00 per vehicle. Extra $1.00-$3.00 added admission for Dolphin show, Family Zoo, Motor Safari and Butterflies! Free general admission on Tuesdays and Thursdays in January, February, March, October, November, and December.
- ❑ Tours: The zoo offers free Zoo Chats several times each day in several areas. Children and parents learn about animals and the keepers get to tell you how they care for their animals - and also share some funny stories about their work. "Ride all day" on the narrated tram, Motor Safari. One ticket lets you hop on and off at any of four stops. They give you the scoop on each area, especially pointing out where the baby animals are.

The largest zoo in the Chicago area (3000+ animals), Brookfield was the first in America to exhibit animals in natural settings vs. cages. Kids love the Dolphin show and Tropic World. Monkeys of all sorts are hilarious to watch here - this was our favorite exhibit area and nice that it's all-weather indoors. Other unique areas are Fragile Kingdom, Seven Seas, Habitat Africa, and The Swamp. Babies are born (even porcupine!) and displayed to the delight of guests (check their website for baby reports - maybe help name babies). Why are zoo keepers glad the sloth bears are tearing up the place? Heard of animal acupuncture? How about a monkey makeover? There is even an unusual smell in some of the zoo's exhibits - the zoo uses fragrant substances like cinnamon and garlic as part of the enrichment program to keep all of the animals stimulated and active. In the Family Play Zoo, youngsters can dress up and pretend to be animals, veterinarians and zookeepers. They even have face-paint and clever outfits to really let the kids get into it. We even pet an albino rat here - even its tail!

LONG GROVE CONFECTIONERY CO. TOUR

333 Lexington Drive, **Buffalo Grove** 60089

❑   Phone: (888) 459-3100, **Web: www.longgrove.com**

❑   Admission: $2.00 per person (Handicapped accessible)

❑   Tour days: Monday through Thursday-year 'round. Hours of
     operation: 9:00am to 1:00pm. Length of tour: About one hour.
     Reservations required.

IN TOWN: Here in Historic Buffalo Grove, the Grosswiller School House, a nostalgic red schoolhouse reminiscent of the one-room variety that once served the village, was built as the first candy kitchen and retail store of the Long Grove Confectionery . One of the store's unique features is a vintage beveled glass window, which still allows visitors today to view some candy production; mostly notably fresh strawberries being dipped in creamy milk chocolate.

FACTORY TOUR: Gather under the Antique Stained Glass Dome in the 85,000 square foot Long Grove Confectionery to begin your tour of our specialty chocolate kitchen. The tour guide will present a short video on how cacao (ca-cow) is grown and processed into "chocolate". It will also include a brief history of the family-owned business (presented by a grandpa talking to his granddaughter, very effective and endearing). Following the video, guests will see the giant sculpted chocolate on display before entering the walkway to view production and packaging of chocolates. The first thing you'll notice - the strong chocolate scent wafting in the air. They say that workers are always happy here because they get to sample all the time. Highlights are the chocolate painted Monets and watching the ladies hand-decorate seasonal "pops". The best part are the samples! Finally, stop at the factory store where purchases can be made with great discounts. This is really a delightful tour - your kids will "ohh and ahh" at every stop!

CHICAGO PROFESSIONAL SPORTS TEAMS

CHICAGO CUBS BASEBALL - (Wrigley Field, home games - see Listing for Wrigley Field for directions). (800) THE CUBS or **www.chicagocubs.com**. The Chicago Cubs' mission is to put the most competitive team on the field, continually reaching toward the goal of a World Series title for the city of Chicago. Off the field the Cubs are dedicated to making a positive impact on Chicago through Cubs Care and the community programs it funds. Admission: Ranges $6.00-$18.00 for the "cheap seats." (April-September)

CHICAGO WHITE SOX BASEBALL - (US Cellular Field, 333 West 35th Street). **http://chicago.whitesox.mlb.com** or (312) 742-PLAY. Join the White Sox Kids Club, the official youth fan club of White Sox Baseball. Look for the mascot, South Paw, at the games. (April-September)

CHICAGO BEARS FOOTBALL - (Soldier Field, 1600 S. Lake Shore Drive, just south of the Museum Campus). (847) 615-BEAR or **www.chicagobears.com**. (September-December)

CHICAGO BULLS BASKETBALL - (United Center, 1901 W. Madison). **www.nba.com/bulls**. (312) 559-1212 or (312) 455-4000. Meet Benny the Bull and watch his antics and the BullsKidz dancing. (October-April)

CHICAGO BLACKHAWKS HOCKEY - (United Center, 1901 W. Madison). **www.chicagoblackhawks.com,** (312) 559-1212 or (312) 445-4500 or Family Nights (kids free with adult ticket). (October-April)

CHICAGO FIRE SOCCER - (Soldier Field, 425 E. McFetridge Drive) (312) 559-1212 or (888) MLS-FIRE or **www.chicago-fire.com**. Meet HUMO (Spanish for "Smoke"), a live Dalmatian dog, perform his tricks to entertain the fans. (June-early September)

CHICAGO TROLLEY & WATER TAXI TOURS

Hop on, Hop off. Day-long fully narrated tour stops at all of Chicago's top attractions every 15-20 minutes. See the highlights of downtown and lakefront areas including Museum Campus, Magnificent Mile and Navy Pier. Unlimited boarding. Admission. **CHICAGO TROLLEY COMPANY** - departs from Sears Tower and various other nearby locations. **www.chicagotrolley.com**. (773) 648-5000. Summertime: Non-narrated, just transport trolleys have stops everywhere and many different routes to all attraction areas in the city. And, it's all FREE - the city foots the bill for this wonderful service. **SHORELINE WATER TAXI**, **www.shorelinesightseeing.com**. (312) 222-9328. For around $5.00 per person, you can taxi to/from the Navy Pier and the Museum complex without having to walk that distance. They also offer sightseeing tours that only last 30 minutes. Daily summer, weekends only late spring and early fall.

CHICAGO NEIGHBORHOOD TOURS

Chicago - *77 E. Randolph Street (Chicago Cultural Center departure by motorcoach), 60601. Web: www.chgocitytours.com. Phone: (312) 742-1190. Admission: $25.00 adult, $20.00 senior and student including refreshments. Special tours: $45.00-$50.00 including lunch.* Guests have a chance to explore 17 different neighborhoods of Chicago. Each tour takes the visitor off the beaten path and provides an insider's look at the traditions, stories and people of the city with tours to the neighborhoods of Andersonville and Lincoln Square, Chinatown, Hyde Park, Little Italy, the Pullman Historic District, Ukrainian Village, Uptown, and many others. Special Interest tours have themes on Ireland, Literary Chicago, tasty Neighborhood Sampling, Chicago's Hidden Murals, Greek Chicago, Great Chicago Fire and Polish Chicago. People who know the areas serve as guides and share their stories with you. Tours are 4-6 hours long.

GRANT PARK & BUCKINGHAM FOUNTAIN

Chicago - *(Grant Park at Congress Parkway - up to Millennium Park on Michigan Avenue), 60601.* Dubbed "Chicago's Front Yard," Grant Park consists of the Museum Campus to the south and Millennium Park to the north. The site of many annual festivals, the park is also home to Buckingham Fountain and many huge sculptures (must see is the "Bean"). The Fountain is modeled after Latona Fountain basin at Versailles in France, but twice its size. During the summer, evening light shows enhance the spectacle of view and rushing water. These parks, and the greenery found plentifully on many downtown streets, adds beauty to the swarm of skyscrapers. You'll be surprised how comfortable this big city feels as you wander from site to site!

METRO DUCK TOURS

Chicago - *(Boarding Point: McDonald's, 600 North Clark Street (Clark & Ohio), 60601. Phone: (312) 642-DUCK, **Web: www.metroducks.com**. Hours: Departures between 10:00am-4:00pm, daily and last approximately one and a half hours. Admission: $10.00-$20.00 per person.* A wet, wild and wonderful duck tour on this WWII amphibious vehicle is sure to "quack" up its riders. Fully certified by the U.S. Coast Guard, riders enjoy a scenic and informative city tour while learning about its rich history. They also discover many points of interest, and hear lots of corny jokes. The funky vehicles drive directly into, and out of, Lake Michigan, giving riders a thrill they won't soon forget.

ART INSTITUTE OF CHICAGO

Chicago - *111 South Michigan Avenue, 60603. Phone: (312) 443-3600, **Web: www.artic.edu**. Hours: Weekdays 10:30am-4:30pm, Weekends 10:00am-5:00pm. Until 8:00pm on Ford Free Tuesdays. Admission: $12.00 adult, $7.00 senior, child.* The museum is one of the world's leading art museums with a great impressionist and post-impressionist collection of works by Monet, Renoir, Degas, Van Gogh, and others. Other collections include sculpture; photography; textiles; and arms and armor. The Kraft Education Center helps young visitors appreciate art from around the world with interactive computers, videos and games.

ADLER PLANETARIUM & ASTRONOMY MUSEUM

Chicago - *1300 Lake Shore Drive (Museum Campus), 60605. Phone: (312) 922-STAR, **Web: www.adlerplanetarium.org**. Hours: Monday-Friday 9:30am-4:30pm, weekends open one-half hour earlier. Summer hours extended. Admission: $11.00-$13.00 (age 4+). Admission plus one show.* The first museum of its kind in the Western Hemisphere has three floors of exhibits on astronomy, space exploration, telescopes and navigation. The museum allows guests to lean back and relax as the Planetarium sky show takes them on a journey into outer space. The Sky Theater and StarRider Theater shows transport visitors to planets, moons, and distant galaxies, and cover the latest topics in space news. They offer a special Sky Show for Kids. Learn about the secrets of giants in space.

CHICAGO PLAYWORKS

Chicago - *60 E. Balbo Drive (just off Michigan Avenue, DePaul's Merle Reskin Theatre), 60605. Web: http://theatreschool.depaul.edu. Phone: (312) 922-1999,* Each season they produce plays for families and young audiences. It may be an adaptation from favorite children's books (ex. Boxcar Children or Grimm's Tales). Some are original cultural productions.

FIELD MUSEUM, THE

1400 South Lake Shore Drive (Roosevelt Rd. at Lake Shore Drive)

Chicago 60605

- ❑ Phone: (312) 922-9410, **Web: www.fieldmuseum.org**
- ❑ Hours: Daily 9:00am-5:00pm. Open every day except Christmas. Varying hours in December.
- ❑ Admission: $19.00 adult, $14.00 senior (65+) or student (w/ ID), $9.00 child (ages 4-11). $1.00-$2.00 discount for Chicago residents. Add $2.00-$3.00 for upgrade packages (more exhibits). The Field Museum offers 52 days a year when admission is discounted for all visitors.
- ❑ Parking lots charge from $8.00-$13.00 per day. On the FREE Trolley route (Museum Campus stop).
- ❑ Tours: Free Highlights Tours - Get the inside stories on some of the fascinating objects on display at the Museum. Monday – Friday: 11:00am and 2:00pm.

Dinosaur buffs will be impressed with "Sue" - the largest, most complete, and best preserved Tyrannosaurus rex discovered yet, at the Field Museum. Considered one of the world's greatest natural history museums, they offer a variety of permanent exhibit spaces. Inside, Ancient Egypt explores two of the original chambers from a real tomb; experience the rich culture of the Pawnee people of the central Plains in the Pawnee Earth Lodge; Underground Adventure is where you enter a whole new world - the soil beneath your feet; or, the Laboratory features research visible to the public while experts study artifacts from the Pacific Ocean island regions. Parents, you'll enjoy taking your kids through the many rooms full of taxidermied animals behind glass - looking like they did in museums when we were kids. We even found skeletons of our beloved guinea pigs.

SHEDD AQUARIUM / OCEANARIUM

1200 S. Lake Shore Drive, **Chicago** 60605

❑   Phone: (312) 939-2438, **Web: www.sheddaquarium.org**
❑   Hours: Daily 9:00am-5:00pm. Open later summer holidays &
     weekends.
❑   Admission: $6.00-$8.00 general admission (age 3+). Discount of
     $2.00-$3.00 for residents. Add $8.00-$15.00 per person for
     special exhibit areas like Wild Reef and the Oceanarium. (Pass
     pricing). Discount Days occur about 50 days/year.

The Shedd offers the world's largest indoor collection of aquatic
mammals, reptiles, amphibians, invertebrates and fish. Wild Reef -
Sharks at Shedd totaling more than 750,000 gallons of water, this
exhibit allows guests to have an intimate encounter with more than
30 sharks, one of the largest and most diverse shark exhibits in
North America, and a coral reef exhibit housing more than 500
aquatic species demonstrating the crucial role coral reefs play in
the health of oceans. Guests can watch one of the Aquarium's daily
feedings in the Coral Reef exhibit, where a diver feeds the fish by
hand and describes their different species. Also, the museum's
magnificent Oceanarium is the world's largest marine mammal
pavilion. The Oceanarium is home to Beluga whales, dolphins,
Alaskan sea otters, seals and penguins in habitats replicating their
natural environments. The Dolphin and Beluga whale "shows" are
a must see! Although they were educating (snuck it in!), these
shows are very entertaining and the mammals were so amusing!
Amazon Rising takes guests on a journey through time in the
Amazon River. There is a set fee for each exhibit area.

FEDERAL RESERVE BANK OF CHICAGO

Chicago - *230 S. LaSalle Street, 60606. Phone: (312) 322-2400. Hours:
Monday-Friday 9:00am-5:00pm. Closed major holidays. Admission:
FREE.* Visit the Chicago Feds Visitors Center and see what a million
dollars looks like. You can try your skill at detecting counterfeits. Learn
how money and banking have evolved in the United States.

SEARS TOWER SKYDECK

233 W. Wacker Drive (bounded by Wacker Drive, Franklin Blvd.,
     Adams Street, Jackson Entrance), **Chicago** 60606

❑   Phone: (312) 875-9696, **Web: www.theskydeck.com**

❑   Hours: Daily 10:00am-10:00pm (May-September) or 10:00am-
       8:00pm (October-April). Last ticket sold ½ hour before closing.

❑   Admission: $9.95 adult, $7.95 senior (65+) or child (3-11).

Get up here and view the world! Breathtaking 360-degree views
from North America's tallest building (1,450 feet). Opened in
1974, Sears Tower consists of black aluminum and bronze-tinted
glass on a structural steel frame. The skydeck, which was
renovated in 2000, offers an elevator to the 103rd floor and includes
the "Above Chicago" a short multi-image presentation movie.
Really, this is an intro to Chicago. The movie and the exhibits both
share highlights of historical and modern downtown Chicago.
They even have "Knee-high" peep holes for the kids to peer
through. You'll learn about each side of the tower and what to look
for. This might be a good place to start your tour of town -
especially if you have a strong interest in history.

NOBLE HORSE THEATRE

Chicago - *1410 N. Orleans, 60610. Phone: (312) 266-7878,* **Web:**
www.noblehorsechicago.com. *Hours: Dinner performances are 1 hour
and 45 minutes. The dinner is catered. The matinees are 70 minutes and
there is no meal served. A snack bar is open for the matinees. Shows are
generally on Fridays and weekends. Admission: $24.00-$38.00 (dinner
show); $14.00-$18.00.* The Theatre castle enhances the mood as you
experience the beauty and grace of the elegant dancing horses performing
shows like Cinderella or the Nutcracker. The horses perform indoors all
year round in this elegant site in Chicago's Old Town (restored 1871
stables). All the guests are close to the horses and every seat provides a
clear view of the show.

AMERICAN GIRL PLACE

111 E. Chicago Avenue (just a few feet west of Michigan Avenue shopping district), **Chicago** 60611

❏ Phone: (877) AG-PLACE, **Web: www.americangirlplace.com**

❏ Hours: Generally open 10:00am-7:00pm daily, except Thanksgiving and Christmas. Extended hours on performance nights and summertime hours.

❏ Admission: $16.00-$18.00 per person for either brunch, lunch, tea or dinner. Scheduled, reserved meals. Theater performances are $28.00 per person. Packages available. Browsing is Free.

❏ Miscellaneous: Boys tagging along? They loan out Game Boys (when available) to male visitors - FREE. Photo Studio (get your picture put on the cover of AG Magazine) and AG Movies behind-the-scenes.

A destination that celebrates everything that's great about being a girl. Dine in the café, see a live musical in the theater, have your doll's hair styled in the doll hair salon, or browse the many entertaining displays and stores about dolls and places/times in history. This is a sweet, feminine place where girls can be girls (moms, too) as they immerse themselves in the art of female-ess" for several hours.

❏ CAFÉ: A fun and fanciful place for girls and their families to dine with their dolls (doll-sized Treat Seat) in a whimsical setting. The café serves family-friendly full meals (brunch, lunch, dinner) or afternoon tea daily. Start with warm cinnamon buns and end with Chocolate Mousse Flowerpot and cakes/cookie. Everything is mildly flavored. They have party favors you get to take home as a souvenir. Conversation starters at each table prompt girls and their guests to share stories.

❏ THEATER: An American Girls Musical or Revue - This lively show brings the stories of the American Girls characters to life through ten original songs. Each one-hour musical celebrates the value of friendship and teamwork, yet sneaking in education and history. Appropriate for girls/families ages 6 and up.

❑   DOLL HAIR SALON: Let their specially trained stylists give
your doll a new hairdo. $10.00-$20.00. Watch them brush out the
"rats" and style the doll's hair into a silky, shiny "do".

❑   PEEK INTO THE PAST: Peek into life-size re-creations of
rooms from the American Girls' homes, including Kaya's tepee,
Josefina's adobe sala, Kirsten's log cabin, Addy's garret,
Samantha's Victorian parlor, Kit's attic, and Molly's living room.

CHICAGO CHILDREN'S MUSEUM
700 East Grand Avenue at Navy Pier, Chicago 60611

❑   Phone: (312) 527-1000, **Web: www.chichildrensmuseum.org**

❑   Hours: Sunday-Wednesday & Friday: 10:00am-5:00pm;
Thursday & Saturday: 10:00am-8:00pm; Target Free First
Mondays: 10:00am-8:00pm

❑   Admission: $6.00-$7.00 per person. Kraft Free Thursday nights
and Target Free First Mondays - look on website for details.

❑   Miscellaneous: Kids on the Fly, a satellite Children's Museum
has been created at O'Hare International Airport to entertain and
educate children during layovers or anytime they are waiting at
the airport.

This museum is a "don't miss" destination for families with
children. "Hands-on" is the logo and the logic for this museum.
Children can explore the Climbing Schooner; take the Flying
Machine Challenge in The Inventing Lab (make your wings and
test them on the flight tower); become junior paleontologists on a
Dinosaur Expedition; PlayMazes and WaterWays; and follow BIG
Backyard to experience the beautiful outdoors - oversized! Become
a bee or butterfly and fly over the city (virtually). Play it Safe has
enticing displays like the Bathroom Theatre. Do you remember
your first words? Check out Now You're Talking. We liked the
clean, well-maintained exhibit spaces and the diversity of each
station - you can even play giant chess and checkers here.

HANCOCK OBSERVATORY

875 North Michigan Ave (John Hancock Center), **Chicago** 60611

- ❑ Phone: (888) 875-VIEW, **Web: www.hancock-observatory.com**
- ❑ Hours: Daily 9:00am-11:00pm.
- ❑ Admission: $9.95 adult, $7.50 senior (62+), $6.00 child (5-12).

A 39-second elevator ride takes you to the 94th floor observatory of the John Hancock Center for a panoramic view of Chicago, Lake Michigan and up to four surrounding states. The large panel windows allow a tremendous view of the city. We also loved the Sky Walk area - a screened in outdoor walk where you can see and hear the city. Count how many roof-top pools you see. Includes two innovative, interactive features: Windows of Chicago and Soundscope (extra $1.00 fee) using virtual reality technology and virtual audio experience. Finally, pose as a Big John construction worker or window washer with amusing trick photography backgrounds and props - go ahead, ham it up! This is the best tower for views.

NAVY PIER

600 East Grand Avenue (off Lakeshore Drive), **Chicago** 60611

- ❑ Phone: (312) 595-PIER, **Web: www.navypier.com**
- ❑ Admission: To individual activities, FREE to roam around.
- ❑ Miscellaneous: Fireworks displays take place every Wednesday and Saturday from Memorial Day to Labor Day.

Navy Pier, a mile-long complex of shops and restaurants, juts into Lake Michigan near the south end of the Magnificent Mile. With an old-fashioned Ferris wheel spinning overhead, the massive old military dock is buzzing all year long with concerts, fireworks and special events. The pier is home to the Chicago Children's Museum and many sightseeing boat docks. You can also roam the children's indoor maze of mirrors, take the Time Escape 3-D thrill ride; attend an IMAX film, or ride an old-style "swing" carousel. Even kids enjoy the Stained Glass walk-thru museum admiring the art of painted or mosaic glassworks for FREE. You can spend hours here - grab a treat and walk and play in the old-fashioned carnival atmosphere.

O' LEARY'S CHICAGO FIRE TRUCK TOURS

505 N. Michigan Avenue, **Chicago** 60611

❑   Phone: (312) 287-6565, **Web: www.olearyfiretours.com**

❑   Admission: 60-90 minute tours run $20-$25.00 adult, and $10-
$15.00 child. Firework night tours are the higher price because of
extra stop at Navy Pier. Scheduled Summer & Fall. Groups only
Winter & Spring.

Take a 1965 Mac Pumper (or another old model) real fire engine
truck tour with REAL firemen! What a great way to learn about the
sites and the history behind the great Chicago Fire - stories from
firemen who know the scoop. At one stop, you can actually stand
on the spot where Mrs. O'Leary's infamous "Betsy the cow"
accidentally tipped over the lantern. Besides the many views of
great architectural buildings, you'll pass several engine houses
(even the oldest one in Chicago). Occasionally, the driver will
blow one of many sirens he has on board. You'll learn about fire
safety advancements, too. And, how the fire pole and Fire Safety
Week initiated at the Chicago fire department. What a unique and
special tour!

"SPIRIT OF CHICAGO" CRUISE

600 E. Grand Street (docks at Navy Pier), **Chicago** 60611

❑   Phone: (312) 836-7899 or (866) 211-3804
Web: www.spiritofchicago.com

❑   Admission: Highly recommended for families, the Lunch Cruise
rates from $25.00-$35.00 per person. Daily Noon-2:00pm
departures. Walk ups welcome but reservations are strongly
recommended.

The luxurious way to view Chicago's skyline on city's most
entertaining cruise ship. Lunch, brunch and sunset cruises. They
have a DJ playing oldies, in between sightseeing pointers and live
entertainment. Their singers and dancers put on a Celebration
Show. Diners can dance, too. Get your groove on OR head up the
stairs and out on the deck. By the way, the food (chicken, beef and
fish) is very good. This was one of the best lunch boat cruises
we've done!

WRIGLEY FIELD TOURS

1060 W. Addison Street (Lake Shore Drive to Irving Park Rd. Head west to Clark. Turn left (south). Wrigley Field is ahead on the left (east), **Chicago** 60613

❑   Phone: (773) 404-CUBS, **Web: www.chicagocubs.com**

❑   Admission: Tickets are $20.00 per person.

❑   Tours: Limited to 46 people per tour. Tours are scheduled every half-hour, beginning at 10:00am with the last tour scheduled for 4:30pm on each date. Basically offered 4 days/month. Tours do sell out. To ensure your tour, tickets must be purchased in advance.

❑   Miscellaneous: The Cubs Gift shop will be open during tours. Personal cameras and video cameras are welcome. If traffic is heavy on Lake Shore Drive, take Broadway or Clark to Addison.

Each 90-minute tour provides an insider's look at 90 years of history in this legendary ballpark. Tour stops include:

Cubs Clubhouse, Press Box, Visitors Clubhouse, Bleachers, Dugouts, Playing Field, And Mezzanine Suites. The Wrigley Field bleachers and scoreboard were constructed in 1937 when the outfield area was renovated to provide improved and expanded seating...the original scoreboard remains intact...the score-by-innings and the pitchers' numbers are changed by hand. One of the traditions of Wrigley Field is the flying of a flag bearing a "W" or an "L" atop the scoreboard after a game ... a white flag with a blue "W" indicates a victory; a blue flag with a white "L" denotes a loss. Most importantly, this is a behind-the-scenes look at the famous history of the 2nd oldest MLB ball field.

CHICAGO HISTORICAL SOCIETY

Chicago - *(North Avenue and Clark Street), 60614. Phone: (312) 642-4600, Web: www.chicagohistory.org. Hours: Monday-Saturday 9:30am-4:30pm, Sunday Noon-5:00pm. Admission: $5.00 adult, $3.00 senior and student, $1.00 child (6-12). FREE admission on Mondays.* The Chicago Historical Society is the oldest cultural institution and keeper of Chicago memories. Visit the museum to trace Chicago's growth from wilderness outpost to the architectural, cultural and social mecca of the midwest. Through artifacts, photographs, paintings and video presentations, the museum tells the story of this town using Hands-on History Galleries with "please touch" artifacts; an exhibit on the Great Chicago Fire; and an American History wing that ties in U.S. history with Chicago.

LINCOLN PARK ZOO & CONSERVATORY GARDENS

Chicago - *2200 N. Cannon Drive (Lake Shore Drive and Fullerton Pkwy.), 60614. Phone: (312) 742-2000 zoo or (312) 742-4838 Web: www.lpzoo.org. Hours: Daily 9:00am-5:00pm. Admission: FREE. Parking $12.00 plus. Miscellaneous: Adjacent to the zoo is the Gardens where the wonders of nature bloom year-round. Exotic plants from around the world.* One of the last free zoos in the country. Where else can you see so many animals right in the center of a city? Thousands of exotic and endangered species fill animal houses, habitats, pools and exhibits. Visit the African Journey exhibit featuring elephants, rhinos, giraffes, wild dogs and hissing cockroaches. The Children's Zoo includes live animal presentations, a petting zoo, a zoo nursery, and a hands-on learning center for kids. Families will get a taste of country life at the Farm-in-the-Zoo, a model Midwest farm in the heart of the city.

NOTEBAERT NATURE MUSEUM

Chicago - *2430 North Cannon Drive (I90 to northwest corner of Fullerton Parkway and Cannon Drive in Lincoln Park), 60614. Phone: (773) 755-5100, Web: www.naturemuseum.org. Hours: Weekdays 9:00am-4:30pm, Weekends 10:00am-5:00pm. Closed on major winter holidays only. Admission: $7.00 adult, $5.00 senior (60+) or student w/ID, $4.00 child (3-12). Thursdays – FREE.* Set along the lakefront in Lincoln Park, this indoor and outdoor museum invites guests to reconnect with nature. This state-of-the-art museum explores the biodiversity of the Midwest through interactive exhibits. From the Great Lakes to the prairies - natural to the urban areas. Hands-on Habitat: This engaging two-story hands-on, body-on exhibit takes budding naturalists (age 3 to 7) on an exploration of the secret world of animal homes. Examine your relationship with nature and the impact humans have on the environment in the Butterfly Haven, River works, Marsh and Wilderness.

GARFIELD PARK CONSERVATORY

300 North Central Park Avenue (I-290 exit at Independence Blvd
(Exit 26A), head north. Turn east (right) onto Washington Blvd.
Turn left (north) onto Central Park (3600W), **Chicago** 60624

❑   Phone: (312) 746-5100, **Web: www.garfieldconservatory.org**

❑   Hours: Daily 9:00am-5:00 pm, Thursdays till 8:00 pm.

❑   Admission: FREE. Free Parking is just south of the
Conservatory's main entrance.

Visit the Children's Garden, which is open during all conservatory
hours, or visit during weekend Discovery Area hours, and let the
staff introduce you to the giant soil table. Inside the Garden, a
gigantic vine beckons children to trace it from root to blossom,
while a 7-foot-tall seed waits to be climbed. The adventurous can
hunt for some of the most unusual specimens found in the Garfield
Park Conservatory (some of which are included on their
downloadable Eye Spy Conservatory Hunt). Young explorers will
encounter the Sensitive Plant, so shy that it cringes when touched,
and the Balsa Tree, which emits a hollow sound when the trunk is
tapped. Up on the mezzanine, children can befriend a larger-than-
life bee and assist it in pollinating the largest flower in the room
before taking a ride down the twirling stem of a green slide. Young
toddlers and babies are invited to explore the colors and textures of
soft-form blocks and play rings in the special permanent Crawling
Area, and can slip down their own miniature green slide. Jungle
climate and a botanical garden under glass.

ELI'S CHEESECAKE WORLD

6701 West Forest Preserve Dr (corner of Montrose), **Chicago** 60634

❑   Phone: (800) ELI-CAKE, **Web: www.elicheesecake.com**

❑   Store Hours: Monday-Friday 8:00am-6:00pm, Saturday 9:00am-
5:00pm, Sunday 11:00am-5:00pm.

❑   Tours: Sneak Peek Tour - Take a guided tour through the bakery
on Chicago 's northwest side, and then enjoy a sample of Eli's
Cheesecake. Monday-Friday at 1:00pm. $3.00 for adults and
$2.00 for children (under 12). Special educational tours available
for school and scout groups.

❑   Miscellaneous: Please Note: For your safety, Eli's requires that
      rubber-soled, low-heeled, close-toed shoes must be worn by each
      guest, no exceptions. Children under two years of age will not be
      allowed in the operating bakery portion of the tour. Also, children
      may not be carried in certain areas of the bakery. All tour guests
      will be required to walk approximately 400 feet. Sorry, no cameras
      or video cameras are allowed in the bakery. Afterwards, shop for
      Sweet Imperfections discounted product in the café store.

Eli's huge cheesecake bakery, retail store and dessert café is the
only place where you can see Chicago's favorite dessert being
made. Years ago, Eli needed a better dessert to offer his guests in
his steak restaurant. Begin a tour watching an informative slide
show that reviews all the cake-making stations. Then, don a hair
net and sneak a peek through the R&D bakery window - what new
flavor are they working on? Did you know they bake an average of
30 new styles of cheesecake each year (some are not for retail, but
wholesale customers). Now, take a tour of the bakery where
30,000 cheesecakes are made everyday. You walk in and Oh does
it smell good! We discovered their number one ingredient is cream
cheese - their most expensive ingredient is vanilla from overseas.
Watch pans filled with cookie-crust bottoms and topped with cake
batter travel through a 70-foot-long baking tunnel (look at all those
cakes). The desserts then spiral slowly up a dizzying two-story
tower to give them time to cool (it looks like a spiral parking lot).
The cakes are then decorated by hand. Tiramisu cakes are dunked
in giant coffee vats. Can you believe those workers do most
everything by hand? They're so skilled at making the desserts look
so appealing. Finally, return to the café and sample a favorite
cheesecake (who can choose just one favorite?), purchase a
gourmet lunch sandwich or browse in the company store. Small
groups can add Cheesecake Decorate & Take for an additional fee.
What fun to spend an hour in a cake factory!

DUSABLE MUSEUM OF AFRICAN-AMERICAN HISTORY

Chicago - *740 E. 56th Place, 60637. Phone: (773) 947-0600,* **Web:** *www.dusablemuseum.org. Hours: Monday-Saturday 10:00am-5:00pm, Sunday Noon-5:00pm. Miscellaneous: Special events such as Kwanzaa workshops and African American History month celebrations are offered throughout the year.* Families can learn about the culture, historical experience, and achievements of African Americans at this museum. Named for Chicago's first settler Jean Baptiste Point DuSable, the museum features over 10,000 pieces in its permanent collection. Using art forms that trace African-American history, including the Works Progress Administration period of the 1930s and the Civil Rights movement. Performances of music and dance, film presentations, and educational seminars are also offered.

MUSEUM OF SCIENCE & INDUSTRY (MSI)

5700 S. Lake Shore Drive (57th St & Lake Shore Dr) **Chicago** 60637

- ❑ Phone: (773) 684-1414, **Web: www.msichicago.org**
- ❑ Hours: Monday through Saturday 9:30am to 4:00pm.
- ❑ Sunday 11:00am to 4:00pm. Extended hours until 5:30pm on school break days.
- ❑ Admission: $9.00 adult, $7.50 senior (65+), $5.00 child (3-11). Discounts for residents. Special exhibits, Omnimax, Body Worlds and on-board submarine extra fee. Parking $8.00-$12.00.

This museum invites children to push buttons and pull levers on its exhibits which explore contemporary science and technology. Families can walk through a beating heart, tour a captured German submarine, and visit a subterranean coal mine. The Submarine exhibition features audio narratives from war veterans as well as the discovery of two original periscopes, which were hidden beneath one of the Navy's most secret research facilities. Let your imagination run wild at the museum's Idea Factory, look at the Tools of Science, or see how toys are made. In the Space Center, visitors can blast off in a simulated space shuttle ride and view the Apollo 8 spacecraft. A museum within a museum, the National Time Museum is located in the North Court and documents how people have measured time throughout history.

ORIENTAL INSTITUTE MUSEUM, THE

Chicago - *University of Chicago, 1155 East 58th Street, 60637. Phone: (773) 702-9514. Web: www.oi.uchicago.edu. Hours: Tuesday - Saturday 10:00am-6:00pm, Sunday Noon-6:00pm. Open until 8:30pm on Wednesdays. Admission: FREE. Suggested Donation: $5.00 for adults, $2.00 for children under 12.* The Oriental Institute Museum is a showcase of the history, art and archaeology of the ancient Near East.

The galleries showcase artifacts that illustrate the power of these ancient civilizations, including sculptural representations of tributes demanded by kings of ancient empires, and some sources of continual fascination, such as a fragment of the Dead Sea Scrolls--one of the few examples in the United States. Visitors begin in Assyria, move across Anatolia and down the Mediterranean coast to the land of ancient Israel. In Mesopotamia: A wealth of objects from what may be the world's first urban civilization are displayed, including pottery, clay tables, stone sculptures, and vessels made of luxurious stones and metals. It includes exhibits explaining how scholars from the Oriental Institute have conducted excavations and research since the end of the nineteenth century until today, plus two computer kiosks that currently house interactive programs for visiting families. Artifacts from Persia, Egypt and Iraq, too.

CHICAGO KIDS COMPANY

Chicago - *5900 W. Belmont / 111th & Western (St. Patrick's Performing Arts Centre - N / Beverly Arts Center - S), 60641. Phone: (773) 205-9600. Web: www.ChicagoKidsCompany.com. Showtimes: Weekdays at 10:30am, Saturdays at 12:30pm. Admission: $8.00 per person.* Celebrating 15 years of Fairy Tale Fun, this company performs at a North Side and South Side location. Productions like fables of the Tortoise and the Hare or Little Red Riding Hood are done with comical costumes and scenery for the kids to enjoy.

MCDONALD'S #1 STORE MUSEUM

400 N. Lee Street (Des Plaines exit towards downtown off I-294 toll road), **Des Plaines** 60016

❑   Phone: (847) 297-5022

    Web: www.mcdonalds.com/corp/about/museum_info.html

❑   Hours: Open Seasonally (Memorial Day to Labor Day). Call for hours. Thursday, Friday, Saturday 10:30am-2:30pm.

McDonald's #1 Store Museum *(cont.)*

❑   Admission: FREE
❑   Miscellaneous: An operating McDonald's restaurant is located
      across the street from the museum.

McDonald's #1 Store Museum is a recreation of the first McDonald's
Restaurant opened in Des Plaines, Illinois by McDonald's
Corporation founder, Ray Kroc, on April 15, 1955. The original red
and white tiled restaurant building featuring the Golden Arches
underwent several remodels through the years and was finally torn
down in 1984. The present facility was built according to the
original blueprints with some modifications to accommodate
Museum visitors and staff. The "Speedee" road sign is original.
The customer service and food preparation areas contain original
equipment used in the days when fresh potatoes were peeled,
sliced, blanched and fried; milkshake mix and syrup were whipped
up on the Multi-mixers; Coca-Cola® and root beer were drawn
from a barrel, and orangeade from the orange bowl. The all male
crew is represented by mannequins dressed in the 1955 uniform -
dark trousers, white shirts, aprons and paper hats. The basement
features a historical display of photos, memos, early advertising,
memorabilia, and a short video presentation.

HAEGER POTTERY

East Dundee - *Seven Maiden Lane (two blocks south of Rt. 72), 60118.
Phone: (847) 783-5420, **Web: www.haegerpotteries.com**. Hours: Monday,
Thursday, Friday 10:00am-6:00pm. Saturday and Sunday 11:00am-
5:00pm. Closed on Tuesday and Wednesday. Closed on New Year's Day,
Easter, Memorial Day, Labor Day, Thanksgiving, Christmas Eve,
Christmas Day, and December 26th. Admission: FREE. Miscellaneous:
the store offers one of a kind pieces, discontinued items and overstocks at
savings of 20% to 50% on Haeger Artware everyday low prices.* Start in
the Museum: On display are many unique pieces from the past 134 years
of Haeger craftsmanship. You may watch the historical video that details
The Haeger Potteries under four generations of family leadership. They
also are continuously showing our video that leads you through the many
steps of ceramic production.

SANTA'S VILLAGE & RAGING RAPIDS

(I-90 exit Route 25 near Elgin. Go north to intersection of Rte. 72)

East Dundee 60118

❑ Phone: (847) 426-6751, Web: www.santasvillageil.com

❑ Hours: Generally open daily 11:00am-7:00pm (June, July August). Weekends only in May and September.

❑ Admission: Santa's Village Day Pass - $23.50 per person. Racing Rapids Day Pass - $12.95 per person. Combo Day Pass to both Parks - $32.00 per person.

SANTA'S VILLAGE: The Three Worlds of Santa's Village has been a favorite family tradition for over 40 years. Choose Old McDonald's Farm, Coney Island or Santa's World areas filled with over 30 rides in a country setting. Check out the shows like: Boardwalk Magic Review or Santa's Snowstorm Game Show.

RAGING RAPIDS: Adjacent to Santa's Village, this wet and wild adventure park provides splashing fun, bumper boats, water slides and go-carts.

CHILDREN'S THEATRE OF ELGIN

Elgin - *1700 Spartan Drive, VPAC 141A (Hemmons Cultural Center performance hall), 60123. Web: www.cteelgin.com. Phone: (847) 214-7152,* Their mission is to provide high quality theatrical experiences for children and young adults...by children and young adults. They encourage family support and participation in theatre with familiar productions like Sleeping Beauty and Cinderella. Most performances are under $7.00 general admission, making live theatre affordable and accessible.

ELGIN PUBLIC MUSEUM

Elgin - *225 Grand Boulevard (Lords Park area), 60123. Phone: (847) 741-6655, Web: www.elginpublicmuseum.org. Hours: Tuesday-Sunday Noon-4:00pm (summers). Weekends only (rest of year). Admission: $1.00-$2.00.* This 1907 building is the oldest building in the state built as a museum and still serving as a museum. Its exhibits focus on natural history and anthropology with highlights of TyRex, fossils, Ice Age and Native Americans. A discovery room allows for hands-on learning and they have weekly programs for kids and groups. Lords Park is the 120-acre park, adjoining, & host to several festivals (Bubblefest, Native American Fest).

PIRATE'S COVE THEME PARK

Elk Grove Village - *999 Leicester Road (I-290 (IL-53): exit at Exit 4, Biesterfield Road, and head east 1/2 mile to Leicester   Road and turn right), 60007. Web: www.parks.elkgrove.org/pages/piratescove.asp. Phone: (847) 437-9494. Hours: Monday-Saturday 11:00am-5:00pm (mid-June thru mid-August). Admission: $6.00-$8.00.* Take a train ride through the property on Safari Express. (Parents can ride too). In the Castle of Camelot, children can climb through a maze of tunnels, nets, tires, and tubes ... or take a ride down the back of Misty, The Smoking Breathing Dragon. Scale the Smugglers Crag, Pirate's Coves 20-foot high climbing wall. The wall is designed with different skill levels in mind. The Eureka Train Ride directs you around a train track, through a dark tunnel, and past the old Eureka Mine. Paddle Boats take you through Pebble Pond, where you and your friends can ride and splash. There's also a carousel and an authentic 18th Century Pirate Ship - perfect for picnicking or just taking a gander at the Theme Park.

GROSSE POINT LIGHTHOUSE

2601 Sheridan Road (I-94 to the Old Orchard exit turning East to Crawford Avenue then North to Central Street and East to Sheridan Road), **Evanston** 60201

❏   Phone: (847) 328-6961, **Web: www.grossepointlighthouse.org**

❏   Admission: $5.00 adult, $3.00 child (8-12). To go into the lighthouse tower, you must have a reservation and you must be at least 8 years old. You must also be able to hoist yourself up onto the final platform to reach the very top. School groups tours do not allow for the tower climb.

❏   Tours: Saturday and Sunday afternoons at 2:00pm, 3:00pm or 4:00pm (June - September). Grosse Point Lighthouse is not open on holiday weekends.

❏   Miscellaneous: Evanston Beaches - five beaches (Clark St, Greenwood St, South Blvd, Lee St, and Central Street) with bike paths, swimming, boating, picnicking and tennis along Lake Michigan. **www.cityofevanston.org**.

Grosse Point Lighthouse was built by the United States Government in 1873 as the lead lighthouse marking the approach to Chicago after several shipwrecks demonstrated its need. While the grounds around the lighthouse are open on a daily basis, tours of the keepers' quarters museum are open only summer weekends. As part of the tour, visitors get a chance to climb the 141-steps to the top of the light tower for a panoramic view of the Lake Michigan shore and Chicago's soaring skyline. Evanston Beach is just beyond the lighthouse and a popular spot. You may have trouble finding parking nearby on summer weekends.

WILLOWBROOK WILDLIFE CENTER

Glen Ellyn - *525 South Park Boulevard (east side of Park Blvd. Across from College of DuPage, one mile south of Rte. 36, one mile north of Rte. 56), 60137. www.dupageforest.com/education/willowbrook.html. Phone: (630) 942-6200. Hours: Daily, except major holidays 9:00am-5:00pm. Winter hours end at 4:00pm.* When you visit the main building at Willowbrook Wildlife Center, you will be able to view close up over 30 native species of wild animals. Windows provide a view of the Center's kitchen and nursery where baby animals are cared for and fed during spring and summer. Children and adults will enjoy discovering an indoor museum where all the exhibits can be touched. Large permanently disabled animals are displayed outdoors along the nature trail including a golden eagle, bald eagle, hawks, owls, raccoons & foxes. The paved trail is open year-round.

CHICAGO BOTANIC GARDEN

Glencoe - *1000 Lake Cook Road ((I-94) and U.S. Route 41. Exit at Lake Cook Road and travel 1/2 mile east to the Garden), 60022. Phone: (847) 835-5440, Web: www.chicagobotanic.org. Hours: Daily 8:00am-sunset. Admission: FREE. Parking fee $12.00 per vehicle. Tours: The Grand Tram Tour is a tram tour around the perimeter of the Garden which provides an overview of all areas. Trams are wheelchair-accessible. (extra $3.00-$5.00).* The Garden's 385 acres are uniquely situated on nine islands surrounded by 81 acres of lakes, 23 gardens and three native habitats. Stroll or take a tram through the fragrant rose garden, the sensory garden and the stunning three-island Japanese garden. A walking and biking trail borders the gardens.

GREAT LAKES NAVAL MUSEUM

Great Lakes - *Building 158, Camp Berry, U.S. Naval Station (main gate, take Farragut Street to Sampson Street, turn right on Barry Road. Look for signs directing you to the museum and Camp Barry), 60088. Web: www.nsgreatlakes.navy.mil/museum/. Phone: (847) 688-3154 Hours: Friday 1:00-4:00pm, Saturday-Sunday 7:00am-3:00pm. Photo ID required for security. Admission: FREE.* The Naval Training Center Great Lakes Museum Exhibit is a small government-owned and operated museum dedicated to telling the story "boot camp" training in the United States Navy. Although originally one of four boot camps, it is now home to Recruit Training Command, the only Navy recruit training command. A special section of the museum is dedicated to the expanding role of women in the United States Navy.

SERPENT SAFARI

Gurnee - *6170 West Grand Avenue (Exit I-94 at Grand Avenue West to Gurnee Mills. Located at Entry C), 60031. Hours: Daily 10:00am-9:00pm, except Sunday only until 7:00pm. Admission: $6.95 adult, $4.95 child (3-12). Tickets valid all day.* Guided safari tours to visit the world's greatest collection of rare and exotic reptiles, including "Baby," the largest snake in the world, weighing over 400 pounds! See a Nile crocodile, rare albino alligator, 350-pound Anaconda and more. All live and on display. A huge, docile python drapes around kids' shoulders for photo ops.

SIX FLAGS GREAT AMERICA AND HURRICANE HARBOR

(I-94 and Grand Avenue, IL 132 east), **Gurnee** 60031

❑   Phone: (847) 249-INFO, **Web: www.sixflags.com**

❑   Hours: Generally the park opens at 10:00am and closes between 8-10:00pm summers. Water park hours are 11:00am-7:00pm (Memorial Day weekend - Labor Day weekend only). Spring and Fall weekends only, closing at dusk. Fridays in October are 5:00-11:00pm only.

❑   Admission: Generally $30.00-$45.00 per person (age 4+). Admission is good for entrance into both parks. Discounts and season passes available.

Six Flags Great America boasts 13 world class coasters, exciting shows spread throughout the day (relax and cool off) and over 100 rides or attractions. Hurricane Harbor is a lush, tropical setting featuring 25 water slides, the world's largest interactive water playground, a massive wave pool, and a ½ mile long adventure river.

SPRING BROOK NATURE CENTER

Itasca - *130 Forest Avenue (behind the Itasca Library and Water Park at Catalpa Avenue and Irving Park Road), 60143. Phone: (630) 773-2239, Web: www.itasca.com/index1.htm. Hours: Nature Center Tuesday-Sunday 1:00-5:00pm (September-May); 11:30am-5:00pm (June-August). Grounds open sunrise to sunset year round. Admission: FREE.* Park at the Water Park and follow the path south across the bridge to the red barn. Visit their raptor aviary (bald eagles and barn owls) and Visitor Center with an aquarium and interactive displays. Over two miles of trails provide hiking opportunities through a marsh, prairie, woodland and arboretum.

CHICAGOLAND/ ROUTE 66 SPEEDWAY

Joliet - *500 Speedway Blvd., 60431. Phone: (815) 722-5500, Web: www.chicagolandspeedway.com.* This state-of-the-art motor sports facility features a 1.5 mile track that hosts NASCAR, Winston Cup and Indy Racing events. Look for occasional Kid Country events.

JOLIET AREA HISTORICAL MUSEUM

204 N. Ottawa Street (I-55 exit Rte. 52 east on Jefferson to downtown. Over the DesPlaines Bridge, turn left on Joliet Street to Ottawa), **Joliet** 60432

❑   Phone: (815) 722-7003, **Web: www.jolietmuseum.org**
❑   Hours: Tuesday-Saturday 10:00am-5:00pm, Sunday Noon-5:00pm. Closed on Mondays, except for School Holidays.
❑   Admission: $5.00 adult, $4.00 senior (60+) and student w/ ID, $3.00 youth (4-17).
❑   Miscellaneous: Free parking is available in the Museum parking lot located 1 block north of the Museum at the corner of Ottawa and Webster Streets. During your visit stop in the Route 66 Welcome Center.

Begin with a short orientation video. Walk through a life-size replica depicting the building of the historic Illinois Michigan Canal. Stroll down a turn-of-the-century street past store fronts. Take in a silent film at the Rialto Theatre (kids think this is hilarious). Take a virtual ride on a replica trolley that takes you on a tour of the city. Along the way, meet life-size models and interact with touch-screen visuals. Talk of the Town is the award-winning video interactive of virtual conversations with historical townsfolk. The past comes alive as you travel through distinct zones depicting the stages of this area's growth. They include: I&M Canal, City of Stone and Steel, and War history. Check out the Resource and Discovery Room which is packed with activities for children. Try an I Spy Game and loads of crafts. Just a city museum, this is an example of modernizing historical artifacts to engage the kids dramatically. Great job.

JOLIET IRON WORKS HISTORIC SITE

(Located .10 miles east of Route 53 (Scott Street) and .10 miles east of the Ruby Street Bridge, on Columbia Street in downtown Joliet), **Joliet** 60433

❑   Phone: (815) 727-8700, **Web: www.fpdwc.org/ironworks.cfm**
❑   Hours: Summer 8:00am-8:00pm, Winter 8:00am-5:00pm.
❑   Admission: FREE
❑   Miscellaneous: The site is also the access point for the 11.4 mile I&M Canal Trail. This trail - of which portions are paved or crushed stone - connects Joliet's City Center to the Centennial Trail at 135th street in Romeoville.

Joliet is known as the City of Steel and Stone. Rich deposits of limestone led to a thriving quarrying industry. In the years following the Civil War, a huge iron producing industry would employ thousands at the Joliet Iron Works until the 1930s. Follow a 1-mile walkway through the site on a self-guided tour through exhibits explaining the iron making process and describing the men who worked there. Walk among the ruins.

SPLASH STATION WATERPARK

Joliet - *2780 US Route 6 (I-80 E to the Houbolt Road exit. Turn right. Take Houbolt to Route 6 and turn left), 60436. Phone: (815) 741-7275,* **Web: www.jolietsplashstation.com.** *Hours: Daily 11:00am-8:00pm (peak summer break). Weekends 11:00am-6:00pm (border summer weekends). Evenings 4:00-8:00pm (weeknights very end/beginning of school year). Admission: $11.00 general, $7.00 under 48" tall (ages 4+). Resident* *discount about $3.00 each. Twilight (after 5pm) is half price.* Experience the thrill of racing your friends down a 200 foot tower of speed as you glide head first down the track. Stay on track through a series of twists and turns on open or enclosed body and tube slides. Relax and meander along the 850 foot river. But don't be fooled, the rapids lurk ahead! All ages will enjoy a fun afternoon in the 250,000 gallon zero depth pool or sandy play area.

LAMBS FARM

Libertyville - *14245 West Rockland Road (intersection of I-94 and Route 176, you can see it from the highway), 60048. Phone: (847) 362-4636, Web: www.lambsfarm.org. Hours:10:00am to 5:00pm daily during season – closed during winter months. Restaurant closed Mondays.* Lambs Farm is a place that, most importantly, empowers an extraordinary group of more than 250 people with developmental disabilities to lead personally fulfilling lives. Uniquely, Lambs Farm is also a place where families gather to enjoy their many shops and attractions. The fun, affordable family destination features a Farmyard with animals to pet, a large Pet Shop, Country Store & Bakery, Thrift Shop, and the Country Inn Restaurant - serving breakfast and lunch. Enjoy a variety of attractions like mini-golf, a mini-train ride, cow bounce house and an Old World carousel. A great idea.

MORTON ARBORETUM

Lisle - *4100 Illinois Route 53 (I-88 Route 53 exit north), 60532. Phone: (630) 968-0074, Web: www.mortonarb.org. Hours: Daily 9:30am-5:00pm. Admission: $7.00 adult, $4.00 child (3-11).* Morton Arboretum has a great Children's Garden & new Maze Garden, focusing on trees and plants of the Midwest. The special garden is geared towards kids ages 2-10. Let kids lead you through the space after you enter the garden at the Kid's Tree Walk, which leads to Tree Finder Grove. Several of the garden areas include water play areas and play equipment to climb on. One garden highlights backyard nature, another encourages kids to look, listen, feel and smell plants. Play in a corn crop or sand and water play areas. The Adventure Woods highlight wetlands, prairie and forest settings. Kids can hop across a shallow pond on stepping stones or cross a kid-sized bridge leading to a tiny island. Play equipment, treehouses and netted bridges turn one garden into a climbing adventure. It leads to a secret stream where kids can play, then crawl in a net above. The prairie flows into another garden that gives kids access to a rope bridge nestled in the treetops.

GAYLORD BUILDING NATIONAL TRUST HISTORIC SITE

200 West Eighth Street (I-80; take Briggs Street north and turn left on Division Street, right on IL 171 (State Street), then left to the 8th Street parking lot), **Lockport** 60441

- ❑ Phone: (815) 588-1100
  Web: www.canalcor.org/gaylord/index.html
- ❑ Hours: Tuesday-Saturday 10:00am-6:00pm, Sunday Noon-6:00pm.
- ❑ Admission: FREE
- ❑ Miscellaneous: Public Landing Restaurant open for lunch & dinner.

Here, more than 150 years ago, the Gaylord Building played a major role in creation of the Illinois & Michigan Canal. The I & M Canal linked Lake Michigan with the Mississippi River, creating a waterway that opened a prosperous trade route from New York to New Orleans. Shortly after its completion, the railroads dominated the transportation industry. Today the Gaylord Building is a gateway to the I&M Canal National Heritage Corridor. Explore the building's canal exhibits. Relax with a stroll or bike ride along the scenic canal trail.

ILLINOIS STATE MUSEUM LOCKPORT GALLERY.

Lockport - *201 West 10th Street (Historic Norton Bldg) (near the crossroads of IL 7 and 171, downtown), 60441. Phone: (815) 838-7400. Web: www.museum.state.il.us/ismsites/lockport/. Hours: Tuesday-Saturday 10:00am-5:00pm, Sunday Noon-5:00pm. Admission: FREE. Miscellaneous: The facility is directly adjacent to the Illinois & Michigan Canal, the Gaylord Donnelley Historical Trail, as well as other nearby historic sites and shopping opportunities.* This branch site of the Illinois State Museum features many works created by past and contemporary Illinois artists. The rotating exhibits showcase paintings, drawings, sculpture, textiles, and decorative objects.

KIDDIELAND

Melrose Park - *8400 West North Avenue (corner of First and North), 60160. Phone: (708) 343-8000. Web: www.kiddieland.com. Hours: Generally opens at 11:00am, closing at dark (summer months). Weekends only in May and October. Admission: $17.25-$20.25. $3.00 off after 5:00pm. Free Pepsi drinks and parking.* Open for over 75 years, the park offers fun for the whole family with more than 30 rides and attractions including classic 1925 carousel, a Ferris wheel, the Pipeline water coaster, many classic kiddie rides and midway games.

DUPAGE CHILDREN'S MUSEUM

Naperville - *301 North Washington Street, 60540. Phone: (630) 637-8000. Web: www.dupagechildrensmuseum.org. Hours: Monday 9:00am-1:00pm, Tuesday-Saturday 9:00am-5:00pm, Sunday Noon-5:00pm. Thursdays until 8:00pm. Admission: $6.00-$7.00 (age 1+).* The DuPage Children's Museum has 3 floors made up of different exhibit neighborhoods - each one special in its own way. Each neighborhood is packed with exciting ways to explore art, math, science and how they work together in the world. Explore Your Home, Airways, Waterways, Build It, Make It Move and Creativity Connections.

NAPER SETTLEMENT

523 S. Webster Street (I-355 or I-88/290, follow signs to entrance located at Aurora Ave. and Webster St.), **Naperville** 60540

❑   Phone: (630) 305-4044, **Web: www.napersettlement.museum**

❑   Hours: Tuesday-Saturday 10:00am-4:00pm, Sunday 1:00-4:00pm (April-October). Tuesday-Friday only (November-March). Closed New Year's, Thanksgiving and Christmas.

❑   Admission: $7.00 adult, $6.00 senior, $4.50 youth (4-17) - peak. $4.25 adult, $3.75 senior, $3.00 youth - winter.

❑   Tours: Optional Audio Tour available for $3.00.

Naper Settlement tells the story of how life changed for people in towns such as Naperville throughout the 19th century. From frontier to bustling town, costumed villagers interpret life and answer questions or tell stories that bring the past to life. The paths of the 13-acre village are dotted with more than 30 structures that range from an early log house to a Victorian mansion. Climb aboard a Conestoga wagon, visit Fort Payne, drop in for class at a one-room schoolhouse or tour a working print shop. Stop in the History Connection to participate in hands-on activities such as building a log cabin or dressing up in old-fashioned clothes.

FULLERSBURG WOODS ENVIRONMENTAL EDUCATIONAL CENTER & GRAUE MILL

3609 Spring Road (between York Road and 31st Street (Oak Brook Road), **Oak Brook** 60523

❑   Phone: (630) 850-8110 or 630-655-2090 (mill)
    Web: www.grauemill.org

❑   Hours: The entry gate opens one hour after sunrise and closes one hour after sunset. The visitor center is open daily from 9:00am-5:00pm except on the Fourth of July, Thanksgiving, Christmas Eve, Christmas Day and New Year's Day. Graue Mill is open daily except Monday 10:00am-4:30pm (mid April to mid-November).

❑   Admission: FREE for Visitors Center. Fee for Mill ($1.50-$3.50).

The newly remodeled Fullersburg Woods Visitor Center is a modern, interactive facility that provides an introduction to the local environment. Visitors can examine the reconstructed remains of a 13,000-year-old woolly mammoth to learn about DuPage County's natural history or can use microscopes and spotting scopes to examine some of the creatures that call the forest preserves home today.

INTERPRETIVE TRAIL - Taking a self-guided tour of this 1.3 mile trail through lowland woods and restored prairies by foot, bicycle or cross-country skis is a good way to learn about DuPage County's natural history. Most of the trail follows Salt Creek, providing visitors with the chance to see beavers, various waterfowl and other creatures.

GRAUE MILL - Travel the 0.5-mile walk along the banks of Salt Creek to visit Graue Mill. Along the way, stop to read the signs that highlight the area's cultural history. The Mill is the only water-powered grist mill in Illinois that still grinds corn daily. Catch a live demonstration or look over exhibits. Iron clothes or try to decide what to purchase from Sears and Roebuck catalogs. After the miller's demo, maybe purchase some ground corn meal to use at home (recipes included). The Mill recently opened an expanded exhibit entitled "The Graue Mill and the Road to Freedom." This new exhibit, using photographs, documents, video, books, music, a computer interactive system and additional displays relates the importance of the Graue Mill and DuPage County in assisting fugitive slaves to escape to freedom.

FRANK LLOYD WRIGHT HOME AND STUDIO

Oak Park - *951 Chicago Avenue (I290 west to Harlem Ave/Rte 43 exit. Head northwest 1.5 miles to right on Chicago Ave. Head 3 blocks east), 60302. Web: www.wrightplus.com/homestudio/homestudio.html. Phone: (708) 848-1976. Hours: Closed Thanksgiving, Christmas, New Year's, and the last week in January for Preservation in Action. Admission: $10.00-$12.00 per person (age 7+). Tours: Weekdays 11:00am, 1:00pm, 3:00pm. Weekends Approximately every 20 minutes from 11:00am to 3:30pm. Tour length 45-60 minutes. All tours start at Gingko Tree Book Shop @ the Home. Interior photography is not permitted. Miscellaneous: Historic District Self-Guided Exterior Audio Tour available for additional $6.00-$8.00.* Tour the place where Frank Lloyd Wright lived and worked for the first 20 years of his career. Wright used his home as an architectural laboratory, experimenting with design concepts that contain the seeds of his architectural philosophy. Here he raised six children with his first wife, Catherine Tobin. In 1898, Wright added a studio, described by a fellow-architect as a workplace with "inspiration everywhere." In the Studio, Wright and his associates developed a new American architecture: the Prairie style, and designed 125 structures, including such famous buildings as the Robie House, the Larkin Building and Unity Temple. The restored early 1900s building has a light-filled octagonal drafting room and an adorable barrel-vaulted playroom. We'd recommend this for older kids who have studied architectural styles.

HEMINGWAY BIRTHPLACE HOME & MUSEUM

339 N. Oak Park Avenue, **Oak Park** 60302

❑   Phone: (708) 848-2222

   Web: www.ehfop.org/birthplace/index.html

❑   Hours: Sunday- Friday 1:00pm-5:00pm, Saturday 10:00am–
   5:00pm. Closed New Year's, Christmas Day, Easter Sunday,
   Fourth of July and Thanksgiving.

❑   Admission: $5.50-$7.00 per person (age 6+).

HOME: Take a moment and stand in front of this beautiful Queen Anne style residence, with its expansive porch and grand turret and be prepared to take a small step back into time. The museum and home focus on Hemingway's first 20 years spent in Oak Park through the collection of photographs, letters, memorabilia and his earliest writings. The home, designed by architect Wesley Arnold and built around 1890 for Ernest Hall, Hemingway's maternal grandfather, maintains many of its original features that even Ernest would find familiar.

MUSEUM: Just a short walk from the birthplace, the Ernest Hemingway Museum is host to permanent and temporary exhibits that explore the author's life. Kiosks fashioned from historic doors hold exhibits of rare photos and artifacts, including Hemingway's childhood diary and the famous letter from nurse Agnes von Kurowsky-later portrayed in "A Farewell to Arms" - terminating their engagement.

WONDER WORKS

Oak Park - *6445 West North Avenue (Harlem Avenue North. Turn east on North Avenue and go approximately 0.4 miles), 60302. Phone: (708) 383-4815,* **Web:** *www.wonder-works.org. Hours: Wednesday-Saturday 10:00am-5:00pm, Sunday Noon-5:00pm. Admission: $5.00 per person.* Wonder Works is a children's museum with permanent exhibits such as Lights, Camera, Action; Farm to Market; Build it; Arts Area; and the Great Outdoors. Become royalty, a dancer or a wild animal on stage or man the lights and sounds to create a never-before-seen production. Pick apples and buy, sell and barter fruits and vegetables the farm stand. Camp out in a tent or climb up in the tree house as you experience the secrets of the great outdoors.

ILLINOIS PHILHARMONIC ORCHESTRA

Park Forest - *377 Artists Walk (performances at Performing Arts Center and High School venues), 60466. Phone: (708) 481-7774,* **Web:** *www.ipomusic.org.* Plan a field trip to the Illinois Philharmonic Orchestra's Annual Concert for Kids! Enjoy a 45 minute kid-friendly symphony concert featuring the award-winning Illinois Philharmonic Orchestra, and hear lively commentary Maestro Carmon DeLeone! All attendees receive complimentary program book complete with music games, and educational factoids. The ensemble also performs a series of chamber, pop and orchestral music - some served with ice cream. Student tickets around $15.00.

ISLE A LA CACHE MUSEUM

Romeoville - *501 E. Romeo Road (.5 miles east of Route 53), 60441.* Phone: (815) 886-1467, **Web:** *www.fpdwc.org/isle.cfm.* Hours: Tuesday-Saturday 10:00am-4:00pm, Sunday Noon-4:00pm. Admission: FREE. "Island of the Hiding Place" - this mysterious title is the translation of the French phrase Isle a la Cache. Inside the Museum, explore exhibits of the French fur trade. Find out about a voyager's day on the river; examine a real birch bark canoe; see the trade items of metal, beads, and cloth that changed the Native American's lifestyle. Step inside a Native American wigwam where you can play native games or dress-up in period clothing. Touch the soft, silky fur of a beaver and realize for yourself why Europeans desired this waterproof coat. Children can take part in a "trade" and understand the value of items for different cultures and experience Native American life while visiting an 18th Century replica longhouse. Isle a la Cache Museum. Find out how cultural history shaped the region and you can picnic, fish and canoe on the property.

ATCHER ISLAND WATER PARK

Schaumburg - *730 S. Springinsguth, 60193.* Phone: 847-985-2135 **Web:** *www.parkfun.com/dir/fit/ww/atcher.html.* Hours: Monday-Friday 11:00am -8:30pm, Weekends Noon-8:00pm (mid-June thru 3rd week in August). Admission: $7.00-9.00 per person. $2.00 per person discount for resident. Each summer, spend some time relaxing on a tropical island. Atcher Island is the Schaumburg Park District's all-new tropical themed water park with water slides, a unique circular drop slide (we call them toilet bowls), children's spray ground (doesn't that just sound like fun?) and more. Remodeled from the ground up with a Polynesian feel, forget your worries and lounge poolside, or feel the rush of plunging down a slide. Refreshments and concessions are available on site.

SCHAUMBURG FLYERS

Schaumburg - *Alexian Field, 1999 S. Springinsguth Road, 60193.* **Web:** *www.flyersbaseball.com.* Phone: (847) 891-2255 or (877) 691-2255. Catch the fun and bat-cracking action of minor-league pro baseball played May through September. Small admission charged. Lots of fun games & antics after each inning.

SPRING VALLEY NATURE CENTER & HERITAGE FARM

1111 E. Schaumburg Road (farm @ 201 S. Plum Grove Road)

Schaumburg 60194

❑ Phone: (847) 985-2100, **Web: www.parkfun.com**
❑ Hours: Trails open 8:00am-5:00pm (open until 8:00pm summers). Farm open Monday-Friday 9:00am-2:00pm, Weekends 10:00am-4:00pm (April-October).
❑ Admission: FREE

Step back in time and see the landscape as the first pioneers saw it...tall grass and wildflowers. Listen to the sounds of frogs and gliding blue heron at the edge of the marsh...help to milk a cow...prepare a meal on a wood cookstove. Walk the 3 miles of accessible trails viewing wildflower-studded prairies, quiet woodlands, and wetlands bustling with wildlife. We'd highly recommend the .7 mile trail between the Farm and Nature Center. You feel immersed in a tall prairie - probably the best example we've seen in the whole state - that you could walk through. The nature center (open 9:00am-5:00pm) museum contain exhibits and trail guide booklets. On a visit to Volkening Heritage farm, you can help with seasonal farm chores, participate in family activities and games of the 1880s or simply visit the livestock and soak in the quiet. Authentically dressed interpreters welcome and guide visitors through the site. Many programs are held at the re-created 19th century farm, complete with antique farm equipment and a furnished farmhouse.

MEDIEVAL TIMES DINNER & TOURNAMENT

2001 North Roselle Road (I-90 Roselle Road, north of tollway)

Schaumburg 60195

❑ Phone: (847) 882-0202 or (888) WE JOUST
   Web: www.medievaltimes.com
❑ Shows: Generally Wednesday-Friday at 7:30pm (summers). Evening and/or Matinee show on weekends and holidays. School year only weekends and holiday shows.

For updates & travel games, visit: **www.KidsLoveTravel.com**

❑   Admission: Adults: $50.95 adult, $35.95 child (12 & under). Tax
    & gratuity not included. Includes dinner, beverages, & live show.

❑   Miscellaneous: Due to some choreographed fighting scenes in the
    tournament, small children may be frightened by the bashing
    sounds of sword against sword (*it appears very real!*).

You'll know you've arrived when the European-style castle front
appears on the horizon. This show transports guests back 900 years
to a time when chivalry was honored and knights performed daring
feats to entertain the lords and ladies of the court. As you are
assigned seating, you'll also be assigned a knight to cheer for and a
"take home" crown to wear to show your support. You will sit with
others who join cheers of support for your chosen knight of the
realm. Serfs and wenches dressed in period costumes serve guests a
feast of fresh vegetable soup, roasted chicken, spare rib, herb basted
potato, a pastry and beverages. In order to honor medieval tradition,
guests eat their meals without silverware (your kids will love *having
to eat with their hands!*). As the lights dim, the story begins with the
battle-weary King and his Knights returning to the Castle. The King
calls for a grand tournament to determine the realm's new champion.
As everyone is feasting, the Knights spar in tournament games and
jousts. As the plot unfolds - we all hope truth, honor and love will
eventually triumph over evil, and peace restored. The villain is
revealed in the final minutes of the show bringing the crowd to their
feet - cheering for the brave hero who defends the castle! The
beautiful Andalusian horses and quick displays of choreographed
sword and jousting ability make this show so engaging!

SKOKIE NORTHSHORE SCULPTURE PARK

Skokie - *(east side of McCormick Blvd between Dempster St and
Touhy Ave), 60076. Web: www.sculpturepark.org. Phone: (847) 679-
4265, Hours: Daily during daylight hours. Admission: FREE.* This unique
facility combines recreational features with an outstanding exhibition of
large scale contemporary sculpture. Plan a visit to walk, bike or jog on
our two miles of pathways and enjoy the more than 72 world class
sculptures you will see along the way. Is it a plant, an animal, or a robot?
What materials were used? Many of these are made (recycled) from found
objects put in the trash. With names like "Weee" and the terribly unusual
shapes - your kids will run to see the name of the next sculpture on the trail.

FOX RIVER TROLLEY MUSEUM

South Elgin - *361 South LaFox Street (IL 31) ((I-90) or US Route 20 west to Elgin. Exit on Illinois Route 31 southbound), 60177. Phone: (847) 697-4676. Web: www.foxtrolley.org. Hours: Saturdays, Sundays and Holidays - seasonally, afternoons. Admission: $2.00-$3.50.* Celebrating more than 100 years of electric trolleys, experience the sights and sounds of this unique part of American history aboard a genuine old-time trolley car which takes you on a four mile trip along the banks of the scenic Fox River and the Blackhawk Forest Preserve. The museum operates a variety of antique trolleys, many from lines long vanished, over tracks that once connected Carpentersville, Elgin, Aurora, and Yorkville.

SAND RIDGE NATURE CENTER

South Holland - *15891 Paxton Avenue (On Paxton Ave. two blocks north of 159th St), 60473. Phone: (708) 868-0621, Web: www.fpdcc.com. Hours: Daily, except Fridays. Basically 9:00am-4:00pm. Later hours in the summer. Closed Friday and Saturday in winter.* Sand Ridge Nature Center is a 235-acre preserve with four well-marked trails offering easy hiking, from under a mile to 2 miles long. Each trail features different habitats, including prairies, oak savannas and woodlands, marshes, a pond, and ancient sand dunes. Within the modern Nature Center building, the Exhibit Room houses interpretive displays, as well as native local wildlife including snakes, turtles, and fish. A Kids Corner features hands-on activities, displays and animal puppets, and puzzles. Outside, visitors can stroll through a colorful butterfly garden, and enjoy a vegetable garden and herb garden displaying plants used by pioneers and Native Americans. There are several reproduction log cabins on site, which depict the lifestyles of early 19th century settlers in Illinois. Pioneer demonstrations are held most Wednesday mornings (May-November).

ST CHARLES BELLE AND FOX RIVER QUEEN

St. Charles - *Potawatomie Park (four blocks north of Route 64 and three blocks west of Route 25), 60174. Phone: (630) 584-2334 www.st-charlesparks.org/links/paddlewheelriverboats.htm. Tours: Public Afternoon Sightseeing Trips: Four-Mile sightseeing trips of the scenic Fox River Valley are about 50 minutes long and depart from Pottawatomie Park. No reservations are necessary. $4.50-$6.00 per passenger. Daily afternoons in summer, weekends /holidays only in spring and fall.* Come aboard and enjoy travel from the era of Mark Twain on one of the daily afternoon sightseeing trips. Two double-decker paddle wheelers that you can ride are replicas of steamboats that ran on the river a century ago. Both boats have open-air upper decks for unobstructed sightseeing and the lower decks have windows that can be closed in cool or rainy weather.

VOLO AUTO MUSEUM

Volo - *27582 Volo Village Road (Route 12 on Highway 120, 13 miles west of I-94), 60073. Phone: (815) 385-3644, Web: www.volocars.com. Hours: Daily 10:00am-5:00pm except Easter, Thanksgiving and Christmas. Admission: $7.95 adult, $5.95 senior, veteran, military (w/ID), $3.95 child (6-13). FREE for any kid under 6 and military personnel in uniform.* After purchasing tickets, the first building you walk is the Kids Hollywood Museum, which is probably the kids favorite space (Scooby Doo Mystery Machine, Batmobile, General Lee and such). They claim the world's largest collection of muscle cars on exhibit and they have a nice growing tribute to military called Military Adventure.

TEMPEL LIPIZZANS STALLION SHOW

Wadsworth - *17000 Wadsworth Road (I-94 exit Rte. 173), 60083. Web: www.tempelfarms.com. Phone: (847) 623-7272 or (847) 244-5330. Shows: Wednesdays at 10:30am or Sundays at 1:00pm (late June - August). Admission: $16.00 adult, $14.00 senior (65+), $9.00 child (4-14). Off season guided tours $9.00 adult, $6.00 child. Tours: Off season Tours: Tuesday and Thursday mornings throughout the off-season between 9:00 and 10:00am.* Watch the famous Lipizzan stallions of Europe (WWII fame) perform their intricate, controlled 70 minute performances followed by a self-guided tour of the farm. Held outdoors on a beautiful farm in an arena with bleacher seating (held in the indoor arena if poor weather), you'll see how 4-year olds train and older horses dance. How did they inherit their high step? This is a slow, quiet performance for the horse lover to really enjoy. Consider your child's age and interest level (younger children may find this type of formal show boring).

LAKE COUNTY DISCOVERY MUSEUM

Wauconda - *Fairfield Road and IL 176 (Lakewood Forest Preserve), 60084. Web: www.lakecountydiscoverymuseum.org. Phone: (847) 968-3400. Hours: Monday-Saturday 11:00am-4:30pm, Sunday 1:00-4:30pm. Admission: $6.00 adult, $2.50 youth (4-17). Admission is $2.50 for seniors after 2:00pm. Discount Tuesdays.* Visit the Discovery Museum and take a ride through 10,000 years of Lake County history at the Vortex Roller Coaster Theater. This award-winning museum provides the same experience you'd expect from a big-city museum. Hands-on interactive exhibits educate and entertain. Learn about the Native American and pioneer families who first settled the area. Be sure to look for the nation's largest public collection of postcards.

BILLY GRAHAM CENTER MUSEUM

500 East College Avenue (I-355 south at Schaumburg. West on Roosevelt Road thru Glen Ellyn, past President Street, to Washington Street. Turn north towards campus), **Wheaton** 60187

❑   Phone: (630) 752-5909

     Web: http://bgc.gospelcom.net/museum/index.htm

❑   Hours: Monday-Saturday 9:30am-5:30pm, Sunday 1:00-5:00pm. Closed Thanksgiving Day and between Christmas & New Years. Call on other holidays.

❑   Admission: $1.00-$4.00 suggested donation. $10.00 family.

A visit to the Billy Graham Center Museum begins in the reception area, which houses a Temporary Exhibit gallery for changing displays. As you journey through the Museum, your first stop will be in the Rotunda of Witnesses, which houses nine displays of great witnesses for the Gospel. From here, you'll proceed to the History of Evangelism in America section, where you will see an array of historical images and artifacts that the museum has collected over the years. At the end of this section, you'll encounter the lovely presentation of the basic Christian message in the Cross of the Millennium. From here, you'll enter a major section of the Museum which highlights the Life and Ministry of Billy Graham. As you leave the Billy Graham display, you'll encounter a powerful depiction of the needs of our world and be challenged to personal evangelism. A final theater presentation in this section captures the highlights of crusades from around the world. What path will you choose? The last leg of your journey through the Museum takes you on a Walk through the Gospel, with a stirring three dimensional presentation of the Christian message. A small chapel and bookstore greet you as you end your tour.

KLINE CREEK FARM

Wheaton - *600 S County Farm Road (Entrance on County Farm Rd.,north of Geneva Rd. on west side (just south of St. Charles Rd.), 60187. Web: www.dupageforest.com/education/klinecreek.html. Phone: (630) 876-5900. Hours: Thursday-Monday 9:00am-5:00pm. Admission: FREE, donations accepted. Tours: The house and summer kitchen are available for guided tours only. Those tours are available from 9:00am – 4:00pm daily when the farm is open.* The Forest Preserve District of DuPage County has combined original structures, authentic re-creations, livestock and historically accurate activities into a realistic 1890's DuPage County working farm. Costumed interpreters depict lifestyles around each building. The self-guided tour brochure is available at the entrance and at the farmstead. Kline Creek Farm offers 50 weekends of theme-based programs and activities each year. These activities are seasonal in nature. Activities include sausage and butter making; canning and processing garden produce; hay making; and the social occasions of holidays.

WHEATON HISTORY CENTER

Wheaton - *606 North Main Street (between North Avenue and Roosevelt Road), 60187. Phone: (630) 682-9472. Web: www.wheaton.lib.il.us/whc. Hours: Monday - Wednesday 10:00am - 4:00pm. Admission: $5.00 (age 9+).* The past comes alive with tours and hands-on activities. The museum's highlighted exhibit is "The Liberty Line: The Slaves' Road to Freedom" depicting the hazardous journey from a southern plantation to freedom in the North. Many other exhibits focus on abolitionists of that time in Illinois.

ILLINOIS BEACH STATE PARK

Lake Front (Take I-94 to Rt.173 east. Follow Rt. 173 to Sheridan Rd.), **Zion** 62863

❑ Phone: (708) 662-4811

   Web: http://dnr.state.il.us/lands/landmgt/parks/r2/ilbeach.htm

❑ Admission: Admission to Illinois State Parks is free. Camping fees range from $6.00-11.00 per night, depending on amenities; a $5.00 fee is charged for camping reservations.

❑ Miscellaneous: North Point Marina, located north of the state park, is a full-service marina. Considered one of the finest and largest floating docks in North America, the site also has restaurants, swimming beaches, charters, sport courts, picnic areas and access to bike or hiking trails. (847) 746-2845.

Illinois Beach stretches for six and a half miles along the sandy shore of Lake Michigan in Northern Illinois. Illinois Beach State Park encompasses the only remaining beach ridge shoreline left in the state...including dunes. The Dead River winds through the preserve creating a unique wetland habitat for many endangered species. Nature walks and guided tours through the preserve are available to the public on the weekends all summer long. 4,160-acres of beauty provide visitors with an opportunity for swimming, boating, picnicking, hiking, fishing, or just enjoying the beauty of nature. Illinois Beach also offers camping in a beautifully wooded campground where both tent and RV camping are welcome. (see separate listing for the resort accommodations).

SUGGESTED LODGING AND DINING

HAMPTON INN & SUITES. 2423 Bushwood Drive, **Aurora**. (I-88 exit Orchard Rd. south one block). **www.hamptoninnandsuitesaurora.com**. (630) 907-2600. This is a wonderful place for kids to stay with their parents when staying overnight in Chicagoland. Not only are the rooms spacious, but they have a frig, microwave and huge free breakfast offering fresh pastry, fruit and hot items that change each morning. The staff even comes around and serves coffee cake just out of the oven. The best part, though, is the pool area. They have a gated area just for kids - a mini water park with a soft frog slide, a water umbrella and water spouts. The other warm pool is for laps or noodle fun (they supply the noodles) with a large, very hot adjoining hot tub for parent relaxation. Most rooms under $99.00 per night. Family Value Package - add $10.00-$20.00.

BUBBA GUMP SHRIMP COMPANY - 700 E. Grand Avenue, Navy Pier area, **Chicago**. **www.bubbagump.com**. (312) 252-GUMP. Step into the world of Forrest Gump and enjoy barbeque ribs, fish and chips, and lots of shrimp! Casual, fun atmosphere with down-home southern bayou cookin'. Order the Hush Pups as an appetizer and finish your meal with the Warm, Giant Chocolate Chip Cookie dessert (share as a family). Order anything Cajun or with shrimp as an entrée. See how many "words of wisdom" you can catch while viewing Forrest Gump movie or looking for sayings around the themed restaurant. Kids menu is around $5.00. Daily lunch & dinner.

GIORDANO'S - Throughout town. **Chicago**. (more than 40 locations - if you're visiting the Sears Tower, there's one across the street on Jackson that really captures the aura of the city). **www.giordanos.com**. Pioneer of the famous stuffed pizza. You have to try this pizza! Be sure to order more than just cheese. Try to order something like their Special or another choice with several fresh ingredients. Pastas, sandwiches and assorted salads, too. Open for lunch and dinner.

MARCHE - 833 W. Randolph Street, **Chicago**. (west on Randolph from downtown, just past I-90/94). **www.marche-chicago.com**. (312) 226-8399. French fare amid whimsical designs and a circus-like atmosphere. You'll love the funky music and décor - which umbrella is your favorite? Classics include steak (most with demi-glaze that is outstanding!) but they also serve escargot, rabbit and lamb prepared in a classic French style. So, why bring kids? They do have a large kids menu with most items around/under $5.00. They serve American items such as grilled cheese or spaghetti. Probably 8-10 items total. We'd highly recommend the Mac 'n Cheese - French creamy style - so smooth! If your family likes to try new things in an eclectic atmosphere, you'll want to try Marche. Most of our food was the best we've ever had! Weekday lunch, Daily (except Sunday) dinner. Gourmet entrée pricing. Note: When making reservations, be sure to check that no special "adults only" events are scheduled that day. Lunch and early dinner seating are the best times for families.

SHERATON CHICAGO HOTEL & TOWERS - 301 E. North Water Street (& Columbus Street), **Chicago**. **www.sheratonchicago.com** (312) 464-1000. Gorgeous view of Navy Pier, Lake Michigan and the Chicago River! Indoor pool and very puffy beds to come back to each evening. Several restaurants are on the property and Walgreens is across the parking lot. This location is within blocks of the Magnificent Mile and Navy Pier. Just a trolley or water taxi from the Sears Tower and the Museum Campus. Great central location to base from. $129.00-$189.00.

HILTON GARDEN INN. 2425 Barrington Road, **Hoffman Estates**. (I-90 exit Barrington Rd, head north). **www.hoffmanestates.gardeninn.com**. (847) 277-7889. The hotel offers comfortable, spacious guest rooms, heated indoor pool and whirlpool, and a refrigerator/micro oven in every room. Great location to base from for shopping/dining at Woodfield Mall, Medieval Times, Nature Centers, waterparks and the zoo. Average $149+.

RAINFOREST CAFÉ. Woodfield Shopping Center (near Mall), **Schaumburg**. (847) 619-1900 or **www.rainforestcafe.com**. A theme restaurant and wildlife preserve filled with live and mechanical animals; ongoing rainstorms; hand-sculpted cave-like rock; a caw from tropical birds; many colored live fish (in tanks) and watch out for the large animals "rumbles." Order anything tropical (we especially recommend chicken and the Appetizer Adventure) and save room for the Sparkling Volcano dessert! They even give groups (pre-arranged) educational tours uncovering misconceptions and mysteries about the rainforest. Educators - they offer discount meals for groups and curriculum, too!

DELL RHEA'S CHICKEN BASKET, Willowbrook. (I-55 & Rte 83, behind the Holiday Inn). (630) 325-0780 or **www.chickenbasket.com**. "Get you chicks on Route 66." It got its humble beginnings sometime in the late 1930's or early 1940's in an old gas station lunch counter. One day two local farm women came in and overheard the owner (Irv Kolarik) talking about selling more food. Having a wonderful recipe for fried chicken they approached him and offered to teach him how to cook fried chicken if he would buy his chickens from them. Because the fried chicken was so good and the highway so busy, the Chicken Basket outgrew its lunch counter and the 2 car repair bays were turned into a dining room. Not long after that, with the restaurant still growing, the adjacent land was purchased and a brand new restaurant was built. The Chicken Basket as it is today opened in the summer of 1946 on Illinois Route 66. Burgers and fried fish are on the menu but the people come for the chicken, on the bone or off, breaded, fried and served with homestyle sides. Average $8.00 meal or $4.00 kids meal. Lunch and dinner every day but Mondays.

ILLINOIS BEACH RESORT. Zion. (847) 625-7300 or (866) ILBEACH or **www.ilresorts.com/index.html**. The Illinois Beach Resort and Conference Center was recently renovated and is located on a portion of our South Unit beach to provide guests with a beautiful view over the waters of Lake Michigan. It offers a restaurant (with the best view), large indoor pool, whirl pool, and weight room. Resort guests also have 24-hour access to the beach. We recommend morning and early evening walks - so beautiful and peaceful. Note: even in the summer, the water only gets to about 70 degrees - too cold to swim for most adults, but a great way to cool off. Other amenities include a gift shop, game room, in-room movies and video games, miles of nature trails, sandy beach, and bicycle trails for your enjoyment. Rooms run $85.00-$129.00 per night. Lake View Suite (upcharge): Suites include a king bed, separate living room with sofa, a lake view and balcony. Also included in the rooms are a refrigerator, microwave, large bathroom, and Jacuzzi jets in the tub.

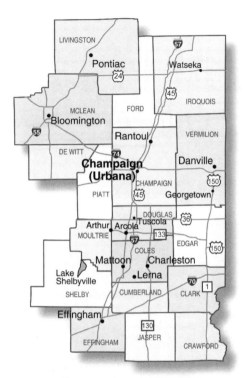

Chapter 3
East Central Area (EC)

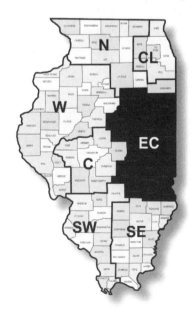

Our Favorites...

* Raggedy Ann & Andy Museum - Arcola

* Amish Country - Arcola / Arthur

* Lincoln-Douglas Debate Museum - Charleston

* Lincoln Log Cabin State Historical Site - Lerna

* Hardy's Reindeer Ranch - Rantoul

Anybody seen my missing reindeer?

BALLARD NATURE CENTER

Altamont - *5253 East US Highway 40 (east of town), 62411. Phone: (618) 483-6856. Web: www.ballardnaturecenter.org. Hours: Center open Monday-Friday 8:00am-4:00pm. Trails open daily dawn to dusk. Admission: Donation suggested.* The Ballard Nature Center consists of 210 acres, including 100 acres of woodland, 15 acres of restored prairie, 10 acres of shallow water wetlands and 85 acres of agricultural land. The 4,300 square foot handicapped accessible building includes a library, bird viewing area, and an exhibit room, featuring interpretive displays on various interesting "bits of nature" relevant to the area. Walking trails through prairie, woodlands, and wetlands are available, and interpretive trails are being developed.

ILLINOIS AMISH INTERPRETIVE CENTER

111 South Locust St (I-57 exit 203, head west to town), **Arcola** 61910

❑ Phone: (888) 45-Amish, **Web: www.amishcenter.com**

❑ Hours: Monday through Saturday 9:00am-5:30pm. Closed Sundays and some holidays.

❑ Admission: $2.25-$2.75 (age 6+).

❑ Miscellaneous: Curious still? Make your own tour by asking for the Amish Country map highlighted by staff here, or at the visitors center next door. Stop in at various Amish businesses, look around, watch them work, & maybe purchase items homemade.

This is the first museum in Illinois dedicated to the Amish culture. It traces the history of the Amish religion and provides a glimpse into the lives of the Illinois Amish. A fifteen minute video on the Amish helps to separate fact from myth about their culture. The Simple People feel the way to heaven is to be in this world, not of this world. The People of the Book cherish their books, especially the Bible. They use horses vs. machinery and keep their farming costs down. One of the oldest known Amish suits and a rare 100 year old buggy are on display along with a view of the inside of a typical Amish home. This is a good way to start a visit to Illinois Amish Country. Next, arrange for a group tour. The Amish work the rich farmland of the area with teams of six to eight horse hitches, and the Amish's horse-drawn, black buggies are a common sight around the Amish country. Sit at long tables as one big, happy family and enjoy the warmth of a country meal at a real

Amish Home. Traverse the Countryside with a ride-along tour guide. Tour the Home of an Amish family. Check out hardwood floors, gas lighting, gas stove and refrigerator. Houses are sparsely furnished, furniture is plain colored, with no prints.

RAGGEDY ANN AND ANDY MUSEUM, JOHNNY GRUELLE'S

110 East Main Street (I-57 exit 203, west on SR 133, right on Locust, left on E. Main), **Arcola** 61910

❑   Phone: (217) 268-4908, **Web: www.raggedyann-museum.org**
❑   Hours: Tuesday-Saturday 10:00am-5:00pm. Closed Sunday, Monday, major holidays and winter.
❑   Admission: $1.00 donation.

While you're here in Amish country, why not learn about Johnny Gruelle, the imaginative storyteller who originated Raggedy Ann & Andy. This wholesome, old-fashioned site is the only officially licensed Raggedy Ann & Andy museum in the world! The Country Store displays many decades of Raggedy merchandising (even canned goods) and "For the Heart's Sake" tells the story of the five generations of Gruelle artists and what their creative philosophy was. Now, wander through some rooms portraying aspects of the doll or creator's life. Marcella's Room is the imagined corner of a girl's bedroom from 1908-1912. It is based on Johnny's drawings of bedrooms in the Raggedy Ann Stories. Visit Johnny's Studio set in time at 1930-1932 and an interpretation of the one he had in his Miami Beach home. Using the Deep Deep Woods theme, display cases give the chronology of Raggedy Ann showing the creation, development, and use of the character from her earliest prototypes in 1914 to the present. In 2005, this adorable and interesting museum celebrated Raggedy Ann's 90th anniversary! Be sure to bring some spending money, girls.

ROCKOME GARDENS

125 North Country Road 425 East (I-57 exit 203, head west)

Arcola 61910

❑ Phone: (217) 268-4106, **Web: www.rockome.com**

❑ Hours 9:00am to 5:00pm weekdays & 9:00am to 5:30pm weekends. Restaurant Hours 11:00am - 7:00pm. (early May - mid-October) Closed on Mondays & Tuesday except during summer.

❑ Admission: $5.00 adult, $4.00 senior (62+), $3.00 child (4-12). Each activity requires an additional fee: Buggy Ride $4.00; Train Ride $3.00; Haunted Cave $2.75; Amish Home $2.75. Save $4.00-$5.00 with combo pricing.

❑ Miscellaneous: Our favorite part - the Horse Powered Buzzsaw - ride the horse as the action cuts a piece of wood that you can take over to the blacksmith and have your name burned into it. A great souvenir! Or, play a game of Tic-Tac-Toe with a live chicken *(...be ready, this chicken is really good!).*

Visitors aren't likely to have seen anything like the "stones" at Rockome Gardens. Using native rock and cement, as well as some odds and ends (old pop bottles and pieces of glass), the Yoders have crafted fences, archways, large hearts, cups and saucers, birdhouses, and a variety of other designs throughout the park to delight and amuse visitors. The adjoining gardens display formal flower gardens, herb gardens, and cacti gardens, as well as the water gardens at the south end of the park. Guests to Rockome Gardens can experience that simpler life firsthand by visiting a house modeled after a true Amish home of the 1950's, with sparse furnishings and a focus on living for the Lord rather than for worldly things. Paths are provided throughout the park, perfect for a leisurely stroll, and children can spend the day riding a horse that provides power for the saw, petting animals in the petting zoo, playing in the tree house, creeping through the haunted cave *(very scary, parents use caution...),* or watching the G-gauge model train as it winds through the hills, flowers, and buildings. If your feet get tired, just hop on a horse and buggy for a ride through the park or climb aboard the train and wind your way through the fields and woods that border the east side of the park.

ARTHUR'S VISITOR INFORMATION CENTER

Arthur - *106 E. Progress Street, 61911. Phone: (800) 72-AMISH Web: www.IllinoisAmishCountry.com.* Arthur has been central to life in Illinois' largest Amish Settlement for more than a century and offers you a year-round look at the way life was and how life is today. Explore the community, enjoy a homemade drumstick ice cream cone at Dick's Pharmacy (118 Vine Street, 217-543-2913) - an old-fashioned soda fountain displaying a collection of over six hundred painted soda bottles. Sample baked goods and cheese. Sit down to a buffet or off-the-menu down-home cooked meals at the Dutch Oven (116 E. Illinois, 217-543-2213). Their specialty is chicken and pies but we liked their soups and meatloaf, too. All of this within easy walking distance downtown Arthur.

BRYANT COTTAGE STATE HISTORIC SITE

Bement - *140 E. Wilson Street, 61813. Phone: (217) 678-8184. Hours: Thursday-Sunday 9:00am-4:00pm. Open until 5:00pm (March-October). Admission: FREE. Donations accepted.* In 1858, Bryant found himself playing a role in one of the country's most famous political debates. That summer, both Abraham Lincoln and Douglas planned to talk to area residents in nearby Monticello. The chance meeting turned into a discussion about their campaign plans and many believe the two politicians formed their platforms for the Lincoln-Douglas Debates, held later that year. The Cottage still stands in Bement and is a state memorial. Look and see a glimpse of a typical residence of that time and shows how Bement's early settlers lived and carried on with their daily activities.

MILLER PARK ZOO

Bloomington - *1020 S. Morris Avenue (Morris Avenue exit off of Veteran's Parkway, turn right onto Wood St., and then take the first right), 61701. Web: www.millerparkzoo.org. Phone: (309) 434-2250, Hours: Daily 9:00am-4:30pm. Admission: $3.00-$4.00 (age 3+).* Miller Park Zoo offers many exhibits and Zookeeper interaction opportunities that are enjoyed by the whole family. Some highlights include: sun bears, reindeer, Sumatran tiger, sea lions, snow leopard, red panda, lynx, Galapagos tortoise, bald eagles, pallas cats, and red wolves. The Zoo features many large exhibits such as a Wallaby WalkAbout, Zoolab, Children's Zoo, Animals of Asia, and the animal building. The Zoo's newest exhibit is the Tropical America Rainforest.

BEER NUTS FACTORY

Bloomington - *103 N. Robinson Street, 61704. Phone: (309) 827-8580.* **Web:** *www.beernuts.com.* *Hours: Monday-Friday 8:00am-5:00pm.* *Admission: FREE.* Originating in the 1930s by Edward and Arlo Shrink, this family-owned manufacturing plant produces redskin nuts, which are exclusive to the company Beer Nuts. The ancestors of today's BEER NUTS Peanuts were known as "Redskins" because they were prepared with their red skins intact. They were processed by hand in the back room of the store and sold over-the-counter by the scoop. "Redskins" were occasionally offered at no charge to entice patrons to buy homemade orange drink. Ten varieties of nuts are produced at this plant including original and glazed peanuts, almonds, cashews, macadamias, and pecans. Visitors can observe the manufacturing process via a short video and can also participate in nut tasting at the gift store (the fun part!). The video is mostly educational explaining that peanut plants flower above the ground, but grow under the sandy soil. Watch as peanuts are washed, roasted and then coated with that special "lightly salty, slightly sweet." *Please Note: No beer is ever used in the making of the product.*

PRAIRIE AVIATION MUSEUM

Bloomington - *2929 East Empire Street (Bloomington-Normal Airport), 61704. Web: www.prairieaviationmuseum.org. Phone: (309) 663-7632. Hours: Tuesday-Saturday 11:00am-4:00pm, Sunday Noon-4:00pm. Admission: $1.00-$2.00 (age 6+).* See the history of aviation technology and get up-close looks at the cabins, cockpits and exteriors of their signature 1942 Douglas DC-3 or more modern Corsair or helicopters. The headquarters houses a theater, an engine, aircraft models, photos and uniforms.

CHILDREN'S DISCOVERY MUSEUM OF CENTRAL ILLINOIS

101 East Beaufort St (downtown), **Bloomington (Normal)** 61761

❑   Phone: (309) 433-3444
     Web: www.childrensdiscoverymuseum.net
❑   Hours: Tuesday-Saturday 9:00am-5:00pm, Sunday 1:00-5:00pm.
     Open until 8:00pm on Thursday and Friday.
❑   Admission: $4.00 per person (ages 2 & over).

Explore, imagine, create and play with three floors of easy hands-on exhibits. Visitors can: "Shop" the Main Street Market; Climb the two story Luckey Climber; Explore a Compost Pile in Oh Rubbish; pretend play on the Train Table or Water Play areas; or explore The Arts. My Place is an endless Brio Plan Table where children can create their own city and travel from place to place. Older children enjoy the simulated computer games where they create their own neighborhood or learn map-making skills using fun computer activities. Mr. Bones and the Medical Center might teach you a few science facts.

ILLINOIS STATE UNIVERSITY MUSEUMS

College Avenue, **Bloomington (Normal)** 61761

❏   Phone: (309) 438-INFO

ISU was founded in 1857 with much of the original legal work completed by Abraham Lincoln. ISU was the first public university in the state and the tenth oldest state teacher's school in the nation.

❏   <u>ISU ART GALLERIES</u>: 110 Center for the Visual Arts. (309) 438-5487. Three art galleries hold nearly 20 annual exhibitions .

❏   <u>ISU EYESTONE ONE-ROOM SCHOOLHOUSE</u>: corner of College Avenue and Adelaide Street. (309) 438-5415. Elementary students can experience a typical day in an authentic McLean County one-room schoolhouse as it was in 1899 (slate boards and wooden desks). Tours by appointment only.

❏   <u>ISU PLANETARIUM</u>: College Avenue and School Street. (309) 438-5007 or **www.phy.ilstu.edu/planet.html**. The majesty of a night sky is recreated in a celestial theater in the round. Tours by appointment. Public showings are 60 minutes.

❏   <u>ISU FARM RESEARCH FACILITY</u>: 25578 ISU Farm Lane. (309) 365-2211or **www.agriculture.ilstu.edu**. Book your tours of a working farm. See dairy operation, beef cattle, swine, sheep and the Aquaculture Research Facility where they raise fish in an indoor, controlled environment. Computers feed animals here - How? FREE.

ORPHEUM CHILDREN'S SCIENCE MUSEUM

Champaign - *346 N. Neil Street, 61820. Phone: (217) 352-5895.* **Web:** *www.orpheum.science.museum. Hours: Tuesday 9:00am-6:00pm, Wednesday-Sunday & various school holidays 1:00-5:00pm.* Walk through the doors of the 1914 Orpheum Theatre now converted to a museum with more than 20 interactive science exhibits. With a giant, 14-foot lever, children balance their body with 300 pounds of lead. A mirror takes the images of two and makes them one. Meet Wendy the box turtle, a tarantula or Irene the Hissing Cockroach. The courtyard outside allows for a Dino Dig or searching for polished rocks at the Gem Mine.

PRAIRIE FARM

Champaign - *2202 W. Kirby Avenue (Centennial Park), 61821. Phone: (217) 398-2550.* **Web:** *www.champaignparkdistrict.com. Hours: Daily 1:00-7:00pm (Memorial Day-Labor Day). Admission: FREE. Fee for trolley ride and some programs.* Traditional farm animals (like sheep, pigs, horses, cows, chickens) mixed with recreation. Visitors are welcome to pet the farm's animals in the petting area. Kids can cross the footbridge that spans the farm's miniature duck pond, then take a trolley ride around the farm. Recreation includes sport courts, picnic areas, waterslide, & pool.

STAERKEL PLANETARIUM

Champaign - *2400 West Bradley Avenue (Parkland College's Cultural Center), 61821.* **Web:** *www.parkland.edu/coned/pla/. Phone: (217) 351-2200 Hours: The Staerkel Planetarium is open year-round on Friday and Saturday evenings. A variety of show types are presented. Admission: $3.00-$4.00.* The second-largest planetarium in Illinois uses a Zeiss Star Projector to project thousands of visible stars on the 50-foot dome. State of the art audio visual equipment and special effects help visitors learn about the planets and stars of the universe. One popular program, Prairie Skies, delivers a live-night tour of the wonders of tonight's sky, accompanied by some of the legendary stories of the ancient sky. Find out what constellations and planets are visible tonight and how to find them. This show is updated seasonally and is intended for all ages. In addition to regular features, the dome offers children's shows, rock-and-roll light shows & seasonal presentations.

ANITA PURVES NATURE CENTER

Champaign (Urbana) - *1505 N. Broadway (Route 45 South, north end of Crystal Lake Park), 61801. Web: www.urbanaparks.org. Phone: (217) 384-4062, Hours: Monday-Saturday 8:00am-5:00pm, Sunday Noon-4:00pm. Admission: FREE.* This environmental education facility is a natural resource to families learning more about the outdoors. The Nature Center features an exhibit field station, an Observation Room and a Nature Shop. The adjacent Busey Woods is perfect for hiking and bird-watching.

SPURLOCK MUSEUM

Champaign (Urbana) - *600 S. Gregory (Univ. of Ill. Campus, I-74, Rte. 45 exit, south. East on University, south on Lincoln. Look for Krannart and you're there), 61801. Web: www.spurlock.uiuc.edu. Phone: (217) 333-2360. Hours: Tuesday Noon-5:00pm, Wednesday-Friday 9:00am-5:00pm, Saturday 10:00am-4:00pm. Admission: FREE.* The museum highlights the lives of people from six continents through the exploration of food, clothing, shelter, communications, technology, conflict, art, religion, and ethics. Learn by looking at objects used by people around the globe and how it was used. See suites of armor or a 2,000 year old mummy of a young child in Ancient Egypt. Walk around a tipi in the American Indian Culture gallery. To engage the kids, make sure you've studied Ancient cultures and religions (esp. the Middle Ages). Also, be sure to pick up a scavenger hunt - be a Spurlock Sherlock - as there are really not any hands-on areas to interact with.

FOX RIDGE STATE PARK

Charleston - *18175 State Park Road (I-70, take Exit for Rt. 130 North. Go approximately 11 miles), 61920. Phone: (217) 345-6416 www.dnr.state.il.us/lands/landmgt/parks/r3/fox/fox.htm. Admission to Illinois State Parks is free. Camping fees range from $6.00-11.00 per night, depending on amenities; a $5.00 fee is charged for camping reservations. Miscellaneous: Fishing, boating and camping.* Fox Ridge State Park is known for its steep, thickly wooded ridges, broad, lush valleys and miles of rugged, scenic hiking trails and covers 2,064 acres. In sharp contrast to the flat prairies of most of this section of Illinois, Fox Ridge is set amidst rolling hills along the forested bluffs of the Embarras ("Ambraw") River. Fox Ridge is a ravine of glacial moraine and many of these trails are steep but has 18 picturesque wooden bridges and numerous rest benches. The staircase to Eagle's Nest requires 144 steps to get you to the deck overlooking the river, providing a wonderful view during the fall, winter & spring.

LINCOLN-DOUGLAS DEBATE MUSEUM

416 West Madison Avenue/126 E. Street (Coles County
Fairgrounds, E. Street @ Madison Avenue), **Charleston** 61920

- ❑ Phone: (217) 348-0430
- ❑ Hours: Daily 9:00am-4:00pm.
- ❑ Admission: FREE, donations accepted.
- ❑ Miscellaneous: The museum participates in a State of Illinois
  Heritage Tourism project called "Looking for Lincoln." While in
  downtown Charleston, view outdoor murals that have been
  created by local artists.

Tour the only museum in Illinois retracing the senatorial debates of
1858 between Abraham Lincoln and Stephen A. Douglas. Just a
few hundred feet away (signs direct you two hundred steps to the
actual spot) from the museum, 12,000 people gathered to hear
Lincoln and Douglas debate their positions on issues including
slavery and interpretation of the Constitution. They show a video
of re-enactors creating scenes from the long debate. The museum
includes a Children's Hands-On Area, a Gift Shop, and a life-size
sculpture of Lincoln and Douglas. This is an absolutely awesome
place for Lincoln photo ops - indoors and out!

WELDON SPRINGS STATE RECREATION AREA

Clinton - *1159 County Road 500 North, 61727, Phone: (217) 935-2644.
www.dnr.state.il.us/lands/landmgt/parks/r3/weldonra.htm Admission to
Illinois State Parks is free. Camping fees range from $6.00-11.00 per
night, depending on amenities; a $5.00 fee is charged for camping
reservations.* More than a museum, Union School Interpretive Center is a
"hands-on" learning center with a "please touch" philosophy. Both science
and local history are emphasized. A collection of taxidermist-mounted
mammals which make their homes in the park encourages visitors to pet a
squirrel's tail, feel a badger's claws, or examine a beaver's teeth. Discovery
boxes are filled with natural treasures grouped around a central theme to
stimulate students' curiosity about the natural world. Insect cards
demonstrate many of the basic concepts of ecology with magnified
specimens. Additional natural history exhibits examine the park's variety of
habitats, the eastern bluebird nestbox trail, forestry, animal builders, and
raptors. During the milder seasons, you are invited to fish, boat, picnic,
camp, hike, and view wildlife. Or, you might want to pitch horseshoes at the

park's tournament-quality horseshoe pits. When the snow flies, hardier outdoors persons may add sledding and tobogganing on a one-eighth mile hill, ice fishing and cross-country skiing to the itinerary of their visit.

VERMILION COUNTY MUSEUM & FITHIAN HOME

Danville - *116 North Gilbert Street, 61832. Phone: (217) 442-2922 or (800) 383-4386. Web: www.vermilioncountymuseum.org. Hours: Tuesday-Saturday 10:00am-5:00pm.* The museum is a replica of the courthouse where Abraham Lincoln practiced law from 1841 to 1859. It houses an exhibit of the Lincoln Law Office, as well as natural history displays, a one room school house, and a coal mine shaft. Also on site is the 1855 Fithian Home. Dr. William Fithian was a friend of Lincoln's. You can see the original room where Lincoln spent two nights in 1858, and the balcony where he gave an informal speech.

CLINTON LAKE STATE RECREATION AREA

Dewitt - *725 1900 East (Turn left at corner of Rt 54 and Co Hwy 14, three miles east of town), 61735. Phone: (217) 935-8722. www.dnr.state.il.us/lands/landmgt/parks/r3/clinton.htm. Admission to Illinois State Parks is free. Camping fees range from $6.00-11.00 per night, depending on amenities; a $5.00 fee is charged for camping reservations. Miscellaneous: Camping, horseback trails, boating and waterskiing.* If just getting out and about is your interest, try the park's three hiking trails. The 5 mile Houseboat Cove Trail north of the beach follows the shoreline and comes back through the woods. It is easy to moderate in difficulty. A beautiful, 1,000-foot white sand beach awaits swimmers in the warm waters of the lake. The beach is open from Memorial Day weekend through Labor Day. Located close to the swim beach or accessible by car, you will find Mascoutin Grill. This concession, with indoor and outdoor dining, serves sandwiches, beverages, snacks and its ever popular fish dinner. You can also purchase bait, camping supplies and ice. Mascoutin Grill is a seasonal operation open during warm weather. Ice fishing, ice skating and snowmobiling are allowed on the lake when the ice is thick enough.

RAILSPLITTER, THE

Divernon - *(I-55 exit 82), 62530. Phone: (217) 628-3338.* Located on historic Route 66 at Pawnee, this is reportedly the world's largest covered wagon. FREE to look around.

CROSS AT THE CROSSROADS

Effingham - *(I-57 & I-70), 62401. Phone: (217) 347-2846. Web: www.crossusa.org. Hours: Daily 10:00am-7:00pm (May - October), Daily 10:00am-4:00pm (November-April).* Soaring nearly 200 feet into the midwestern sky along one of the country's most traveled interstates, the cross has an arm span of 113 feet. It's made of 848 yards of concrete and has nearly 34 tons of reinforced steel footings at its foundation. The visitors center features a reception area, restrooms, refreshment center, a chapel, and a media room where guests can view a video of the construction and dedication of the Cross. Hosts an Easter sunrise service.

LAKE SARA & EFFINGHAM BEACH

Effingham - *Lake Sara Road (Illinois Routes 32 & 33, exit 160), 62401. Phone: (217) 868-2964. Hours: Daylight. Admission: FREE.* Lake Sara offers the outdoor enthusiast water skiing, swimming, beaches, fishing, boating and camping. Large beach, picnic areas, docks, & pavilion rentals.

MY GARAGE R & D CENTER/ CORVETTE MUSEUM

Effingham - *One Mid America Place (north Route 45), 62401. Phone: (217) 347-5591 or (800) 500-1500. Hours: Monday-Friday 8:00am-5:00pm, Saturday 9:00am-3:00pm.* The "MY Garage R & D Center /Museum" features Mike Yager's continuously expanding showcase of classic and low-mileage Corvettes, in addition to a wide array of Corvette Memorabilia. The entire collection is displayed in a unique 1950's-60's style backdrop, complete with storefront settings and jukebox music. Of the 30+ Corvettes on display, highlights include the "Last C4", the CERV 1, SCCA Challenge Race Cars, and a 1954 Roadster.

SCULPTURE ON THE AVENUES

Effingham - *201 E. Jefferson Avenue (begin here at Effingham CVB). 62401. Phone: (800) 772-0750.* In 1997, Effingham took the first steps to creating a popular public art event. The first piece was created by Leonardo Nierman, an internationally renowned sculptor, titled Flame of Hope - a work of polished steel. Eight sculptures by Midwestern artists later, Sculpture on the Avenues was born. There's fun, whimsy and stark lines and edges. The pieces are placed to be accessible, to be touched and viewed from every angle. A dozen sculptures have found permanent homes in Effingham and the surrounding area. Childlike pieces include Joy and Balancing Boy. An informative brochure, which facilitates a walking tour, is available at area hotels, downtown businesses, the tourism office at City Hall and in a convenient display outside City Hall.

EAGLE CREEK STATE PARK

Findlay - *(Hwy 121 to Dalton City, then Hwy 128 south to east of Findlay), 62534. Phone: (217) 756-8260 or (800) 876-3245 resort Web: www.eaglecreekresort.com. Admission to Illinois State Parks is free. Camping fees range from $6-11.00 per night, depending on amenities; a $5.00 fee is charged for camping reservations.* Nestled on the shores of Lake Shelbyville, Eagle Creek offers miniature golf, hiking, fishing, waterskiing, bicycling, archery, and horseback riding. On the lake's west shore sits a luxurious resort with furnishings inspired by the nearby Amish community. The 138 rooms have outdoor patios overlooking the lush forest and lake. The resort amenities include indoor and outdoor pools, pontoon rentals, boat docks, and sport courts. In addition to the small, friendly wooded campgrounds and the action on the lake, large herds of deer frequent these areas and are always an exciting and inspiring sight.

HOMER 500 SNOWMOBILE/ATV GRASS DRAG RACING

Homer - *202 E. 4th Street, 61849. Phone: (217) 896-2635. Web: www.fastgrass.itgo.com.* Bring the entire family out to the races to watch snowmobiling like you've never seen! The grass drag strip starts with a packed clay start line. Machines go from zero to 100 mph in just a few seconds. Race season runs from late June-October.

LINCOLN LOG CABIN STATE HISTORIC SITE

South 4th St/ 400 South Lincoln Hwy Road (I-70 exit 119. Route 130 north. Follow signs. 8 miles south of Charleston), **Lerna** 62440

❑   Phone: (217) 345-1845, **Web: www.state.il.us/hpa/hs/log.htm**

❑   Hours: Wednesday-Sunday 9:00am-5:00pm. Living History Program open daily (mid-April to Labor Day). Closes one hour early in winter.

❑   Admission: FREE, donations appreciated.

❑   Miscellaneous: Picnic shelters, playgrounds, restrooms available. One mile north is the Moore Home State Historic Site, a reconstructed frame home where Abraham Lincoln bid his stepmother farewell in January of 1861 before leaving to assume the Presidency. Also, many visit the Lincoln cemetery (open dawn to dusk) to see the burial site of Abraham Lincoln's father and stepmother, Thomas Lincoln and Sarah Bush Lincoln. The church is open to the public.

Lincoln Log Cabin Historic Site was the 1840's home of Thomas and Sarah Bush Lincoln, father and stepmother of our 16th president. Abraham Lincoln was a lawyer living in Springfield by the time his parents lived here, but he did visit them periodically. The site includes a working, living history farm developed around a two-room cabin. A second farmstead, the Stephen Sargent Farm, has been moved to the site to help broaden visitors' understanding of 1840's rural life in Illinois. Be sure to watch the 14-minute film about the Lincolns, Sargents, 1840s life, and the site's living history program. This film prepares visitors for their visit to the farms. Compare the two types of farming: lifestyle farming (Lincolns) vs. profit farming (Sargents). The excellent Museum has many "TRY IT!" interactives. How many cords of wood do you need to stack? Design a pattern of scraps for a quilt. Even try running your own farm (by computer). Upland Southern dialect is spoken with first person interpreters in the outdoor village. They are really good actors!

MORAINE VIEW STATE PARK

LeRoy - *27374 Moraine View Park Road (I 74, Exit #149 at LeRoy. Follow signs into LeRoy), 61752. Phone: (309) 724-8032. www.dnr.state.il.us/lands/landmgt/parks/r3/moraine.htm. Admission to Illinois State Parks is free. Camping fees range from $6.00-11.00 per night, depending on amenities; a $5.00 fee is charged for camping reservations.* With fully developed facilities for picnicking, camping, hiking, swimming, fishing, boating, horseback riding, and winter sports, the 1,687-acre Moraine View State Recreation Area, with its 158-acre lake, is a beautiful, convenient and accessible locale for relaxation and recreation. The Black Locust picnic area includes a public, sandy beach where swimming is permitted from Memorial Day to Labor Day. The half-mile Tanglewood Self-Guiding Nature Trail winds around the lake finger in a wooded area and will take you within sight of a thriving beaver dam and lodge. Tall Timber Trail is a 1.5-mile backpack and hiking trail over moderate terrain. The Timber Point Handicapped Trail is a half-mile long opportunity for the disabled visitor to enjoy the pleasures of the woods as well.

EARLY AMERICAN MUSEUM

North Route 47 (1 mile north of I-74, Lake of the Woods
Forest Preserve), **Mahomet** 61853

❑   Phone: (217) 586-2612, **Web: www.earlyamericanmuseum.org**
❑   Hours: Daily 1:00-5:00pm (March-December); Monday-Saturday
     hours extended 10:00am-5:00pm (summer).
❑   Admission: Donations accepted.
❑   Miscellaneous: Complemented by Mabry Gelvin Botanical
     Gardens.

A full size wigwam, the tooth of a wooly mammoth or crank the
working model-T engine. With many hands-on exhibits and
programs, the museum lets visitors experience life on the Grand
Prairie in Champaign County during the 1800s and 1900s. Two
floors of exhibits present architecture, trades and occupations and
childhood life of the time. The Discovery Room offers hands-on
opportunities to interact.

LINCOLN TRAIL STATE PARK

Marshall - *16985 East 1350th Road (just west of IL 1, 2 miles south of
town), 62441. www.dnr.state.il.us/lands/landmgt/parks/r3/lincoln.htm.
Phone: (217) 826-2222 Admission to Illinois State Parks is free. Camping
fees range from $6-11.00 per night, depending on amenities; a $5.00 fee is
charged for camping reservations.* Within the thickly wooded land of this
park lies a nature preserve with ravines holding a beech-maple forest just as
they did in the pioneer days. The Lincoln passed through this area en route
from Indiana to Macon County in 1830. The focal point of the park is
Lincoln Trail Lake, which covers 146 acres in the southwest corner of the
park. Enjoy camping, fishing and hiking trails and power boating, as well as
an on-site restaurant. The Beech Tree Trail is just a half-mile long, extending
from the boat dock parking lot and concession stand, past the large picnic
shelter, and to Lakeside Campground. The trail includes a series of stairways
and foot bridges, which provide an excellent view of the beech maple forest.

MONTICELLO RAILWAY MUSEUM

Monticello – *P.O. Box 401 (I-72 at Market Street. Exit 166. Turn at the
stoplight onto Iron Horse Place), 61856. Phone: (217) 762-9011. **Web:**
www.prairienet.org/mrm. Admission: Fees charged based on trip. Tours:
Trains depart the museum site on Saturdays and Sundays, three to four*

times per day. weekends and holidays May-October). The train pulls up to the depot and the call "All Aboard" echoes in your ears and prepares you for your trip back to the olden days of railroading. Allow yourself to enjoy the sights of the Illinois countryside. As you travel, the conductor will punch your souvenir ticket, call attention to the points of interest along the way and answer any questions you might have. Make an afternoon of it with a picnic at the grove near Camp Creek Yard.

DR. HIRAM RUTHERFORD'S HOME

Oakland - *Pike Street, 61943. Phone: (217) 346-2031. Hours: Open select days each summer. Call first. Admission: Small donation.* Some 110 years ago, rural folk with ailments came from miles around to see Dr. Hiram Rutherford in his Oakland home office. Rutherford was Oakland's first doctor. The interior of the home offers a look into 19th-century life, complete with a summer kitchen and drying shed. Largely because his life coincided with Abraham Lincoln's days as a lawyer – and because Rutherford played a part in a lawsuit that Lincoln lost – the doctor's house, & even his desk, have been preserved.

WALNUT POINT STATE PARK

Oakland - *2331 East County Road 370 North (within a few miles of Interstate 57, U.S. Highway 36 and Illinois Route 133, just north of town), 61943. www.dnr.state.il.us/lands/landmgt/parks/r3/walnutpt.htm. Phone: (217) 346-3336 Admission to Illinois State Parks is free. Camping fees range from $6.00-11.00 per night, depending on amenities; a $5.00 fee is charged for camping reservations.* Enjoy camping, fishing, hiking and boating in this park. Paddle-boat, row-boat and canoe rentals are available, as well as a concession store. Hear live music on weekends. The 59-acre, multi-fingered Walnut Point Lake is the focal point of the park. Hiking and nature-study enthusiasts will find 2.25 miles of trails weaving through the timber. By using the main park road and the Gray Squirrel-Twin Points connection trail, walkers and joggers can complete a 3-mile exercise loop. All trails are restricted to foot traffic only. The Lakeside Nature Trail (.5 mile) is handicapped accessible.

KICKAPOO STATE PARK

Oakwood - *10906 Kickapoo Park Road (off I-74 near Danville), 61858. www.dnr.state.il.us/lands/landmgt/parks/r3/kickapoo.htm. Phone: (217) 442-4915 Admission to Illinois State Parks is free. Camping fees range from $6.00-11.00 per night, depending on amenities; a $5.00 fee is charged for camping reservations.* This park was the first in the country to be built on strip-mined land. The park offers many types of camping, miles of hiking trails, fishing, canoeing, guided horseback riding, and more than 10 miles of mountain biking trails. The Middle Fork State Fish and Wildlife Area winds through a mixture of forests and prairies.

HARDY'S REINDEER RANCH

1356 CR 2900N (I-74 exit 184, Rte 45 N approx. 16 miles. Head west on Rte. 136. Just past I-57, turn left at Evans Road and follow signs), **Rantoul** 61866

❑ Phone: (217) 893-3407, **Web: www.reindeerranch.com**

❑ Hours: Open July-December, call for seasonal hours. Generally 10:00am-8:00pm, especially September & October.

❑ Admission: FREE (fee for corn maze, hayrack ride & pedal carts).

❑ Miscellaneous: Great place for groups to come - chuckwagon packages range from $6.00-$20.00. In the banquet hall, play dress up as the "characters" in your group dress for the wild west - great photo ops!

The North Pole has moved to Central Illinois! From August thru October the theme is "BEST IN THE midWEST." Pick a pumpkin in the pines, browse through the general store gift shop, or try your luck at figuring out the mysteries of the 6-acre Cornfusion maze. Experience the Kid's Corral, take a hayrack ride, play in a realistic Indian tepee or the straw fort, pedal your way through the new Grand Prix style race track, and of course, see the Reindeer! Wait until you see them! Try on some antlers (they shed them every year) and feed them apples. The staff will teach you so much. From November through December, the reindeer ranch is transformed into a Christmas wonderland. Hear that clicking sound? The reindeer do click when they walk (Up on the Housetop, click, click, click...) and they really do leap and dance (if it's snowing!) The general store is reminiscent of days gone by with a pot-bellied stove, period costumes, twinkling lights and wonderful smells. The western style banquet facility was recently renovated and is available for "Wild West" BBQ or outdoor weenie roast. "Howdy partner" - this place is so...o....o endearing!

OCTAVE CHANUTE AEROSPACE MUSEUM

1011 Pacesetter Drive (Rte 45 N to turn right at Welcome to Rantoul sign, follow around until you see planes by the side of the road), **Rantoul** 61866

❑ Phone: (217) 893-1613, **Web: www.aeromuseum.org**
❑ Hours: Monday-Saturday 10:00am-5:00pm; Sunday Noon-5:00pm.
❑ Admission: $8.00 adult, $6.00 senior, $4.00 child (over 5).
❑ Miscellaneous: Skydiving events held on campus are a big thrill to watch or do!

Located in and out of a hanger of the former Chanute Air Force Base, this museum is the largest aerospace museum in Illinois and home to more than 40 aircraft and missiles. From the old biplane, prop plane, and high performance World War II fighter planes right up through modern jet aircraft. In the hanger, kids will awe over the greeting from a giant planes! Ever seen an ejection seat? Go down to missile storage or see the missile platform base. How does a motor work? Push a button and watch. If you like memorabilia, check out the diaries and uniforms paying homage to all veterans, prisoners of war, and those missing in action. End indoors at the simulated repair shop with sight and sound. This place really appeals to the guys.

LAKE SHELBYVILLE

Rte 4, Box 128B (between Rtes 121, 32 & 128), **Shelbyville** 62565

❑ Phone: (217) 774-3951
   Web: www.mvs.usace.army.mil/Shelbyville
❑ Miscellaneous: Folks tell us they love annual family reunions at Lithia Resort (217-774-2882 or **www.lithiaresort.com**). Air-conditioned rooms with refrigerator, rooms with kitchen or rooms with adjoining kitchen. Luxury Cabins: large kitchen and family room, bath and bedrooms - some are log cabins. The property has a large picnic shelter, grills, campfire rings, catch and release ponds, arcade, and are close to the Lithia Springs Marina.

The US Army Corps of Engineers lake offers sparkling waters, sheltered coves, and sandy beaches. Shelbyville Visitor Center is located in the Dam East Recreation Area. The center is one mile east of Shelbyville just off Rte 16. Tour the exhibit area, stay for an introductory video about the lake, or take a guided tour of the Lake Shelbyville Dam. All tours begin at the visitors center and are held each weekend from Memorial Day to Labor Day. The visitor center is open daily in the summer, weekends spring and fall. The Corps offers trails ranging in length from 1/2 mile to the 11-mile Chief Illini Trail. As snow approaches, so do the sledders and cross-country skiers. Ice fishing and ice-skating are also very popular activities.

HIDDEN SPRINGS STATE FOREST

Strasburg - *Rural Route 1, Box 200 (5 miles southwest of town, Illinois Route 32), 62465. Phone: (217) 644-3091 www.dnr.state.il.us/lands/landmgt/parks/r3/hsforest.htm.* Miscellaneous: *Timbers Restaurant and Lodge (adjacent) features a dining room and accommodations in a log building, horse-drawn surrey rides and pony leads for kids. Chuckwagon dinners for groups. (www.timberslodge.com or 217-644-3130).* The name Hidden Springs was selected to designate this particular state forest because of the seven known springs on the property which were used for drinking water by the early settlers. Most of the springs are covered over with vegetation but two spring trails remain: Rocky Spring and Quicksand Spring. Possum Hollow Nature Trail, 3/4 mile in length, provides access to Park Pond and the pine seed orchard. Trail guides, available at the headquarters, campground, and picnic area, guide the visitor to the 35 interpretive stations. The Big Tree Trail, one mile in length, features a sycamore 78 inches in diameter, one of the largest to be found in Illinois. Facilities for picnicking, camping, fishing, and wildlife watching are here, too.

LITTLE THEATRE ON THE SQUARE

Sullivan - *12 E. Harrison Street, 61951. Phone: (217) 728-7375 or (888) 261-9675. Web: www.thelittletheatre.org. Hours: Matinees: Wednesday & Sunday at 2:00pm; Saturday at 4:00pm. Theatre for Young: 6 days each month (summer) at 10:30am. Admission: $20.00-$25.00 per person for matinees. Theatre for Young Audiences: $7.00 per person.* The Little Theatre features name artists and many talented amateurs. In addition to traditional theatre and musicals (ex. Beauty and the Beast), the Theatre produces children's theatre (ex. Sleeping Beauty) and a Christmas holiday show.

WOLF CREEK STATE PARK

Windsor - *Rural Route 1 (on Lake Shelbyville's eastern shore), 61957.* *www.dnr.state.il.us/lands/landmgt/parks/r3/wolfcrek.htm.* *Phone: (217) 459-2831. Admission to Illinois State Parks is free. Camping fees range from $6.00-11.00 per night, depending on amenities; a $5.00 fee is charged for camping reservations.* The Wolf Creek/Eagle Creek sites, facing each other across the central portion of Lake Shelbyville, provide the perfect setting for outdoor recreation and natural relaxation. This 2,000 acre park offers camping, fishing, horseback riding, hiking trails, swimming and power boating. For refreshing walks in the forests, Wolf Creek contains seven hiking trails. For invigorating winter time activity there is a 16½ mile snowmobile trail, and for the equestrian there is a scenic 15-mile equestrian trail.

SUGGESTED LODGING AND DINING

HOLIDAY INN EXPRESS, AMISH COUNTRY, Tuscola. (I-57 & US 36, exit 212; (217) 253-6363 or **www.holiday-inn.com**) A family-friendly hotel close to Amish attractions, restaurants and shopping. The spacious rooms include micro/frig units and high-speed internet. The hotel offers guests a free deluxe Breakfast Bar each morning and a heated indoor pool and spa. If you've already had your fill of Amish food, try a good Italian restaurant just four lights west of the hotel.

TUSCANY STEAK AND PASTA HOUSE, Tuscola. (217) 253-1030. (on Rte 36, just past Main Street). Good steaks and big portions of pasta. Try the Pasta Sampler Plates for variety. Kids Menu (7 choices) around $4.00 and includes beverage.

AMISHLAND RED BARN, Tuscola. (I-57 exit 212, across from the Holiday Inn Express). Phone: (217) 253-9022. Meals ~$9.00-$10.00 for adults (all you can eat buffet). Children have a reduced rate. Lunch and dinner daily. The Amishland Red Barn is the north gateway to the largest Amish community in Illinois. The Amish Style buffet serves loads of food choices with great chicken and homestyle foods. Oh, and the pies! The quiet, indoor "streets" with cobblestone sidewalks, street lamps, and several individual specialty stores are a great way to walk off all the yummy food served at the Red Barn Buffet. If you still have room, sample Aunt Sarah's Cheese - many varieties.

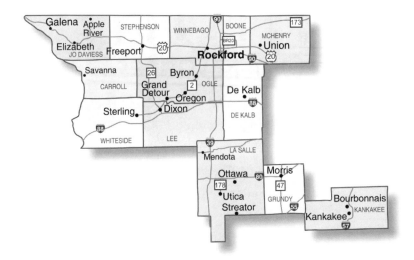

Chapter 4
North Area (N)

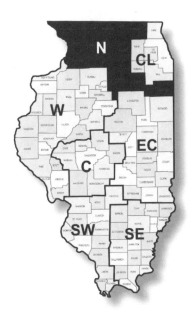

Our Favorites...

* Stagecoach Trails - Apple River (Galena)
* Ronald Reagan Boyhood Home - Dixon
* Apple River Fort - Elizabeth
* Alpine Slide at Chester Mountain - Galena
Downtown Galena - Shops, Dining, Sites
John Deere Historic Site - Grand Detour
* Burpee Museum of Natural History - Rockford
* Historic Auto Attractions - Rockford (Roscoe)
Donley's Wild West Town - Union
* Starved Rock Area Park & Lodges - Utica

A Real Stagecoach Ride - Stagecoach Trails

APPLE RIVER CANYON STATE PARK

Apple River - *8763 E. Canyon Rd (U.S. Highway 20 at Illinois Highway 78, 1 mile east of Stockton. Travel north 6 miles on Illinois 78 and turn west at the park signs), 61001. Phone: (815) 745-3302. www.dnr.state.il.us/lands/landmgt/parks/r1/apple.htm. Admission to Illinois State Parks is free. Camping fees range from $6.00-11.00 per night, depending on amenities; a $5.00 fee is charged for camping reservations.* This scenic canyon area was formed by the action of the winding waters of Apple River. Limestone bluffs, deep ravines, springs, streams and wildlife characterize this area which was once a part of a vast sea bottom that stretched from the Alleghenies to the Rockies. Five hiking trails rated moderately difficult to strenuous wind through the woods and along the scenic river bluffs. Watch for white-tailed deer, raccoons and hawks. Eagles are sometimes seen in winter. Forty-seven varieties of birds, some 14 different ferns and 165 varieties of flowers, including the rare bird's-eye primrose, are found here. The park has four picnic areas along the Apple River and three picnic shelters. Fishing is popular, and Apple River is stocked with trout in the spring. There are 47 primitive campsites (without showers or electricity); reservations are not accepted.

STAGECOACH TRAILS LIVERY

5656 Stagecoach Trail (1/2 mile west of town), **Apple River** 61001

❑   Phone: (815) 594-2423

❑   Admission: $75.00 per hour per group of eight.

❑   Miscellaneous: Also available: wagon train trips, hayrides and sleigh rides. Bunkhouse warming room. Call for reservations.

Stagecoach Trails Livery near Galena, Illinois offers stagecoach rides in a replica of an original Concord Stagecoach. They offer covered wagon trips with or without authentic "chuck wagon" meals. You choose the length of all trips. First, visit the Bunk House looking through pictures of the family of horses; see the goat who rides horseback; pick up a piece of real lead; or try to pick up a stagecoach robbery strong box - filled with gold and such - can you imagine trying to carry it? R.J. Spillane (the proprietor) will weave lots of cowboy tails as he shares his memories! The trails are located on some of the old original stagecoach and wagon trails. It used to take 5 days (1820s) to go from Galena to Chicago. On the trails you may find all kinds of wildlife including small game, deer, or perhaps the magnificent wild turkey. Maybe you'll take the trail over a bridge or cross the racking Apple River and right through prairie tall grass. Sometimes, you may catch a glimpse of an old church, school, barn and general store. Come along, relax, and enjoy God's country. This is truly one of the most unique settings and "historical" tours we've ever taken! Well worth the effort to make the trip out to literally "feel" like you're out west in the early 1800s...and, you get to meet a modern-day cowboy – R.J. Spillane is quite a character!

BOONE COUNTY HISTORICAL SOCIETY MUSEUM

Belvidere - *311 Whitney Boulevard, 61008. Phone: (815) 544-8391. Web: www.boonecountyhistoricalmuseum.org. Hours: Tuesday, Thursday 8:00am-4:00pm; Wednesday, Friday & Saturday Noon-4:00pm. Admission: $1.00-$3.00 (K and up). $5.00 family.* How often have you seen a 160-year-old log cabin inside a building? Walk through the general store, the bank, the barbershop, or the one room school and experience history come alive. Explore this collection of local memorabilia set in themed "rooms." The museum houses a collection of Civil War, agriculture, blacksmithing, tornado, dolls, music, school, sports and toy artifacts from the past (industries through the years). The natural history room showcases many birds and small animals native to Northern Illinois that will surprise you. Also on the premises: an 1904 Eldredge Runabout and the first Chrysler produced in Belvidere.

EXPLORATION STATION CHILDREN'S MUSEUM

Bourbonnais - *1095 West Perry Street, 60914. Phone: (815) 935-5665. Web: www.btpd.org/exploration_station.htm. Hours: Monday-Saturday 10:00am-5:00pm, Sunday 1:00-5:00pm. Open late until 8:00pm on Fridays and until 6:00pm many weekdays. Closed most major holidays. Admission: $4.00-$5.00 (age 1+). Discount for township residents.* At Exploration Station, children can be a clerk in the new grocery store, climb inside the tower of a medieval castle, work in a kid's size emergency room, man an ambulance, create a flying machine, sit in the cockpit of a fighter jet behind the controls, connect pipes and elbows in WaterWorks, view the planets and star constellations, learn about fossils, create their own art project, dance on the floor keyboard like Tom Hanks in "BIG", paint their faces and much more.

KANKAKEE RIVER STATE PARK

Bourbonnais - *5314 West Illinois Route 102 (I-55 north to Dwight Exit (Rte.17 east). Go approximately 20 miles to Warner Bridge Rd. north), 60914. www.dnr.state.il.us/lands/landmgt/parks/r2/kankakee.htm.* Phone: *(815) 933-1383 Admission: FREE.* No reservations for camping. Anglers, canoeists, hunters, campers, hikers, bicyclers, horseback riders (rentals) and other outdoor enthusiasts find the park's recreational opportunities unsurpassed. The naturally channeled Kankakee River, listed on the Federal Clean Streams Register, is the focus of the park's popularity. Recreation seekers from Chicago began using the area as early as the 1890s. The park's Rock Creek Café and Trading Post, near Rock Creek Canyon and the suspension bridge, offers meals and camping supplies. The park's trail system stretches for miles along both sides of the river. Hiking, biking and cross-country ski trails are on the river's north side, while horse and snowmobile trails can be found on the south. A 3-mile route along Rock Creek lets hikers take in the beauty of limestone canyons and a frothy waterfall. A bicycle trail begins at Davis Creek Area and travels 10.5 miles of trails in the form of a linear trail along the river and a loop in the west end of the park. Also, come to the visitor center and learn about the history and wildlife of the park through numerous exhibits and displays. Seasonal concessions.

STRICKLER PLANETARIUM

Bourbonnais - *One University Avenue (I-57 S to exit 315, Bradley/ Bourbonnais. Rte 50 S to right on Armour Road. Left onto Convent Street to Main Street, follow signs), 60914. Phone: (815) 939-5308. Shows: Generally late afternoon or early evening performances - especially near holidays. Admission charge is $1.00 per person/per show. There are no advanced ticket sales. Doors open 10-15 minutes prior to show time.* Named after Dr. Dwight Strickler, a former biology professor at Olivet, the planetarium features a dome presentation screen with specially designed seating. Each year, approximately 8,000 people view astronomy shows in the planetarium, one of only a few planetariums located on private university campuses nationwide and the only planetarium located on a Christian campus. Explore the universe, and learn about the stars, comets and asteroids - even poetry. Special shows take place during holiday seasons.

BYRON FOREST PRESERVE/ JARRETT PRAIRIE CENTER

7993 North River Road, **Byron** 61010

❑ Phone: (815) 234-8535

www.oregonil.com/attractions-jarrett-nature.html

NATURAL HISTORY MUSEUM: the Jarrett Prairie Center's focal point with its prairie, woodlands, and wetland exhibition areas. The museum depicts how the area appeared before the arrival of the European settlers. Kids like climbing through the wolf den. The center has large diorama aquariums - home to the native turtles and snakes you would find in the nearby Rock River area and its tributaries. A glass-sided beehive gives visitors a close-but safe-encounter with honey bees at work making honey, caring for their queen and her unending brood, and protecting their home.

HERITAGE FARM MUSEUM: also located in the Byron Forest Preserve District. This house includes five rooms: a bedroom, a living room, a kitchen, a summer kitchen, and a room showing a section of original grout house. The rooms contain furniture representative of the time period 1843 - 1869. Currently the outbuildings, which include the big barn, the corncrib, the hog barn, and the milk house, are being restored.

WEISKOPF OBSERVATORY

Byron - *7993 North River Road, 61010. Phone: (815) 234-8535*. The J. Weiskopf Observatory, appropriately located on the third highest point in Ogle County, is open for public sky viewing on every Tuesday and Saturday beginning at dusk, weather permitting. Rockford physician, Dr. Jerome Weiskopf, donated the dome and 11-inch reflecting telescope. During the weekly viewing sessions, visitors see the planets, the moon and fainter objects in the sky. Call ahead to confirm viewing conditions.

CHANNAHON STATE PARK & I&M CANAL TRAILHEAD

Channahon - *2 West Story Street (I-55: take the Rte. 6 / Channahon exit; one mile south of US 6 and Canal Street), 60410. www.dnr.state.il.us/lands/landmgt/parks/i&m/east/channaho/park.htm. Phone: (815) 467-4271. Admission: FREE.* This state park serves as the trailhead for the 61-mile I&M Canal State Trail. Channahon is an Indian word meaning "the meeting of the waters" and signifies the joining of the DuPage, Des Plaines and Kankakee Rivers. Historic structures include a canal locktender's house and canal locks 6 and 7. Anglers of all ages will enjoy fishing in either the Illinois & Michigan Canal or the DuPage River. Primitive tent camping only.

GLIDDEN HOMESTEAD AND HISTORICAL CENTER

Dekalb - *921 West Lincoln Highway (I-88 to Annie Glidden Road exit, to Lincoln Highway east), 60115. Web: www.gliddenhomestead.org.* Phone: *(815) 756-7904, Hours: First and third Sundays from Noon-4:00pm (May-first week of December).* The Glidden Homestead & Historical Center is restoring and developing the site where in the 1870s, Joseph F. Glidden invented "The Winner," one of the most widely-used types of barbed wire. It is still a work in progress. Built in 1861, the house and brick barn were constructed for local farmer and barbed wire inventor, Joseph Glidden. It is considered the birthplace of barbed wire, one of several important inventions to encourage homesteading on the prairie.

STAGE COACH THEATRE

Dekalb - *126 South 5th Street, 60115. Phone: (815) 758-1940. Web: www.stagecoachers.com. Shows: Thursday-Saturday evenings, Sunday matinees. Admission: Tickets run $7.00-$12.00 depending on venue. Children under 5 are recommended to only attend matinees.* Attend a drama, comedy or musical in one of the oldest community theaters in Illinois. Productions include family friendly shows like Huck Finn and a Christmas Carol.

RONALD REAGAN BOYHOOD HOME

816 S. Hennepin (look for signs off IL 26 north), **Dixon** 61021

❑   Phone: (815) 288-5176

❑   Hours: Monday-Saturday 10:00am-4:00pm, Sunday 1:00-4:00pm (April-November); Weekends only (February and March); closed December and January.

❑   Admission: Donations accepted.

❑   Tour: Begin at the Visitors Center with a short video, then followed by a 15 minute house tour. Just the right amount of time for kids.

Reagan's parents, Jack and Nelle, moved to Dixon in 1920, when Reagan was 9 years old. The Ronald Reagan Boyhood Home is restored to its 1920 condition and decorated with furniture typical of the period. Family activity extended beyond the house to the barn where "Dutch" and his brother "Moon" raised rabbits. The boys also played football on the side yard with their friends. Listen and watch for the signed football and the secret hiding place for coins (hint: by the fireplace). What was their favorite evening snack? No, not jelly beans! Learn how diverse his interests were and some of his heroics (saving 77 lives as a lifeguard). This is a great way to study a modern-day President as a boy. Excellent presentation.

NATIONAL MISSISSIPPI RIVER MUSEUM & AQUARIUM

350 E. 3rd Street (follow the signs off Rte. 20 west, just over the bridge from IL), **Dubuque (IOWA)** 52001

❑   Phone: (563) 557-9545 or (800) 226-3369
   Web: www.rivermuseum.com
❑   Hours: Daily 10:00am-5:00pm. Open until 6:00pm (summers).
❑   Admission: $9.75 adult, $8.75 senior (65+), $7.50 youth (7-17), $4.00 child (3-6).
❑   Miscellaneous: Boat & Breakfast - stay overnight in bunks on a steam ship dredger. Have a hearty sailors' breakfast.

Take a historic and natural journey on the Mighty Mississippi. Begin with Mississippi Journey - a sight, sound and motion short film - grabs you into the river "scene". Chart a course as you pass floor-to-ceiling glass panels framing gators, otters (so playful), ancient sturgeon and paddlefish. Walk on working riverboats, go into cargo holds in the Barge theatre, touch fish or "Noodle" a catfish! Kids can also roll on logs like lumberjacks, pilot a boat or walk through a lead mine (actually, almost crawl). Finally, watch craftsmen carve a boat in the wood shop. A lot of money and time have produced an excellent site to feel the mighty Mississippi from on, and in, the water. Well worth the trip over the bridge to the Iowa shores.

APPLE RIVER FORT STATE HISTORIC SITE

P.O. Box 206, **Elizabeth** 61028

❑   Phone: (815) 858-2028, **Web: www.appleriverfort.com**
❑   Hours: Wednesday-Sunday 9:00am-5:00pm (March - mid-April);
     9:00am-4:00pm (November-February). Open daily in summer.
❑   Miscellaneous: Living History Weekends are held almost every
     weekend (May-October). Chat with the townsfolk and find out
     what their chores were and what they feared.

Apple River Fort State Historic Site is the site of one of the battles
fought during the Black Hawk War. The discovery of lead in the
Galena area during the 1820's brought many miners to the area.
Black Hawk, a Sauk warrior who had fought with the British against
the United States in the War of 1812, was determined to return to the
land he believed belonged to his people. Black Hawk and his
warriors attacked the hastily erected fort on June 24, 1832. The
Sauk had over 200 warriors, the settlers only 25 men. How did
settler womens' bravery during the fighting help them win and earn
the town's name?   Located a short walk from the fort, the
Interpretive Center relates the story of the Black Hawk War and the
Apple River Fort. A series of illustrated panels tells the story of Sauk
and Fox, the early miners, and the conflict between the two cultures
that led to the Black Hawk War. Other exhibits at the two-story
Interpretive Center include a 15-minute video of the Black Hawk
War (pull up a tree stump chair) and archaeology exhibits telling
how the fort was located and displaying some of the artifacts
uncovered at the site. Exhibits along the trail to the fort explore the
role of Abraham Lincoln and other notables in the Black Hawk War.

FRANKLIN CREEK STATE NATURAL AREA
& GRIST MILL

1872 Twist Road (one mile NW of town, 8 miles east of Dixon, just
north of IL 38), **Franklin** 61031

❑   Phone: (815) 456-2878 or (815) 456-2718 mill
     www.dnr.state.il.us/lands/landmgt/parks/r1/franklin.htm
❑   Hours: Gristmill: Thursday-Sunday Noon-4:00pm (April-
     October).

Franklin Creek State Natural Area & Grist Mill *(cont.)*

❑   Admission: Admission to Illinois State Parks is free. Camping
        fees range from $6.00-11.00 per night, depending on amenities; a
        $5.00 fee is charged for camping reservations.

The beautiful Franklin Creek flows throughout the 664-acre park
and serves to offer fishing, horseback riding, hiking and cross-
country skiing sites. The Mill Springs Trail is a unique, concrete-
surfaced trail suitable for people of all mobility levels. The easy
trail leads to the beautiful Mill Spring. Pioneer Pass is highly
recommended to see the park's unique, natural beauty. The
original early American corn meal and wheat flour producing mill,
constructed in 1847, was the "largest and most complete" grist mill
in Lee County. The newly reconstructed Franklin Creek Grist Mill
became operational in 1999. Along with milling demonstrations,
the building serves as a visitors center for the natural area. All four
levels of the Grist Mill are handicapped accessible.

SILVER CREEK AND STEPHENSON RAILROAD ANTIQUE STEAM TRAIN RIDES

Freeport - *2954 S. Walnut (US 20 west of Rockford, Walnut and Lamm
Roads), 61032. Phone: (815) 235-7329 or (815) 232-2306. Hours:
Typically weekends beginning in May thru October. 11:00am-4:00pm.
Admission: $3.00-$5.00 per person.* All aboard as a 36-ton 1912 Heisler
steam locomotive pulls three cabooses, including an antique red caboose
reported to be the oldest in the state, and two passenger flatcars for a four
mile ride through farmlands and across a bridge 30' above Yellow Creek.
Purchase your ticket at the Silver Creek Depot, a turn-of-the-century
replica filled with railroad artifacts. Browse for novelties in the Freight
House. Visit the 25-room Silvercreek Museum filled with early Americana
and enjoy homemade food served for lunch.

STEPHENSON COUNTY HISTORICAL MUSEUM

Freeport - *1440 South Carroll Avenue, 61032. Phone: (815) 232-8419.
Web: www.stephcohs.org. Hours: Generally weekends Noon-4:00pm.
Summer extended days open. Admission: $1.00-$3.00.* Oscar Taylor built
this mansion back in 1857. Today, exhibits feature over 150 years of area
history, plus a rural schoolhouse, log cabin, farm and industrial museums.
Living History Days are the best time to visit as re-enactors are demonstrating fur
trading, spinning, open-fire cooking, blacksmithing & candle or soap-making.

CHESTNUT MOUNTAIN RESORT ACTIVITIES

8700 W. Chestnut Road, **Galena** 61036

❑ Phone: (815) 777-1320 or (800) 397-1320
Web: www.chestnutmtn.com

❑ Hours: Slide Weekends and Holidays 10:00am-8:00pm (dusk). Weekdays generally 3:00pm-8:00pm.

❑ Admission: $3.00-$5.00 per slide or mini-golf. Unlimited passes available, too. Note: once you go down the Alpine Slide once, you'll want to go again.

❑ Tours: Cruise: Saturday, & Sunday at 10:30am, 12:30pm, 2:30pm, and 4:30pm (Please arrive 1/2 hour early for departure time. Tickets can be purchased at Alpine Slide).

❑ Miscellaneous: Skiing, of course, is their specialty with many chairlifts and slopes to choose from. Lodging rooms are available year-round and chalet atmosphere dining, too. The resort is modest and caters towards skiers and simple accommodations.

ALPINE SLIDE - Fun for all ages. No special skills needed — you control your own speed. Ride your own sled down the 2,050 ft. ofterrain-tailored track to the banks of the Mississippi. What a thrill - go slow the first ride - then, challenge yourself with speed! Travel back up on the scenic chair lift and enjoy a three-state view. Opens Memorial Day Weekend-Labor Day. Spring and Fall hours are weekend only. Children six and under must ride with an adult. $4.00-$5.00 per ride. Unlimited passes available, too.

MISSISSIPPI EXPLORER CRUISES - Jump aboard the Mississippi Explorer's newest cruise and experience all the nature the Upper Mississippi River National Wildlife & Fish Refuge has to offer. This 1½ hour expedition cruise offers explorers an in-depth exploration of the Mississippi River's ecosystem, navigation, and history. It's a slow and lazy tour - good for relaxation but not terribly exciting for active kids. Binoculars are provided. Summer weekends only. Rates run $12.00-$20.00 per person (age 3+). *All cruises include Alpine Slide/Scenic Chair Ride to and from departure area.

GALENA JO DAVIESS COUNTY HISTORICAL MUSEUM

211 S. Bench Street (downtown), Galena 61036

- ❑ Phone: (815) 777-9129, **Web: www.galenahistorymuseum.org**
- ❑ Hours: Daily 9:00am-4:30pm.
- ❑ Admission: Small admission (ages 10+).
- ❑ Miscellaneous: Do you realize that the Field of Dreams Movie Site is just one hour away in Iowa? Go to **www.fodmoviesite.com** to get directions to the site in Dyersville, Iowa. Open daily 9:00am-6:00pm. FREE.

Exhibits include Civil War, mining, steamboating, clothing, geology, dolls, and toys. Shown hourly, watch the 15 minute slide show detailing Galena's history. Learn how early mining, smelting and steamboating made Galena a lead mine boom town. They recently found (during renovations) an opening to a real mine shaft. Now, you can lean over the clear-covered opening and look down. Kids really like this and the hands-on area where kids can pretend to make a pie or weigh lead. Incredibly, nine of Galena's citizens became Union Generals for service rendered during the Civil War, including the most famous of all - Ulysses S. Grant. Keep a watchful eye over the gallery for the famous Thomas Nast painting "Peace in the Union" depicting Lee's surrender to Grant at Appomattox in 1865.

GALENA TROLLEYS

314 S. Main Street, Galena 61036

- ❑ Phone: (815) 777-1248 -9301 or (877) GALENA1
  Web: www.galenatrolleys.com
- ❑ Admission: $11.00 adult, $6.00 child (under 12)-one hour non-stop.
- ❑ Tours: Leaving every hour, except weekends every ½ hr.

Did you know that 85% of the world's lead ore was extruded from this territory by the 1870's (a Lead Rush vs. a Gold Rush)? Galena is Latin for lead. Galena is the most historically preserved 19th century town in the United States and 85% of the buildings are on the National Historic Registry. The lead mining and river boating era left behind evidence of tremendous wealth and prosperity. The trolley tours travel up and down the hills and valleys, passing by the beautifully restored mansions (the biggest and the oldest) and U.S. Grant's pre and post civil war homes. Drive through the flood gates - make sure you're on the right side. See and hear about the first candlemaker; the train depot; a boot company; riverboat captains; a garden with a tin man and a dinosaur; a high school turned into condos; and the oldest continually running Post Office in the U.S. End the tour passing shops and restaurants lining Main Street, which is bustling with pedestrians, horse carriages and adorable window storefronts tempting you to enter. Now that you're armed with information, we recommend walking Main Street, reading many of the historic plaques, trying to find the spot filmed as Chisholm, Minnesota in Field of Dreams (ask about stories from townsfolk), or purchasing treats from Chocolat' or American Popcorn Company. This town is too fun!

ULYSSES S. GRANT HOME & OLD MARKET HOUSE STATE HISTORIC SITES

500 Bouthillier Street/ 123 North Commerce Street, **Galena** 61036

❑   Phone: (815) 777-3310, **Web: www.granthome.com**
❑   Hours: Wednesday-Sunday 9:00am-5:00pm (March-May). Open
     Daily (summer). Museums close at 4:00pm (winter). The sites
     are also closed on New Year's, Martin Luther King, Jr.,
     Presidents, Veterans, General Election, Thanksgiving and
     Christmas Day.
❑   Admission: Suggested donation $1.00-$3.00.

GRANT HOME: In March 1864, Grant was appointed lieutenant general and commanded the Union army to war's end. On April 9, 1865, Confederate General Robert E. Lee surrendered his troops to Grant at Appomattox Court House, and Grant's image as a war hero was complete. On August 18, 1865, Galena celebrated the return of its Civil War hero. Following a jubilant procession with much flag waving and speeches, a group of Galena citizens presented the General with a handsome furnished house on Bouthillier Street. The 1860s brick home is furnished and decorated as it was in 1868. With many masculine touches, you'll see the "presence" of Grant in every room. You'll learn something of his personal life, too.

OLD MARKET HOUSE: The Old Market House, constructed in 1845-1846, was the focal point of community life during Galena's heyday. The Greek revival Old Market House sheltered vendors and shoppers, who gathered in the heart of the river city's business district until 1910. Buyers and sellers would congregate there, wrote Galena's semi-weekly newspaper, The Jeffersonian, and the competition would lower prices. Galenians would no longer be compelled to "traverse half the city to make some paltry purchase." The House is connected to Grant through a special exhibit. In it, look for a "Get Well" letter written by a little girl.

VINEGAR HILL LEAD MINE & MUSEUM

Galena - *8885 N. 3 Pines Road, 61036. Phone: (815) 777-0855. Hours: By appointment and regular summer hours. Call for current schedule and admission.* Mined by an Irishman in 1822 and handed down to following generations, this underground mine is typical of the era. As you visit the Vinegar Hill Lead Mine, your guide will acquaint you with early mining methods. The museum includes primitive tools and early artifacts. The guided tour includes a walk into the mine. Don a hard hat and enter the low passageway (reason for the hard hats) way below the surface. Even pass under a cemetery far above the underground mine.

JOHN DEERE HISTORIC SITE

8393 South Main (take I-88 to IL-26. Continue 1.70 miles north on IL-26, and turn right onto East River Road/IL-2. Continue approximately 6 miles to town), **Grand Detour** 61021

❑   Phone: (815) 652-4551, **Web: www.JohnDeerePavilion.com**
❑   Hours: Daily 9:00am-5:00pm (April-November).
❑   Admission: $3.00 (ages 12+).

Vermont native, John Deere, with a few tools and very little money, struck out on his own towards Illinois. He promised his wife Demarius and their children that he would be back to get them after he made a good start. It didn't take long, Grand Detour was in need of a blacksmith and John Deere was just the man needed. Shortly after arriving in town, Deere learned that the commonly used cast-iron plows of the day performed poorly in the sticky soil of the Midwest.   Convinced that a plow with a highly polished surface would clean, or self-scour as it moved through the field,

John Deere fashioned just such an implement in 1837, using steel from a broken saw blade. It wasn't long before manufacturing plows, not blacksmithing, became the main focus of Deere's livelihood. Visit the Center's exhibits and film, then go onsite through the Deere home and the re-created blacksmith shop where it all began. See the archeological original floor of the actual workshop where he invented the "singing" plow. They present an interesting description and demonstration of how Deere ran his shop - the blacksmith is witty and a good storyteller. How does a blacksmith put a muffler on his anvil? What does the term "beat the daylight out of it" mean? In the home, hear a simulated conversation, John and Demarius Deere talking of daily events. A wonderful place to explore the history of a famous man and his invention.

LAKE LE-AQUA-NA STATE PARK

Lena - *8542 North Lake Rd (IL 73 north and to 2 miles into the town of Lena. Turn left onto Lena Street. 3 miles north of town), 61048. www.dnr.state.il.us/lands/landmgt/parks/r1/leaquana.htm.* Phone: *(815) 369-4282 Admission: Admission to Illinois State Parks is free. Camping fees range from $6-11.00 per night, depending on amenities; a $5.00 fee is charged for camping reservations.* Lake Le-Aqua-Na takes its name from a combination of the words Lena and aqua, the Latin name for water. The family oriented park surrounds a 40-acre, man-made lake offering fishing and boating. Bring your own, or rent a rowboat, canoe or paddleboat at the park concession stand (only electric motors are allowed on the lake). Food and picnic snacks are also available (seasonally). There's a small beach especially for children (open daily 8:00am-8:00pm, Memorial Day-Labor Day (no lifeguards). Campers will find RV, tent, equestrian and youth group campgrounds. Deer are common at Lake-Le-Aqua-Na, and wild turkeys are sometimes seen. Migrating waterfowl frequent the lake in the spring and autumn. The park's 7 miles of wooded trails are rated easy to moderate. Cross-country skiing, sledding & ice fishing are popular in the winter months.

TORKELSON CHEESE COMPANY

Lena - *9453 Louisa Road. 61048. Phone: (815) 369-4265.* **Web:** *www.torkelsoncheese.com.* Duane and Cheryl Torkelson have been involved in the cheese industry for over 30 years. Torkelson Cheese Company manufactures Brick, Muenster, Quesadilla, and Asadero. Torkelson Cheese purchases quality milk from local farmers, helping to produce more than 30,000 pounds of cheese per day. See cheese made, then stock up on award-winning cheese at Factory prices. Generally, weekday mornings are best for viewing. Call ahead for tours or best viewing times.

ILLINI STATE PARK

Marseilles - *2660 East 2350th Road (on the southern bank of the Illinois River south of town), 61341. Phone: (815) 795-2448. www.dnr.state.il.us/lands/landmgt/parks/i&m/east/illini/park.htm.* The 500-acre park is a haven for songbirds, waterfowl and other wildlife. Many of the shelters were constructed by CCC in the 1930s. Birders mention this trail as one of the best sites in the county for viewing migrating vereos, warblers, thrushes, and other songbirds in Fall. Illini State Park is the perfect place for winter fun. An ice skating pool and hills ideal for sledding provide hardy outdoor enjoyment. A shelter offers a comfortable setting for warming fingers and toes after a winter workout. They also have ball fields, fishing, hiking, biking, cross-country, and skiing trails. The LaSalle Lake area features rocky shorelines, a wildlife refuge and power boating.

MORAINE HILLS STATE PARK

McHenry - *1510 South River Road (IL Rt. 12 south to Rt. 176. West to River Road. North on River Road approx. 2 miles to entrance), 60051. www.dnr.state.il.us/lands/landmgt/parks/r2/morhills.htm Phone: (815) 385-1624.* From angling to hiking, from viewing rare plants to observing migratory waterfowl, more than 10 miles of one-way trails make Moraine Hills popular for hikers and bicyclists. Deriving its name from the accumulation of boulders, stones and other debris left by glaciers, the park also includes marsh areas. Pike Marsh, a 115-acre area in the southeast corner of the park, is home to many rare plants. Its outer fen area (a very rare marsh wetland) includes one of the state's largest known colonies of pitcher plants, which attract, trap, and digest insects. McHenry Dam, on the Fox River, is on the park's western border. Boat rentals and concessions are available.

GEBHARD WOODS STATE PARK

Morris - *401 Ottawa Street, 60450. Phone: (815) 942-0796. www.dnr.state.il.us/lands/landmgt/parks/i&m/east/gebhard/park.htm. Admission to Illinois State Parks is free. Camping fees range from $6.00-11.00 per night, depending on amenities; a $5.00 fee is charged for camping reservations.* Dotted with shade trees, the park stretches along the I&M Canal. Today, hikers, campers, picnickers, and canoeists frequent this 30-acre site, making it one of the state's most popular state parks. Gebhard Woods is only a footbridge away from the historic Illinois & Michigan Canal State Trail. This 61 mile trail on the old canal towpath is easy walking and gives access to unparalleled scenic and historic sights. Bicyclists can also take advantage of the groomed towpath to enjoy the natural and manmade wonders. The trail is marked and has various wayside exhibits that describe features of the canal era encountered along the way. Due to the trail's composition, horseback riding isn't allowed, however, winter snow brings out registered snowmobilers.

GOOSE LAKE PRAIRIE STATE NATURAL AREA

5010 North Jugtown Road (southeast of town, midway between Hwy 47 and I-55), **Morris** 60450

❑   Phone: (815) 942-2899

www.dnr.state.il.us/lands/landmgt/parks/i&m/east/goose/home.htm

Visiting Goose Lake Prairie State Natural Area today is much like seeing Illinois as it was 150 years ago, when prairie covered nearly 60 percent of the state. Looking much like prairie you'd see on TV shows, you'll see big bluestem, Indian grass and switchgrass plus broad-leafed flowering plants known as forbs. One of the best ways to experience Goose Lake Prairie is to hit the trails. With 7 miles of hiking trails including a floating bridge, you'll have ample opportunity for viewing the plants and animals that make the area unique.

❑   PRAIRIE VIEW TRAIL, with 3.5 miles of moderate hiking, goes through prairie and farmland. Visible are strip mine reclamation areas, low-lying marshes and farmland.

❑   TALL GRASS NATURE TRAIL is a self-guiding trek that winds through the prairie and the trail's trademark grasses of big bluestem and Indian grass, which can grow to 8 feet in height.

Depending on the route you decide to take, the trail can be 1 or 3½ miles long. One loop offers a hard-packed, wheelchair-accessible surface. Trails are available for cross-country skiing in the winter.

MORRISON-ROCKWOOD STATE PARK

Morrison - *18750 Lake Road (I-88 to IL 78 exit north through town to Damen Road. Turn left on Crosby Road, follow signs about 1.5 miles), 61270. www.dnr.state.il.us/lands/landmgt/parks/r1/morrison.htm#directions.* Phone: (815) 772-4708 Admission to Illinois State Parks is free. Camping fees range from $6.00-11.00 per night, depending on amenities; a $5.00 fee is charged for camping reservations. Boasting an abundant animal population, this State Park offers woodland and water to coyotes, deer, foxes and large birds. The site includes Lake Carlton and offers camping, fishing, horseback riding, hiking trails, and boating. Take the large, two-span Covered Bridge on part of the road to the park. At 148 feet long, it has 32 windows on each side, letting light in and adding to its antique look. Plan a family outing at the Lakeview picnic area, or just do some bird watching among the hickory, ash, oak and walnut trees.

WHITE PINES FOREST STATE PARK

6712 West Pines Road (southwest of town, US 20 west to
Rte. 2 south), **Mt. Morris** 61054

❑   Phone: (815) 946-3717 or (815) 946-3817 lodge

  www.dnr.state.il.us/lands/landmgt/parks/r1/whitepns.htm

❑   Admission: Admission to Illinois State Parks is free. Camping
  fees range from $6.00-11.00 per night, depending on amenities; a
  $5.00 fee is charged for camping reservations.

❑   Miscellaneous: White Pines Dinner Theatre afternoon matinees
  (evening performances in December only) are for those who enjoy
  nostalgic musicals, charming entertainers, lots of laughter, and
  delicious food served in a log cabin lodge. Best of all, it's reasonably
  priced and you can be home before dark (April through mid-Dec.).

The park features the southernmost strand of native white pines in Illinois. It is also noted for its vine-covered limestone bluffs. You can drive through Pine Creek's flowing stream via the concrete fords. History tells us that this was for years the principal route east and west across the northern part of the state. Today, there are plenty of outdoor recreation activities, such as hiking, fishing, camping and picnicking. Whether you choose an easy walking trail or a more difficult path, three of the seven marked trails are less than a mile long and provide ample opportunity to see the beautiful vine-covered limestone bluffs, blossoming spring flowers and whispering pines. Amidst the serene setting, modern lodge facilities, log cabins and camping allow for overnighting. Each cabin sleeps four people and is complete with shower, gas log fireplace, one queen bed and one trundle bed. All cabins are air-conditioned and heated, and have telephones and televisions. The historic lounge area, which is part of the main lodge, is filled with crafts and artwork, including a gift shop.

CASTLE ROCK STATE PARK

Oregon - *1365 W. Castle Rd. (4 miles south of town on IL Hwy 2), 61061. www.dnr.state.il.us/lands/landmgt/parks/r1/castle.htm. Phone: (815) 732-7329. Admission to Illinois State Parks is free. Camping fees range from $6.00-11.00 per night, depending on amenities; a $5.00 fee is charged for camping reservations.* This 2,000-acre, day-use-only park (no camping) is named for a large sandstone wall along the Rock River. Some 700 acres of Castle Rock are designated as an Illinois Nature Preserve, preserving remnants of native forest and prairie. Picnic tables are scattered along the river. There's a boat-launching ramp opposite the park entrance. Castle Rock has 6 miles of easy to moderate hiking trails, including three trails near the south edge of the park. Hikers may spot white-tailed deer or wild turkey. Beaver, great blue herons, indigo buntings and kingfishers are common park residents. The park's namesake lies about one-half mile south of the entrance. It's a healthy hike up the wooden steps to the top of Castle Rock, but the bird's-eye view of the Rock River is worth it. Winter activities include cross-country skiing & tobogganing.

LOWDEN STATE PARK

Oregon - *1411 N. River Rd (I-39, exit #104 on Rt 64 west 16 miles), 61061. www.dnr.state.il.us/lands/landmgt/parks/r1/lowdensp.htm Phone: (815) 732-6828 Admission: Admission to Illinois State Parks is free. Camping fees range from $6.00-11.00 per night, depending on amenities; a $5.00 fee is charged for camping reservations.* Set on high bluffs, the park is best known as the home of Chicago sculptor Lorado Taft's huge concrete statue of an American Indian. Taft named his 50 foot-high, 100-ton creation "Eternal Indian." But it's universally called "Black Hawk," after the famed 19th Century Sauk warrior. Legend has it that Chief Black Hawk, as he left the area after the Black Hawk War, talked of the beauty of the area and admonished his captors to care for the land as he and his people had. The 207-acre park offers splendid views of the Rock River and Oregon. There are several picnic areas with tables, drinking water and park stoves. Individual and group camping sites include limited electricity and a shower building; reservations are not accepted. Four miles of hiking trails rated moderately difficult wander through scenic woods and along the bluff tops. White-tailed deer and many species of birds, including the brilliant red-headed woodpecker, are park residents.

WHITE PINES RANCH

Oregon - *3581 Pines Road (I-90 West to Rockford, West on 20 (towards Freeport), South on IL Route 2), 61061. Phone: (815) 732-7923. Web: www.whitepinesranch.com. Miscellaneous: The dormitories are complete with bunk beds, carpeting, electrical heating and adjoining bathrooms with showers, flush toilets, and vanities with mirrors. The main lodge has a large dining hall where home-cooked meals are served buffet style. A game room and gift shop are on the premises.* White Pines Ranch covers 200 acres of beautiful woods, pastures and horse trails. The buildings are modern structures built with an old west theme. This ranch offers horseback riding, swimming (in season), hiking through a beautiful sandstone canyon, horse studies with grooming, scavenger hunts, mapping, orienteering, outdoor games, fossil hunts, and studying wildlife. Evening activities may include hayrides, bingo, country line dancing and campfire songs. Winter activities include cross country skiing, sledding and lots of hot chocolate. Hours and admission are per package or program offered/scheduled.

BUFFALO ROCK STATE PARK & EFFIGY TUMULI

Ottawa - *Dee Bennett Road, 1300 North 27th Road (banks of Illinois River, two miles west of town), 61350. Phone: (815) 433-2220. www.dnr.state.il.us/lands/landmgt/parks/i&m/east/buffalo/home.htm Admission to Illinois State Parks is free. Camping fees range from $6.00-11.00 per night, depending on amenities; a $5.00 fee is charged for camping reservations.* On the bluffs of the River, stand five earthen sculptures molded from Illinois clay. Called Effigy Tumuli, this unique "earth art" is one of the most prominent displays of outdoor sculpture around. All five subjects - snake, catfish, turtle, frog and insect are native to the area. The park has ball diamonds, picnic areas, biking, canoeing, hiking, snow-mobiling and cross-country skiing trails, too.

ILLINOIS WATERWAY VISITORS CENTER

Ottawa - *950 North 27th Road, Dee Bennett Road (I-80 to Utica and exit south on rt. 178, enter the park from the west; across the river from Starved Rock State Park), 61350. Phone: (815) 667-4054. Web: www.iit.edu/~travel/iww.html. Hours: Daily, daylight hours. Admission:*

FREE. Water is still the least expensive way to transport heavy bulk goods like grain, coal, sand and gravel. In 1933, the US Army Corps of Engineers replaced the I&M Canal with the Illinois River to create a waterway from Chicago to the Mississippi River. Today, one barge can carry 1500 tons - the same freight it would have taken 10 canal boats to carry. One tugboat can push 15 barges at a time. Explore the observation area and visitors center where you can see huge barges going through a lock. Interpretive programs discuss the lock and dam system of the Illinois River and the national waterway system.

SHERRI LYNN RIVERBOAT CRUISES

Ottawa - *(south on LaSalle towards the river, under the Rte. 23 bridge), 61350. Phone: (815) 228-5772. www.ottawariverboat.com. Tours: Sightseeing tours run 90 minutes at 2:00pm ($14.00-$19.00). Lunch tours (lunch at Starved Rock Marina, Captains Cove) run $20.00-$29.00. Season runs Wednesday-Sunday (May-October). Refreshments available on board. Reservations recommended.* Ottawa's miniature paddle wheeler cruises up and down the Illinois River where you will see and hear about Buffalo Rock, Tugboats and Barges, mansions and wildlife along the banks.

PROPHETSTOWN STATE RECREATION AREA

Prophetstown - *Riverside Drive and Park Avenue (south side of Rock River, northeast edge of town), 61277. Phone: (815) 537-2926. www.dnr.state.il.us/lands/landmgt/parks/r1/prophet.htm. Admission to Illinois State Parks is free. Camping fees range from $6.00-11.00 per night, depending on amenities; a $5.00 fee is charged for camping reservations.* Once the site of an American Indian village, the 53-acre park derives its name from the Native American prophet Wa-bo-kie-shiek. This park offers camping, fishing, a boat ramp, canoe access, and hiking. Wa-bo-kie-shiek nature trail follows along the edge of Coon Creek for approximately 1/3 of a mile. It offers access for anglers while also providing a scenic walk for hikers.

KLEHM ARBORETUM & BOTANIC GARDEN

Rockford - *2701 Clifton Avenue, 61102. Phone: (815) 965-8146. **Web:** www.klehm.org. Hours: Daily 9:00am-4:00pm, year-round. Open until 8:00pm in the summer. Admission: $2.00 (age 16+).* Planted initially as a nursery, today, the site showcases spring blossoms, summer flowers, fall foliage and winter evergreens, plus themed gardens (like the Butterfly Garden), sculptures and fountains. All ages can enjoy the maze and interactive sundial in the Children's Garden. Look for the mascot,

Klehmantine, as you take in whimsical sights, sounds and scents. Enjoy the paved figure-eight and many other wood-chipped paths.

BURPEE MUSEUM OF NATURAL HISTORY

737 North Main Street (downtown), **Rockford** 61103

❑   Phone: (815) 985-3433, **Web: www.burpee.org**
❑   Hours: Monday-Saturday 10:00am-5:00pm, Sunday Noon-5:00pm.
❑   Admission: $5.00 adult, $4.00 child (3-17). Wednesdays FREE to all. Free Parking.

The Natural History Museum is housed in three buildings on the west bank of the Rock River. The big attraction: *JANE!* This young dinosaur died in the Montana Badlands. In 2001, a group from Burpee discovered her bones. Experts have called this find "one of the ten most important dinosaur discoveries in the past 100 years." Upon entering the exhibit, visitors encounter a flat-screen television that shows the barren Badlands landscape of today. One by one, the dinosaurs appear on the scene. Next to the TV is a display of fossils that were found near Jane's bones. What did a housewife and professor find first? Tucked in a corner of the exhibit hall is a recreation of a paleontologist rustic cabin camp. Visitors can watch "home movies" that show what camp life was like and tell stories of how the team excavated Jane. Turning a corner, you finally come face-to-face with the fully restored *REAL skeleton of Jane!* What a great story! It's like solving a mystery along with the team of pros and amateurs. And, the area has easy, hands-on displays (for example: tap on the shoulder of a scientist to learn about his experiments). Other wonderful exhibits include: Walking through a Coal Forest - watch out for the thunderstorm; Native American recreated wigwam, tipi and pueblo (even sit a spell listening to storytellers or watch a PowWow); walk into the Woodlands in spring where you hear, touch and smell nature in the noisy season; and an interesting Viewing Lab where you can watch scientists at work as they prepare specimens.

DISCOVERY CENTER MUSEUM

711 North Main St (adjacent to the Burpee Museum), **Rockford** 61103

- Phone: (815) 963-6769, **Web: www.discoverycentermuseum.org**
- Hours: Tuesday-Saturday 10:00am-5:00pm, Sunday Noon-5:00pm; plus Mondays when local public schools are not in session.
- Admission: $4.00 adult, $3.00 child.
- Miscellaneous: Theatre has live science shows during peak times using theatrics. Fun, playful Family Fridays each summer are popular.

Discovery Center is a children's museum with 200+ hands-on arts and science exhibits and an outdoor science park (the play of a Kinetic ball maze, friction slides, pendulum swings, water play and digging for dinos like Jane). There's a Planetarium where kids can pretend they're astronauts; a TV Studio with live broadcasts on a local museum station (be an anchor, cameraman, producer or disappearing weatherman); Team Up where you explore science in sports choosing proper equipment, position and play; a Tot Spot with a huge dollhouse 5-feet high and pretend play; and the special Spiral staircase with a giant mouse-hole maze between the museum's two levels.

TROLLEY STATION & FOREST CITY QUEEN RIDES

324 N. Madion St (Riverview Park, south end), **Rockford** 61103

- Phone: (815) 987-8894
  Web: www.rockfordparkdistrict.org/facilities.html
- Admission: $3.50-5.00 per seat. Slight discount for residents.
- Tours: Trolley: Thursday, Saturday, Sunday afternoons. Queen: Wednesday, Friday, Saturday & Sunday afternoons. Tours depart on the hour, hourly (early June - late August).
- Miscellaneous: Family Fun Nights are offered Wednesdays with pizza and the best seat on the river for Ski Broncs water ski shows. This fun-filled 2 hour cruise is packed with excitement for kids of all ages. Order whole pizzas or by the slice.

All aboard! Departing from downtown Rockford, by rail or by sail, you will discover interesting tidbits about the early history of the community by enjoying a ride on the Track Trolley or the Forest City Queen Riverboat.

TROLLEY CAR 36: Makes its way from the Trolley Station beside the scenic Rock River Recreation Path, makes a stop for a brief visit to the Sinnissippi Greenhouse, then turns around at Symbol and returns to the station.

FOREST CITY QUEEN: The Forest City Queen gives you an up close and personal glimpse of some of the most stately homes on the banks of the Rock River. You'll hear lighthearted stories about Rockford's humble beginnings on the River and its constant influence today. A variety of cruise options are available, from hourly narration tours, family-style picnics, Ski Broncs performances, to elegant dining.

ANDERSON JAPANESE GARDENS

Rockford - *318 Spring Creek Road, 61107. Phone: (815) 229-9390. Web: www.andersongardens.org.* Hours: Monday-Friday 10:00am-5:00pm, Saturday 10:00am-4:00pm, Sunday Noon-4:00pm. (May-October). Admission: $5.00 adult, $4.00 senior, $3.00 student. These Japanese Gardens were named the best Japanese garden in North America. The 12-acre treasure is open for self-guided tours daily featuring waterfalls, ponds, paths, quiet corners and 16th century Sukiya-style structures, including a guesthouse, teahouse and gazebo.

MIDWAY VILLAGE

6799 Guilford Road (I-90 to BR20 west. North on Bell School Rd, west on Guilford Rd.), **Rockford** 61107

❑   Phone: (815) 397-9112 **Web: www.midwayvillage.com**
❑   Hours: Museum Center: Tuesday-Saturday 10:00am-5:00pm, Sunday 11:00am-5:00pm. Village: Tuesday-Sunday 11:00am-4:00pm (June-September); Thursday-Sunday only (May & October).
❑   Admission: $5.00 adult, $3.00 child (3-17). Events ~$1.00 more.
❑   Miscellaneous: Cheer on the Midway Marauders as they play Baseball using rules from 1858 when men were men and gloves were for sissies. Enjoy popcorn, peanuts and old-fashioned root beer. The Museum Gift Shop has prepared Sock Monkeys or make-your-own kits.

Explore stories of ancestors in the Museum Center galleries: Swedish Singers, Rockford Peaches, Industry, and Aviation. Walk the route of soldiers on the floor map. Discover the invention of the sock knitting machine and the famous red-heeled sock - now, the tube sock and the endearing Sock Monkey toy! Now, wander overseas as stories are told in the world of miniatures in the Old Dolls House Museum where the cultures of countries around the world are represented in miniature homes. Kids love this doll museum (even boys) because every house is completely different and everything is much cuter in miniature. Visit the Millhouse located on Lake Severin featuring an exhibition, video presentation, and functioning waterwheel. Finally, experience stories of the Victorian age as you stroll through Midway Village, featuring 26 historic structures including a hardware store, general store, print shop, one-room schoolhouse, fire station, police station, hospital, bank, and homes. Be sure to allow time for a guided tour.

MAGIC WATERS WATERPARK

7820 CherryVale North Blvd. (I-90 exit BR 20 west, Bell School Rd. south, across from Cherryvale Mall), **Rockford (Cherry Valley)** 61016

❑   Phone: (815) 332-3260 or (800) 373-1679

   www.magicwaterswaterpark.com

❑   Hours: Summers opening at 10:00am until 7:00 or 9:00pm.

❑   Admission: $15.50-$18.50. $3.50 (age 2 and under). Residents and youngsters under 48" save $3.00 off. Save $5.00-$6.00 off after 3:00pm. Locker rental $3.00, Tube Rental $4.00.

"Totally Splashtacular Family Fun". Start in the darkness of the Abyss or the light of the water bucket Island. Daring? Try Splashblaster - the Midwest's largest Water Coaster thrill ride. This is really a thrill as it's a combination of the "big hill" to start a coaster ride, combined with the twists and falls being cushioned by water. Breaker Beach wavepool is 650,000 gallons of heated water, alternating between ocean waves and calm. Kick back and tube up, because you'll be set in motion on the 1200-foot floating River. Body slides splash, twist and careen at speeds up to 30 mph. Pipeline tube rides send you on wet, winding fun adventures down a wave of water. Little ones have their own Little Lagoon waterplay area. Clean and nice park for families.

SKI BRONCS WATER SKI SHOW

Rockford (Loves Park) - *Shorewood Park on the Rock River (Forest Grove Street between Junius and McKinley Streets), 61103. Phone: (815) 378-3000. Shows: Wednesdays and Fridays 7:00pm (late June-Labor Day weekend). Admission: FREE, donations collected at intermission.* The Ski Broncs Water-Ski Show Team performs summer shows with a humorous "Around the World in 80 Days" theme or some sort of variation of a sitcom theme. Support local, competitive skiers who are honing their presentation skills.

ROCKFORD SPEEDWAY

Rockford (Loves Park) - *9572 Forest Hills Road (just two miles west of Interstate 90 at the intersection of Forest Hills Road and Highway 173), 61105. Phone: (815) 633-1500. Web: www.rockfordspeedway.com.* Exciting NASCAR stock car races and novelty races take place April through October. They host the National Short Track Championships.

ROCK CUT STATE PARK

Rockford (Loves Park) - *7318 Harlem Road (Go North on Perryville to Hwy. 173, Go East on Hwy. 173 about 1-1/2 miles), 61111. www.dnr.state.il.us/lands/landmgt/parks/r1/rockcut.htm. Phone: (815) 885-3311 Hours: Summer hours (April - October) 6:00am-10:00pm. Winter hours (November - March) 8:00am - 5:00pm. Admission to Illinois State Parks is free. Camping fees range from $6.00-11.00 per night, depending on amenities; a $5.00 fee is charged for camping reservations. Beach swimming $1.00.* Two lakes set off the park's 3,092 acres. Pierce Lake, with 162 acres, is a retreat for people wanting to fish, ice fish or ice skate. A second 50-acre Olson Lake is especially for swimmers. Rounding out the park's recreational options are camping, hiking, horseback trails and cross-country skiing. The trail system at Rock Cut offers opportunities for hiking (40 miles), mountain biking (23 miles), and equestrian (14 miles) and has been completely remarked beginning in 2003. Trail users will find updated trail head/information signs at picnic areas and trail access points for trail information and regulations. Only certain trails are designated for mountain biking and equestrian use and are identified by colored trail markers.

HISTORIC AUTO ATTRACTIONS

13825 Metric Drive (I-90 exit 3 west to Metric. Turn right)

Rockford (Roscoe) 61073

❏   Phone: (815) 389-7917
    Web: www.historicautoattractions.com
❏   Hours: Tuesday-Saturday 10:00am-5:00pm, Sunday 11:00am-
    4:00pm (summers). Weekends only (September-November)
❏   Admission: $8.00 adult, $7.00 senior (65+), $6.00 student (6-15).

More than just a display of historic automobiles - ten huge rooms where history meets entertainment. See several Presidential Limos from Grant to Eisenhower. The Kennedy Day in Dallas presentation represents cars present in the motorcade the fateful day of his death. Or, see Abraham Lincoln's chair from his presidential rail car. On the lighter side, view Cars of the Stars - including Elvis Presley. Movieland has Batmobiles, Ghostbusters and Superman mobiles. TV Land is where you revisit Andy Griffith or Sanford and Son vehicles. There's even a Money Car covered with 120,000 coins. Not just a display of cars, each exhibit area displays era artifacts that are often just as interesting. And, because they are constantly adding to, and changing, the space - it's a new visual experience each visit. Trust us when we say this is a special find - one of those "treats" we discover in our travels that awes us!

MISSISSIPPI PALISADES STATE PARK

Savanna - *16327A Illinois Highway 84 (3 miles north of town), 61074. www.dnr.state.il.us/lands/landmgt/parks/r1/palisade.htm. Phone: (815) 273-2731 Admission to Illinois State Parks is free. Camping fees range from $6.00-11.00 per night, depending on amenities; a $5.00 fee is charged for camping reservations.* On first impression, this park has but two directions--up and down. The rugged, 2,500-acre park sits atop a line of towering bluffs overlooking the Mississippi River. Deep, wooded ravines pierce the un-glaciated landscape. Four developed overlooks provide views of the Mississippi; Oak Point Overlook is accessible by visitors with limited mobility. Mississippi Palisades' 13 miles of trails are rated moderate to strenuous. Trails in the northern part of the park are less strenuous than those in the southern part. The Native American pathfinders along the rock palisades of the Mississippi River did as present-day hikers do - in coursing the bluffs, they took the paths of least resistance. The trails at the Mississippi Palisades, especially the park's southern routes, puts you in touch with the past. Walk them and you'll trace the footsteps of all those natives thousands of years ago. Pileated woodpeckers, wild turkeys, deer, fox and other small animals make their home here. The park has numerous scenic picnic areas and a campground with 241 RV campsites (105 with electrical hookups), showers and a convenience store; reservations are accepted. You can go fishing or boating on the Mississippi River and enjoy cross-country skiing, sledding and ice fishing in winter months.

HOGAN GRAIN ELEVATOR AND I&M CANAL VISITORS CENTER

Seneca - *124 West Williams (off Interstate 80 and onto Route 6, downtown), Web: www.dnr.state.il.us/lands/landmgt/parks/i&m/east/seneca/home.htm. Phone: (815) 357-6197. 61360. Hours: Wednesday-Sunday 8:00am-4:00pm (April-October). Varied winter hours. Tours: Groups of 10 or more:* The Illinois and Michigan Canal invites you to come and enjoy history with "Maggie" - a first person re-enactment of a canal woman. The M.J. Hogan Grain Elevator is the earliest remaining elevator along the canal that was fully operational during the canal's heyday. Built in 1862, the grain elevator allowed farmers to unload their grain locally instead of hauling it to the market in Chicago by wagon. Grain was then loaded onto canal barges and transported to market. The types of grains that were carried by the cargo boats to Chicago on the canal, were corn, wheat, oats, barley and rye. On the return trip, the boats were generally filled with lumber for new buildings. Tour the elevator and look at diagrams of how an elevator of this size operates.

SHABBONA LAKE STATE PARK

Shabbona - *4201 Shabbona Grove Road (off US 30, midway between DeKalb and Peru), 60550. Phone: (815) 824-2106. Web: www.dnr.state.il.us/lands/landmgt/parks/r1/shabbona.htm. Admission to Illinois State Parks is free. Camping fees range from $6.00-11.00 per night, depending on amenities; a $5.00 fee is charged for camping reservations.* Named for the Potawatomi chief who briefly held a small parcel of this land 10 years after the 1832 Black Hawk War, this park offers boating, camping, picnicking, fishing and some neat trails. Just over eight miles of scenic hiking and cross-country skiing trails weave through the wooded areas of the park. A trail brochure is available at the office. A specially developed cassette tape can guide you along on the "Touch the Earth" trail. The tape and a special brochure is available at the park office.

CHAIN O'LAKES STATE PARK

Spring Grove - *8916 Wilmot Road, 60081. Phone: (847) 587-5512. www.dnr.state.il.us/lands/landmgt/parks/r2/chaino.htm. Admission to Illinois State Parks is free. Camping fees range from $6.00-11.00 per night, depending on amenities; a $5.00 fee is charged for camping reservations.* Explore 6,500 acres of water, woods, fields and twisting shoreline. Try cross-country skiing and ice fishing in winter. Enjoy hiking, horseback riding, camping, fishing, and boating the rest of the year. Bike and boat rentals are available. Chain O Lakes has four trail systems. The Nature's Way hiking trail starts at Oak Grove Picnic Area and is 2 ¼ miles in length. The Pike Marsh North Picnic Area has a trail especially designed for disabled users that is ¼ mile long. The park also contains an equestrian trail with three loops and a total length of 8 miles. A biking/hiking trail, 6 miles in length can be accessed at any picnic area between the concession stand and the park office. In the winter all trails can be used by cross-country skiers with the park office doubling as a warming house on weekends with 3" of snow; hours are 10:00am-3:00pm.

CHIEF SHIKSHAK NORTHWEST BISON RANCH

Sterling - *23637 Quinn Road, 61081. Phone: (815) 336-2145.* Native North American bison and red deer graze, surrounded by nature trails and spring fed creeks. Tour the livestock facilities, hike the trails, horseback ride, mountain bike or tour the camp in a Hummer. Camp in a teepee or rent the caretakers house. Friday - Sunday: call for reservations. Admission for activities.

RONALD REAGAN BIRTHPLACE

Tampico - *111 South Main Street (Reagan Apartment and Museum), 61283. Phone: (815) 438-2130. Admission: Donations accepted.* Today, visitors will enjoy a step back in time as they tour the birthplace of President Reagan (40th President). The apartment is decorated as it had been when the Reagans lived there in the early 1900s. Memorabilia of Reagans childhood, acting career, and terms in office can be viewed at the Visitor Center below the apartment. A visit to Tampico would not be complete without a piece of homemade pie at the Dutch Diner located just a few doors down from the birthplace. Also of interest is the Hennepin Feeder Canal where the Reagan boys learned to swim.

DONLEY'S WILD WEST TOWN

8512 South Union Road (I-90 exit US 20 Hampshire/Marengo. Turn left (west), go 4.5 miles to South Union Rd), **Union** 60180

❑   Phone: (815) 923-9000, **Web: www.wildwesttown.com**

❑   Hours: Daily 10:00am-6:00pm (Memorial Day-4th weekend in August). Weekends only (April, May, September & October).

❑   Admission: $14.00 per person (age 3+).

Visit a Wild West town complete with mock gunfights, a blacksmith shop, and pony rides. Try your hand at panning for gold (pyrite); or the shooting range or bow & arrow target practice. Union Jail has original jail cells that once held the local desperados. The Marshal even deputizes upstanding young citizens for special posses. Want to be a miner - try the Hand car rides - see how fast you can ride the line. Visit and play or slide in the playhouse Cowboy's Place. Catch the Magic Show at the Saloon. Board a scale model of a locomotive with special surprises along the way. Visit the Toy Store, Gunshop, Tobacco Shop, Telegraph Office, the Lamp Store, and a collection of toy trains in the Museum. Stop by the Ice Cream Parlor or Steakhouse for supper or sweets. Many shops have personalized souvenirs (like Indian face painting or names engraved on a lucky horseshoe) to purchase. However, most all activities are included in admission making this town a good value. A wonderful, easy to manage family outing awaits you here - too cute!

ILLINOIS RAILWAY MUSEUM

7000 Olson Road (I-90 to US 20 NW, follow signs), **Union** 60180

❑   Phone: (815) 923-4000 or (800) BIG-RAIL, **Web: www.irm.org**

❑   Hours: Weekend operations: 10:30am-5:00pm, grounds 9:00am-6:00pm (usually May-October on Saturdays and most Sundays). Weekday operations: 11:00am - 4:00pm, grounds 10:00am - 5:00pm. (daily, summer)

❑   Admission: $6.00-$12.00 adult, $4.00-$10.00 child

❑   Miscellaneous: Due to damage during a non-fatal accident in the rail yard mid-September, 2005, some trains may not be visible (in repairs) or running. "Day Out with Thomas" is usually held late August.

The Illinois Railway Museum is a Museum in Motion. Watch now, as a little red streetcar clangs across Depot Street on the car line, or as the thundering steam train whistles past on the mainline, or perhaps as the gleaming streamliner simply whispers by. These artifacts don't just sit there, they move! Electric cars operate on weekdays, and the Museum grounds and barns are open to visitors on weekdays. Weekend operations during the season feature a steam or diesel train that departs from the Museum's East Union depot on a posted schedule. During the forty minute round trip to Kishwaukee Grove, the trains roll past a small farmstead, a bit of Illinois prairie and a rural grade crossing before dropping into the Kishwaukee Valley. The demonstration railroad includes a one-mile trolley loop around the property and a five-mile mainline. Your admission ticket entitles you to an unlimited number of train rides, as well as several barns with over two miles of indoor track, and their collection of over 375 pieces of railroad rolling stock.

GRAND BEAR LODGE INDOOR WATERPARK RESORT

2643 N. Illinois Route 178 (I-80 Eastbound and Westbound: Get off at exit #81 (Rt.178, Utica). Go south 3 miles on Route 178 and follow the signs), **Utica** 61373

❑   Phone: (866) 399-FUNN, **Web: www.grandbearlodge.com**
❑   Hours: Parks open from 9:00am-10:00pm.
❑   Admission: Waterpark for guests only. No day passes available. Suites range $139.00-$299.00 (includes passes). Villas (all amenities of home including full kitchen, bedrooms, and washer/dryer) range $259.00-$429.00 and sleep up to 10 people.
❑   Miscellaneous: Parents will appreciate the little things: vanilla-scented soaps, Restonic mattresses (oh, how good that feels!) and an espresso café serving pastries (perk you up and yummy sweets like "Bear Claws").

Grand Bear Lodge offers water and amusement fun all year long right in the beautiful setting of Starved Rock. Their 60 wooded acres offer all of nature's wonders plus a 24,000 sq. ft. indoor waterpark *and* a 36,000 sq. ft. amusement park - all indoors.

Grand Bear Lodge Indoor Waterpark Resort *(cont.)*

❏　**GRAND BEAR FALLS** - Try America's first motion & sound adventure water slide with flashing lights allowing native woods creatures, storms or balloons to appear on the ride. You choose the effects you want on every ride down. They also have a Body Slide chock-full of twists and turns plus a Lazy River, Wave Pool, dumping bucket, a whirlpool, and a little kiddies play area and slide. Life guards are pretty casual here so be sure to keep an eye on young ones and help them play safely. You can bring your own floaties for non-swimmers. Tubes for required rides provided.

❏　**ENCHANTED FOREST** - has 10 full-size amusement rides under roof. It has carnival midway games and vendors with popcorn and cotton candy. A DJ booth looms high above providing music and announcements.

When you're ready to dry off, enjoy resort accommodations. The charming lodge features oversized rooms and guest suites or stay in vacation villas each with all the amenities that make it feel like home. All accommodations have television with cable access, microwave oven, refrigerator, coffee maker and hair dryer. Dining options include Jack's Place, a café or ice cream shop. Bandit's Bar & Grill is in the heart of the outdoor Bear Island and a great place to have a sandwich or snack. Kids will love the large stone fire pit area where storytellers weave yarns of adventure and intrigue about Grizzly Jack and Grand Bear as well as fairy-tales and legends. There is also a beanbag tournament court and other games. Other dry games include a huge Cave Arcade and miniature golf. Behind the Island, catch a wagon ride or trolley to tour the park or sites in town.

LASALLE COUNTY HISTORICAL SOCIETY MUSEUM AND COMPLEX

Utica - *Mill and Canal Streets (I-80 on Route 178 south), 61373. Phone: (815) 667-4861,* **Web: www.lasallecountymuseum.org**. *Hours: Wednesday-Friday 10:00am-4:00pm, Weekends Noon-4:00pm (summer). Friday, Saturday, Sunday Noon-4:00pm. The* museum complex is located on the banks of the Illinois & Michigan Canal. The two-story stone museum was built during the presidency of Zachary Taylor in 1848.

Originally it was a general store serving the needs of early pioneers and the traffic along the canal. The museum complex consists of four buildings. The 1848 stone warehouse is one of three original buildings remaining on the Illinois & Michigan Canal. It displays Lincoln, Civil War and river trade exhibits. Also an 1865 one-room school, an 1874 post-beam barn, and an 1896 working blacksmith shop offer a glimpse of pioneer life in the late 19th century.

STARVED ROCK STATE PARK

P.O. Box 509 (I-80 Eastbound & Westbound: Get off at exit #81 (Rt.178, Utica). Go south 3 miles on Route 178 and follow the signs), **Utica** 61373

❑ Phone: (815) 667-4906 or (800) 868-ROCK
www.dnr.state.il.us/lands/landmgt/parks/i&m/east/starve/
park.htm

❑ Hours: Trail Parking Lots 8:00am to sunset. Visitors Center 9:30am-3:30 or 4:30pm.

❑ Admission: Admission to Illinois State Parks is free. Camping fees range from $6.00-11.00 per night, depending on amenities; a $5.00 fee is charged for camping reservations.

❑ Miscellaneous: The lodge has been refurbished, but still reflects the peaceful atmosphere of yesteryear. The Lodge features an indoor swimming pool, children's pool, whirlpool, saunas and an outdoor sunning patio. The lodge offers 72 luxury hotel rooms and 22 comfortable cabin rooms. The original Great Room is furnished with decorative rugs and art and is centered around a massive stone fireplace. The restaurant is open seven days a week and offers many house specialties. A tour boat company also offers seasonal cruises departing near the Visitors Center.

Starved Rock State Park derives its name from a Native American legend about an Indian Chief who sought refuge on the rock and eventually starved to death versus being slain by enemies below. The backdrop for your activities are 18 canyons formed by glacial meltwater and stream erosion. They slice dramatically through tree-covered, sandstone bluffs for four miles through the park with overlooks at opportune points along the south side of the Illinois River. The park has 13 miles of hiking trails. Evidence of beavers and muskrats can be seen as you walk along the River Trail. During early spring, when the end of winter thaw is occurring and rains are frequent, sparkling waterfalls are found at the heads of all 18 canyons. The Visitors' Center offers displays and information about the area's geology, French and Native American history, flora, and fauna. Orient yourself first watching short videos. Now, you're ready to grab your backpack, water bottle, and maybe a hiking stick (all can be purchased at the gift shop/café) and hit the trails. Boating, fishing, camping, horseback riding, picnicking, and winter sports can all add to your Starved Rock experience. Rental of canoes, boats, horseback rides, and skis are available. No swimming or rock climbing - however, they allow ice climbing!

CHALLENGER LEARNING CENTER

Woodstock - *22 Church Street, downtown, 60098. Phone: (815) 338-7747. Web: www.challengerillinois.org. Admission: $25.00-$75.00 per student. First come, first serve, by deposit reservation only.* Join a crew for a week-long adventure full of interactive activities. Summer 1 to 5-day camps spotlight flight, rocketry, robotics and space travel. Participants have the opportunity to visit the new interactive exhibit area, build rockets and gliders, fly in the Boeing 737 cockpit simulator and experience a simulated space mission. During the school year, school groups (best grade 5+) or organized civic or home-school groups can arrange similar experiences.

DICK TRACY MUSEUM / CHESTER GOULD

Woodstock - *Old Courthouse Arts Center Building (I-90 west to Rte. 47 north to Woodstock Square), 60098. Phone: (815) 338-8281. Web: www.chestergould.org. Hours: Thursday-Saturday 11:00am-5:00pm, Sunday 1:00-5:00pm. Admission: Donations.* Stop in to view and reminisce (invite the grandparents) about Dick Tracy and his cast of characters, as well as Chester Gould, the creator. Check out the Crimestopper Club Room filled with child-friendly hands-on exhibits including forensics, identification measures and drawing techniques. Look to purchase the legacy yellow fedora hat with black trim if you have a budding detective amongst you.

SUGGESTED LODGING AND DINING

BENJAMIN'S. 103 N. Main Street. **Galena**. (815) 777-0467 or www.benjaminsgalena.com. The Historic pub with family atmosphere features a cozy wood-paneled pub that caters to families by offering crayons and paper tableclothes and kids meals served in plastic firefighter hats that kids can keep. Known for their Apple Pork Chops, Salmon, Prime Rib and Burgers. The owners and staff are super friendly here. Try an Arnold Palmer beverage (lemonade and iced tea, mixed) - so refreshing. Finish your delightful meal off with a giant Avalanche Sundae (love the fudge and cinnamon touch) for four! Now, walk it off shopping the addictive, quaint Main Street shops. You'll fall in love with this town. Open daily at 11:00am serving lunch and dinner. Live music Saturday nights. Children's Menu with 8 items to choose from, all under $5.00. Adult dinners run $10.00-$20.00 per entrée.

BOONE'S PLACE. 515 S. Main Street, **Galena**. (815) 777-4488. Made-from-scratch French dips, pita wraps, stuffed potatoes, hearty soups, prime rib and Eli's cheesecakes. Their signature meals are highlighted and we'd recommend choosing them. Children's Menu includes ice cream treat. Outdoor dining. Open daily at 11:00am.

COURTYARD RESTAURANT AT DESOTO HOUSE HOTEL. 230 S. Main Street, **Galena**. www.desotohouse.com. (815) 777-0090. A lovely four-story atrium serving breakfast and lunch daily. Sunday breakfast buffet and weekday lunch buffet.

EAGLE RIDGE INN RESORT, **Galena**. (US 20 west, just a few miles east of town). (815) 777-2444 or (800) 892-2269 or www.eagleridge.com. Spending the week or just a weekend, Eagle Ridge offers a variety of lodging options that will meet the needs of everyone from a well-appointed guest room at the Inn ($149-$199) to the spaciousness of a fully furnished private villa or home (the best way to spend a few overnights). They have a stocked General Store and wonderful food at the restaurants and cafes (or, cook your own meal at your home rental). Lake Galena dominates the setting below the Inn with its 7 miles of shoreline and picturesque marina. In addition to the 80 guest rooms and suites, the main Inn complex houses a spacious common area with a double-sided fireplace and comfortable conversation areas. Golf not your game? Not to worry, the resort also offers the best in outdoor recreational facilities that include fishing, gorgeous hiking trails, horseback riding and kids programs. Often, they have special festivals, hayrides, campfires, crafting, scavenger hunts and movies in tubies. Enjoy cross-country skiing, sledding, skating, and horse-drawn sleigh rides throughout the winter. The resort is friendly, not stuffy and a destination to work from as you explore this adorable town. The Camp Eagle Program is available in half-day and full day (both including lunch), providing children ages 4-12 with a wide variety of supervised Arts and crafts, swimming, pool games, and nature trail hikes. Each day has a different theme including Sports Mania, Alien Adventure, and Bikini Bottom Bash! (reservations required by 6:00pm the day before). The Kids Night Out Program is every Friday and Saturday night from 7:00-10:00pm for children ages 4-12. Pizza, movies, games, boat rides and crafts will fill up their evening while Mom and Dad have a quiet evening alone or out with friends. (reservations required by 2:00pm the day of). HOT AIR BALLOON RIDES - Escape to a tranquil world that is sure to give you a new perspective. What a way to see the Territory. Come for a peaceful journey above the treetops and a celebration upon landing. Flights offered daily at dawn and dusk. $150.00 per person. For additional information or to reserve your flight, contact the Recreation Department at 815-776-5035.

BEEF-A-ROO. Various locations. **Rockford**. Another Rockford original with 7 stores specializing in sandwiches, burgers, salads and seasonal soups and shakes. Love the special flavor shakes. **www.beefaroo.com**.

MARY'S MARKET. Various locations, especially near malls, **Rockford**. Yet another Rockford original with stores decorated in modern tones and serving freshly made breads sided or filled with soup (try cream of Broccoli) of the day and chicken salads. All the ingredients are wafting in the air as you dive into your food. Modern comfort food.

OLYMPIC TAVERN. 2327 N. Main Street, **Rockford**. (815) 962-8758. A Rockford Original that's 60 years old and an easy drive from the Museums. They offer a big menu and kids menu (including steak on it). Baked potato soup, house dressings on salad, giant one-pound burgers, wonderful daily special pasta dishes, chicken and fish. Moderate pricing.

QUALITY SUITES. 7401 Walton Street, **Rockford**. (I-90 at BR20 west to Bell School Rd.) (800) 228-5151 or **www.qsrockford.com**. Each room has a privacy bedroom with remote control TV, living area with a sofa sleeper, microwave, refrigerator, VCR, and coffee maker. The best part: complimentary Quality Beginnings Hot Buffet Breakfast; evening snack reception; and their indoor pool and whirlpool spa.

131

Chapter 5
South East Area (SE)

Our Favorites...

* Cave-in-Rock State Park - Cave-in-Rock

* The Chocolate Factory - Golconda

* Fort Massac - Metropolis

* Superman Museum - Metropolis

* American Flourite Museum - Rosiclare

* Garden of the Gods - Vienna

Garden of the Gods - Superman must live around here somewhere...

CACHE RIVER STATE NATURAL AREA

930 Sunflower Lane (south on Rte. 45 thru Vienna, then west on Belknap. Right on Main, right on Sunflower - Headquarters)

Belknap 62908

- ❑ Phone: (618) 634-9678
  www.dnr.state.il.us/lands/landmgt/parks/r5/cachervr.htm
- ❑ Hours: Visitors Center: Fridays and Saturdays from 8:30am-4:30pm. Park open daylight hours.
- ❑ Admission: FREE
- ❑ Miscellaneous: The Tunnel Hill State bicycle trail travels through eight miles of the Cache River State Natural Area terminating at the Wetlands/Visitor Center.

Among the outstanding natural features found within the area today are massive cypress trees whose flared bases exceed 40 feet circumference. They're surrounded by ancient blackwater swamp. A boardwalk winds its way into the relatively undisturbed depths of this forested swamp, providing visitors a chance to step back in time and observe wetland and aquatic ecosystems (best moderate trail: Lower Cache River Swamp Trail (2.5 miles) or Section 8 Boardwalk (accessible & only 500 ft). Look for the award-winning giant Tupelo tree at the end of the trail. Visitors can experience this lost world while paddling a canoe through 6 miles of trails that meander through rivers, swamps and ponds in a portion of the Lower Cache River known as Buttonland Swamp. Maybe you'll catch a glimpse of a bird-voiced tree frog or a soaring eagle. Heron Pond Trail crosses the Cache River on a new truss bridge. Walk on a floating boardwalk into the middle of Heron Pond.

Located south of Whitehill on Illinois Route 37, the Wetlands Center helps visitors gain a better understanding of the area and learn the importance of wetlands through exhibits, displays, audio-visual presentations and viewing decks. Among the features at the center are a sound amplification system, bird feeders, birdhouses and shrub and tree landscaping to attract wildlife. The sound being amplified allows visitors the chance to hear outdoor wildlife sounds, while standing or sitting inside the wildlife viewing area.

FRANKLIN COUNTY GARAGE/ MUSEUM

Benton - *211 North Main Street, 62812. Phone: (618) 438-2121 or (800) 661-9998. Hours: Monday-Friday 8:00am-4:00pm.* Built in 1910 as a Ford Garage - once housing the county's first automobile dealership. On display are vintage cars and the belt driven machinery used in their repair. The museum features an electronic interpretive tour and depicts items and events with historic connections to the Jail Museum only a block away.

FRANKLIN COUNTY HISTORIC JAIL MUSEUM

Benton - *209 West Main Street (I-57 exit Rte. 14 east), 62812. Phone: (618) 439-0608 or (800) 661-9998. Hours: Monday-Saturday 9:00am-Noon and 1:00-4:00pm. Admission: Donations.* The Historic Jail Museum serves as a tourist information center and headquarters for the Franklin County Tourism Bureau. Visit the 1920s gang era of notorious gangsters. Relive Civil War Days with General John A Logan who was one of the most pivotal Generals in the War, an outspoken Congressman who was the creator of Memorial Day by his general order #11. Follow the careers of Benton's famous natives, actor John Malkovich and NBA basketball star and coach Doug Collins. Discover why Franklin County's WFRX radio station in West Frankfort was the first radio station in the US to play a "Beatles" record in 1963.

CAVE-IN-ROCK STATE PARK

#1 New State Park Rd. (I-57 exit Hwy 13 east to SR 1 south for 22 miles), **Cave-in-Rock** 62919

- ❑   Phone: (618) 289-4325 or (618) 289-4545
  www.dnr.state.il.us/lands/landmgt/parks/r5/caverock.htm
- ❑   Admission: Admission to Illinois State Parks is free. Camping fees range from $6.00-11.00 per night, depending on amenities; a $5.00 fee is charged for camping reservations.
- ❑   Miscellaneous: Boating, camping, fishing, marina and 2 marked hiking trails. Fees for camping.

The heavily wooded park is named for the 55-foot-wide cave that was carved out of the limestone rock by water thousands of years ago. Cave in Rock was a landmark on the maps of the early 1800's. Lewis and Clark knew of the Cave and its reputation for housing pirates and other rogues. Today, you can see the cave by taking a short walk from the ferry landing at Cave in Rock. Trails winding along the riverbank offer views of riverboats, barges and other river scenes. The deep, dark recesses engage images of adventure, mystery, terror, robbers and pirates. The cave served as a backdrop for a scene in the movie "How The West Was Won." The scene was a portrayal of how ruthless bandits used the cave to lure unsuspecting travelers in to rob them. Enjoy the walk down Pirates Bluff into the cave and take in the outstanding view of the river.

Cave-In-Rock Restaurant and Lodging features four duplex guest houses with eight suites, each accommodating up to four people comfortably. The suites contain deluxe baths, a dining area and wet bar, a large bedroom/living room, and a private patio deck overlooking the Ohio River. One suite is handicapped accessible. The Lodge operates on a seasonal basis. Southern-style cooking is presented at the restaurant (8:00am-9:00pm).

MILLSTONE BLUFF

(Hwy 147, ½ east of Robbs, Shawnee Nat'l Forest), **Eddyville** 62928

❑   Phone: (618) 658-2111

❑   Miscellaneous: In the same town, within the Shawnee National Forest, walk through Bell Smith Springs (8 miles west of IL 145 south - 800-699-6637) has cold-water springs and a large natural stone bridge. Indian Kitchen Cave and the 80 to 100 foot sheer bluffs is the remains of an ancient native American stone wall. They were built by prehistoric hunters to stampede the woodland buffalo over the cliffs that intersect the walls at right angles. Lusk Creek & Indian Kitchen, 618-658-2111. (1 mile east of Eddyville on Hwy. 145)

The site has remained relatively undisturbed because it is perched in a high hill surrounded by an 80-foot high bluff. The Mississippian period village is thought to have been active for 500 years, ending about 500 years ago. The paved trail leads to a Native American Cemetery, the remains of a stone wall, and the depressions excavated for buildings in the small town. There were probably two to six individuals per household living here. But the highlights of the site are the petroglyphs (carvings in rock) of a thunder bird, rattle snake, corn stalk on bloom, etc. The figures are actually "pecked" into the stone, and not carved.

ILLINOIS IRON FURNACE

Elizabethtown - *(along Big Creek, north of town above Tecumseh Lake), 62931. www.fs.fed.us/r9/forests/shawnee/recreation/trails/ironfurnace/. Phone: (618) 287-2201. Hours: Daylight. Admission: FREE.* While hiking, you can see the remains of huge 1837 stone furnaces. During the Civil War pig iron was smelted here, then shipped down the river to make the Union iron clad boats. Explore some of the easy hiking trails and you may see coyotes, gray and fox squirrels, little brown and red bats, and many songbirds and woodland flowers in a forest of towering beech and maple trees. The Furnace Trail is a .9-mile trail leading from the back of the picnic area. The trail winds along Big Creek and offers 2 or 3 deep old-fashioned fishing holes. Fishing, hiking and picnicking opportunities are nearby.

ROSE HOTEL

Elizabethtown - *10 Main Street (57 South to I-24 East to 146 East), 62931. Web: www.state.il.us/hpa/rose.htm. Phone: (618) 287-2872.* E-Town (local talk for Elizabethtown) was named for the wife of James McFarland, who ran a ferry business in early years. He also built a beautiful home and lodge for river travelers, and it stands today remodeled, restored and open again for travelers. The historic Rose Hotel dates back to 1812, the oldest lodging still in existence in Illinois. Today you can enjoy the view from the veranda, rest a spell in the old gazebo which sits right on a rocky bluff near the river bank, take a tour inside or reserve a nights lodging.

CHARLIE BROWN PARK/ LITTLE TOOT RAILROAD

Flora - *Old US 50 (County Road 425), 62839. Phone: (618) 662-8313 or (866) 836-8668 railroad. Web: www.littletootrailroad.com. Hours: Weekends morning and afternoon. Admission: $3.00 per person. $4.50 all day pass.* This 100-acre park features a swimming pool, playground, a golf course, fishing, camping, and steam engine rides. Little Toot Railroad is a 15-inch-gauge locomotive that runs through the park. Visitors can ride the rails and wave to passers-by. The depot has a gift shop and party room.

CHOCOLATE FACTORY, THE

Rt. 2 Box 164 (on Hwy 146 east, right across from Dixon Springs State Park), **Golconda** 62938

❑   Phone: (877) 949-3829, **Web: www.thechocolatefactory.net**
❑   Hours: Daily 9:00am-5:00pm, Seasonal Sunday hours.

❑   Admission: FREE. Samples a plenty. Reasonable prices for
      theme chocolates to fit any hobby or interest.

Follow your sweet tooth west on Hwy 146 to the Chocolate
Factory which is right across the highway from Dixon Springs
State Park. There's over 50 kinds of chocolates, in a wide variety
of shapes, hand painted novelties, plus ice cream and the best
chocolate turtles! Ask them, they would love to give you a
demonstration! We watched them paint a tractor and mint
chocolate chip ice cream cone chocolates. The trick is the
temperature of the white chocolate "paint" and the artist using
brushes working from front to back, layering the color for the right
effect. Their ice cream is only $1.00 a scoop, too.

DIXON SPRINGS STATE PARK

Golconda - *RR #2, Box 178, Route 146 (I-24 traveling East, take exit
#16 to Rt. 146. At the stop sign turn left and the park is 13 miles
on the left - near Rte. 145), 62938. Phone: (618) 949-3394.
www.dnr.state.il.us/lands/landmgt/parks/r5/dixon.htm. Admission to
Illinois State Parks is free. Camping fees range from $6.00-11.00 per
night, depending on amenities; a $5.00 fee is charged for camping
reservations. Miscellaneous: The Chocolate Factory is across from the
entrance. You might find some real turtles, not chocolate, at Dixon
Springs, plus 78 acres of unique rock formations, cliffs and waterfalls.*
Dixon Springs takes its name from William Dixon, one of the first white
settlers to build a home in this section, who obtained a school land warrant
in 1848. At one time, a great hotel and spa were here with promises that the
mineral water could cure anything from alcoholism to rheumatism. The park
offers hiking trails, picnic spots, camping areas, and an outdoor swimming
pool (seasonal). Just north of here is Lake Glendale Recreation Area (618-
949-3807) where visitors can fish, swim, camp and horseback ride.

WAR BLUFF VALLEY WILDLIFE SANCTUARY

Golconda - *(north on IL 146 from town. West on Bushwack Road (gravel
road) for a couple miles), 62938. Phone: (618) 457-6367.
www.shawneeaudubon.org/war_bluff_valley_sanctuary.htm. Hours:
Dawn to dusk. Admission: FREE.* This wildlife sanctuary is nestled in the
uplands of the Shawnee National Forest and supports many ancient oak-
hickory woods, river bottom forests, young forests and old field habitats.
Simmons Creek and several ponds provide the water needed to support a
diverse natural community. Look for more than 300 types of plants,

including a rich variety of wildflowers and nine types of ferns. Other features include 7 ponds, historic homestead sites, and interesting geology. There are 10 walking trails or tractor paths allowing access to all areas of the sanctuary.

FERNE CLYFFE STATE PARK

Goreville - *Illinois Route 37, P.O. Box 10 (one mile south of town, between I-57 and I-24), 62939. Phone: (618) 995-2411. www.dnr.state.il.us/lands/landmgt/parks/r5/ferne.htm. Admission to Illinois State Parks is free. Camping fees range from $6.00-11.00 per night, depending on amenities; a $5.00 fee is charged for camping reservations.* Ferne Clyffe has been known as an outstanding natural scenic spot for nearly 100 years. An abundance of ferns, unique geological features and unusual plant communities create an atmosphere that enhances the many recreational facilities offered at the park. Trails wind through the woods, allowing visitors to view unusual rock formations and an intermittent waterfall (Big Rocky Hollow Trail). Ferne Clyffe Lake is open to bank fishing, but boating and swimming are prohibited. Camping, horseback riding and picnicking are available, too.

DEVIL'S BACKBONE PARK, DEVIL'S BAKE OVEN, TOWER ROCK

Grand Tower - *(Grand Tower and Brunkhorst Roads, IL 3 & Great River Road), 62942. Phone: (618) 565-8380 or (618) 565-2454 campground.* When early explorers journeyed down the Mississippi River in 1673, they recorded in their journals a large rock that is known as Tower Rock today. The name was given to the landmark after three French missionaries erected a large wooden cross on the rock's crest in 1678. During the heyday of river travel and exploration, a number of people were killed in the rapids that sometimes run at the base of the rock. Thanks to this, the Native Americans were convinced that evil spirits lurked here, waiting to claim the lives of unwitting victims. Devil's Backbone is an unusual rock ridge that runs along the Mississippi River. Another unusual rock formation called Devil's Bake Oven is at the north end of the park. Pitted with caves, the Oven once harbored river pirates until a U.S. cavalry troop drove them away in 1803. The park also was the site of an Indian massacre in the early 1800s. The foundation walls of an old house still stand atop Devil's Bake Oven. According to legend, the ghost of a young girl who died of a broken heart lingers among the ruins and is sometimes seen on quiet, moonlit nights.

SALINE CREEK PIONEER VILLAGE AND MUSEUM

Harrisburg - *1600 Feazel Street (east on Rte. 13, southwest part of town), 62946. Phone: (618) 253-7342. Admission: Donations.* The village represents a pioneer settlement of the era 1800 to 1840. Here you'll go back in time when you walk through this log cabin village with its school, old Moravian church, general store and post office. Venture through the 1877 Victorian era museum which once served as the county poor farm. Today each room is filled with unique collections. Also, are several log family cabins, a threshing barn filled with tools and other antique items.

SAM DALE LAKE

Johnsonville - *Illinois Route 161 (I-57, take exit #109, turn East on Rt 161, travel approx. 22 miles), 62850. Phone: (618) 835-2292. www.dnr.state.il.us/lands/landmgt/parks/r5/samdale.htm.* The highlight of a visit here will be Sam Dale Lake, a beautiful 194 acre lake with eight and a half miles of shoreline to hike around, swim in, or just sit beside and enjoy. The tall, shady trees and plentiful flowers and greenery beckon picnickers at Sam Dale Lake. One of the picnic areas has shelter. Several picnic areas are available with tables, drinking fountains, and outdoor stoves. Playground equipment, concession stand. In addition, several smaller ponds are home to fish and wildlife.

STEPHEN A. FORBES STATE RECREATION AREA

Kinmundy - *6924 Omega Road (15 miles northeast of Salem, off I-57), 62854. www.dnr.state.il.us/Lands/Landmgt/parks/r5/stephen.htm Phone: (618) 547-3381. Admission to Illinois State Parks is free. Camping fees range from $6.00-11.00 per night, depending on amenities; a $5.00 fee is charged for camping reservations.* As the sun comes up, take a swim at sandy Rocky Point Beach. The rest of the day offers many options, from hiking on the nature trails, softball , volleyball, water skiing and boating. Or, you may want to spend the night at the Oak Ridge Campground.

CRAB ORCHARD NATIONAL WILDLIFE REFUGE

Marion - *8588 Route 148 (IL 148, south of Rte. 13, west of town), 62959. Web: www.fws.gov/midwest/craborchard/. Phone: (618) 997-3344. Admission: FREE. Miscellaneous: Restricted campsites.* Crab Orchard is well-known for hunting, fishing, camping and boating opportunities. This 4,000-acre refuge is especially beautiful in the fall when the geese return for the winter. Every Sunday in October, wildlife enthusiasts drive through sections of the refuge normally closed to traffic, watching for wild turkeys, coyotes, foxes and bobcats. Little Grassy, Devil's Kitchen and Crab Orchard lakes are well-known for fishing opportunities and six small ponds that are open to the public. Crab Orchard Lake is popular for water skiing, swimming and sailboating. The refuge also has about 30 eagles.

HAMILTON COUNTY STATE FISH & WILDLIFE AREA

McLeansboro - *RR 4, Box 242 (8 miles southeast of McLeansboro off Route 14), 62859. www.dnr.state.il.us/lands/landmgt/parks/r5/hamilton.htm.* Phone: (618) 773-4340 Dolan Lake is the main attraction offering fishing and boating. 60 campsites, horseback riding, hiking and boat rentals.

FORT MASSAC STATE PARK

1308 E. 5th Street (I-24 exit 37, follow signs), **Metropolis** 62960

❑   Phone: (618) 524-4712

    www.dnr.state.il.us/lands/landmgt/parks/R5/frmindex.htm

❑   Hours: Daily 8:30am-4:00pm (Winter), Daily 10:00am-5:30pm (April-November)

❑   Admission: Admission to Illinois State Parks is free. Camping fees range from $6.00-11.00 per night, depending on amenities; a $5.00 fee is charged for camping reservations.

❑   Miscellaneous: Picnicking, camping, hiking, and boating. The 2.5-mile Hickory Nut Ridge Trail is one not to miss, as it takes hikers along the scenic Ohio River.

Native Americans, early Spanish DeSoto crews and even the French used this point overlooking the Ohio River as a lookout and fortress. It was rebuilt after the Revolutionary War as George Washington thought it to be a strategic location. Lewis and Clark with their party arrived here on November 11, 1803 and stayed here 2 days. While here, Lewis and Clark recruited several enlisted men and they also hired George Drouillard to act as an interpreter and hunter for the party. It was again re-fortified for part of the War of 1812 and the Civil War. Edward Everett Hale used the setting of Fort Massac and the Burr-Wilkinson plot as basis for his classic historical novel, "The Man Without a Country." Today, Fort Massac is an excursion through the entire course of American history, and the perfect place to relax and explore life as it was lived when our country was young. The historic site is a replica of the 1802 American fort that was on site. The fort area contains 2 barracks, 3 block houses, officer quarters, well, stockade along with a fraise fence. There is also a visitors center and museum with a short video and some artifacts. The site is best to visit during monthly or bi-weekly weekend re-enactments to relive history. If you come during the week, let the kids just play "fort" while parents sit nearby with a nice breezy view of the Ohio River.

SUPER MUSEUM (SUPERMAN)

517 Market Street (Superman Square), **Metropolis** 62960

- ❏ Phone: (618) 524-5518, **Web: www.supermuseum.com**
- ❏ Hours: Daily 9:00am-5:00pm.
- ❏ Admission:$3.00 per person (ages 6+).
- ❏ Miscellaneous: The Americana Hollywood Museum is next to Harrah's at 100 West 3rd Street. Hollywood icons (Elvis, NASCAR, Finding Nemo & John Wayne cowboys). Daily 9:00am-6:00pm. $5.00 ages 6+. Military FREE.

View a collection of Superman memorabilia including the original costume worn by George Reeves, the first Superman in the 1950s. Browse through movie props, rare toys and comic books. The museum is filled with a $2.5 million collection spanning 60 years, honoring the most famous hero of all time. See Lex Luther's Scientific Lab as the mysterious theme music plays and you walk the colorful isles. Get energy from the Krypton - beware of Kryptonite! The gift shop has hundreds of items to buy. The famous Superman Statue is a 15-foot bronze figure that overlooks the uptown area of the city (Market St. & 5th Street). Visitors enjoy having photos made with this famed "Man of Steel."

BEALL WOODS STATE PARK

Mt. Carmel - *9258 Beall Woods Avenue (six miles south of town on Rte. 1), 62863. Web: www.dnr.state.il.us/lands/landmgt/parks/r5/beall.htm. Phone: (618) 298-2442 Hours: Beall Woods is open year-round from sunrise to 10:00pm. The park is closed on Christmas Day and New Year's Day. Admission to Illinois State Parks is free. Camping fees range from $6.00-11.00 per night, depending on amenities; a $5.00 fee is charged for camping reservations.* The forest contains trees over 120 feet tall and as much as 3 feet in diameter. The five established trails offer the hiker an excellent view of this old-growth forest. From the easy 1-mile Tuliptree trail which features a self-guided trail brochure to the 1¼-mile moderately easy

White oak trail, the nature enthusiast can get a sense of what the settlers saw when they arrived at the banks of the Wabash River. Besides hiking, Beall Woods also offers camping, picnicking, and fishing.

JEFFERSON COUNTY HISTORICAL VILLAGE

Mt. Vernon - *1411 North 27th Street (Exit 95 off I-57 at Mt. Vernon onto Illinois Highway 15. Go east to 27th Street and turn north at the traffic light), 62864. Phone: (618) 246-0033. Hours: Saturday 10:00am-4:00pm, Sunday 1:00-4:00pm (first weekend in May - last weekend in October). Admission: FREE.* The village features an 1820s jail, the 1873 log church, a print shop with working machines more than 100 years old, a medical building with Civil War equipment, a general store, a blacksmith, a 1920s one-room school, and a display museum. A nature trail wanders near the village.

MITCHELL MUSEUM AT CEDARHURST

Mt. Vernon - *2400 Richview Road, 62864. Phone: (618) 242-1236. Web: www.cedarhurst.org. Hours: Tuesday - Saturday 10:00a.m.- 5:00p.m, Sunday 1:00 - 5:00p.m. Admission: FREE.* Explore rolling meadows and woods, home to Cedarhurst Sculpture Park, the museum's outdoor gallery with over 60 large-scale sculptures. Visit the Mitchell Museum with contemporary art exhibitions in two galleries, including the Children's Gallery. The hands-on Children's area features Art History and making art like the masters.

AMERICAN FLUORITE MUSEUM

Main Street (across from City Hall), **Rosiclare** 62982

❑ Phone: (618) 285-3513, **www.kcminerals.com/american.htm**

❑ Hours: Thursday, Friday & Sunday 1:00-4:00pm, Saturday 10:00-4:00pm (March-December).

❑ Admission: $3.00 adult, $1.00 child (6-12).

❑ Tours: Tours are available by special appointment. Call or write for information.

❑ Miscellaneous: Although the mines are now closed (China mines most fluorspar now), you can still mine for your own minerals. Search through heaps of rock piles outside the museum digging for fluorite crystals (pay $1.00 per pound of rock to dig through). This isn't gem panning - it's hand-panning.

The American Fluorite Museum is located in the former office building of the Rosiclare Lead and Fluorspar Mining Company.

Once the largest fluorspar mining area in the United States, the specimens were collected from this region. A good many of these are well over a foot across. "Butterball, floating, peppered or oil slicks" are descriptions of some of the unusual formations. Of the colored crystals, purple, blue and yellow are prevalent. One display includes a scale model of one of the mines and shows the workings of everyday mining operations in the district. Fluorspar was mined no where else in the United States. Fluorspar is made from supersaturated minerals at great temperatures and pressures deep in the earth. When driven through faults they congeal into the mineral rich deposits of fluorspar, the state mineral of Illinois. Do you use fluoride toothpaste? It comes from fluorite.

SHAWNEE QUEEN RIVER TAXI

(on the Ohio waterfront at the end of Main St), Rosiclare 62982

❑   Phone: (618) 285-3342 or (877) 677-6123
     Web: www.ridesmtd.com/shawneequeen.htm
❑   Hours: Tuesday-Saturday 8:00am-4:05pm (mid-May - Nov. 1st)
❑   Admission: Fares are determined on boarding and departure
     points. Round trip fares range from $10.00-$20.00 per adult.
     Children (3-10) are ½ price. One way trips run $3.00-$10.00 per
     person. Reservations are required.
❑   Tours: Tours run 2-4 hours roundtrip.
❑   Miscellaneous: May be a little slow for active kids. Be sure to
     only take the 2 hour tour if with children.

If you want to see the area from the water as did Lewis and Clark, you can take a ride on the Shawnee Queen River Taxi. Take a scenic cruise on the historical Ohio River with stops in Golconda, Rosiclare, Elizabethtown, and Cave-In-Rock. Relax and enjoy the shorelines of Illinois and Kentucky, as the crew occasionally points out the natural and man-made wonders of the area. View estate homes, an 1812 historic tavern (Rose Hotel) to Cave-in-Rock (peer inside, how far does it go?), as well as fish (we saw fishermen show off their 50lb. catfish and large spoonbill/paddlefish) and other animal and plant life native to the river. The 48-seat riverboat floats past sandstone bluffs, caverns and stops at river towns. Because of the way the sun hits the water, other boats look like "ghost ships" floating above the water on the horizon.

WILLIAM JENNINGS BRYAN BIRTHPLACE MUSEUM

Salem - *408 South Broadway (I-57 exit 116), 62881. Phone: (618) 548-7791. Hours: Daily, except Thursdays 1:00-5:00pm. Closed holidays.* "Billy," as his friends knew him, was born at this address in 1860. William Jennings Bryan was the son of Judge Silas M. and Maria E. (Jennings) Bryan. Silas was a teacher, lawyer, school superintendent, state senator and circuit court judge. As a devout Presbyterian, he would pray to God for assistance before he made a decision. He had an active political career during his entire life, from a young lawyer entering the House of Representatives to the seasoned prosecuting attorney at the Scopes Trial, where the issue of whether evolution should be taught in school was argued in 1925. William was known as "The Great Commoner" and "The Silver-Tongued Orator" and he ran for president of the United States in three campaigns (never won, though). He became famous at the 1896 Chicago Democratic Party convention when he uttered words which lived on in history - "You shall not crucify the working man upon a cross of gold!" This building is on the National Register of Historical Places.

RED HILLS STATE PARK

1100 N. & 400 E. (midway between Olney and Lawrenceville on U.S. 50, northeast of Sumner), **Sumner** 62466

❑ Phone: (618) 936-2469

Web: www.dnr.state.il.us/lands/landmgt/parks/r5/redhls.htm

❑ Admission: Admission to Illinois State Parks is free. Camping fees range from $6.00-11.00 per night, depending on amenities; a $5.00 fee is charged for camping reservations.

❑ Miscellaneous: The Trace Inn is named for the Cahokia Trace. The restaurant provides seating for 100, and is open year-round. A beautiful canopied deck for warm weather dining is a popular attraction. It also offers a scenic overlook of Red Hills Lake. The restaurant is furnished with maple tables and chairs and the rustic atmosphere is enhanced with antiques. Visitors to the Trace Inn will also enjoy a unique craft and collectibles shop. For more information call (618) 936-2351.

Red Hills is a carefully preserved and maintained 948-acres of high wooded hills, deep ravines, meadows and year-round springs. A satellite area of the park, the 565-acre Chauncey Marsh Nature Preserve, contains the best remaining example of what is called a

Wabash Border Marsh Ecosystem, with marshes, dry and wet prairie, lush bottomland forest and thriving riverline communities. The sparkling 40-acre lake is ideal for fishing and boating. An open-air tabernacle at the base of the tower (financed and constructed by area residents cooperating with an interdenominational council) holds services on Sunday evening during the summer. A popular activity since 1943 has been the annual Easter sunrise services.

GARDEN OF THE GODS RECREATION AREA

Hidden Springs Ranger District/Shawnee National Forest (Rte. 45north) (I-24 exit 16, Rte. 146 east, north on SR 34 to intersection with Rte. 1), **Vienna** 62995

❑   Phone: (618) 658-2111 or (800) MY WOODS

   Web: www.fs.fed.us/r9/forests/shawnee/recreation/trails/gog/

❑   Hours: Daylight

❑   Admission: FREE

As you arrive, you will be in the surrounding 3,300 acre wilderness of the Shawnee National Forest. Garden of the Gods Observation Trail is a .3-mile flagstone moderate loop walk that contains interpretive signs explaining the geological history. A great uplift, and then erosion, formed the unusual shapes of rock peaks. Wooden and rock steps occur at midpoint. Taking one of the many marked paved trails, you'll find yourself standing on sandstone bluffs that are over 400 feet above the forest floor. Rock formations have been given names such as Camel Rock, Devil's Smokestack and Noah's Ark because of their unique shape and size. We named some smaller formations - turtle, frog, lizard and table rock. It's fun to find some new shape around every corner. Many side-views of formations look like faces. Bring your camera to capture the views of the plant and wildlife in this panoramic setting.

POUNDS HOLLOW/ RIM ROCK RECREATIONAL AREA

Hidden Springs Ranger District/Shawnee National Forest (Rte. 45north) (Garden of the Gods, continue east on Karber's Ridge Road to route 1), **Vienna** 62995

❑   Phone: (618) 658-2111 or (800) MY WOODS

    Web: www.fs.fed.us/r9/forests/shawnee/recreation/trails/

❑   Miscellaneous: Also offered in this quadrant of the Shawnee National Forest are camping, picnicking, fishing, boat rentals, and a swimming beach.

At Pounds Hollow/Rim Rock Recreational Area you will view walls almost a ¼ mile long and originally 8 to 10 feet high, believed to have been Indian forts. Several enclosures were thought to have been used to entrap animals and thus the name Pounds. Even after the Indians, the early logger pioneers kept their oxen and horses within the fenced in walls. Rim Rock Trail is a .4-mile difficult trail that leads the hiker around the top rim of the "Pounds," which is a circular 40-acre tract of land isolated from the surrounding terrain by steep sandstone bluffs. Interpretive signs along the trail explain the history of the much-used "Pounds." The trail meanders past an old Indian Wall, the Ox-Lot Cave and Fat Man's Misery, a narrow passage through massive cliffs and boulders.

TUNNEL HILL STATE TRAIL

Vienna - *Illinois Route 146, 62995. Phone: (618) 658-2168. Hours: Dawn to dusk daily. Miscellaneous: Bicycles can be rented from Peddles and Paddles @ 618-658-3641.* Tunnel Hill State Trail stretches for 45 miles from Harrisburg to Karnak, with 2.5 mikes being managed by the city of Harrisburg. The trail is so named for a 10-mile stretch from Tunnel Hill to Vienna. It passes through a 540-foot railroad tunnel that was built in the 1870s. Several high trestles pass over deep-narrow valleys in the hilly southern Illinois countryside. The trail continues on a trails spur for 2.5 miles from Karnak to Cache River State Natural Area - Henry Barkhausen Wetlands Center on the old Chicago and Eastern Illinois railroad bed. The 9.3-mile section between Tunnel Hill and Vienna crosses trails already known to outdoor recreationists, including the Trail of Tears, the primary route the Cherokee Indian tribe took in the winter of 1838-39 during their forced move from the Great Smokies to Oklahoma. A Visitors Center in

Vienna features a reception and interpretive area highlighting features of the region's communities. Most of the landscape is flat farm country or wetlands (no more than 2% grade). Each trailhead has parking areas from which hikers, runners and cyclists can access the trail.

COWBOY WORLD WESTERN TOWN

West Frankfort - *Seventh Street, 62896. Phone: (618) 932-8801. Hours: Daily except Monday 9:00am-5:00pm. Miscellaneous: Nearby is Mike's Drive In.* Since 1953, this popular drive-in restaurant has featured its own home-made root beer & barbeque sandwiches. An adventure-interactive attraction showcasing wild west atmosphere, complete with horseback riding, gift shop, carriage rides & year-round activities. Pre-arrange a trail ride and chuckwagon dinner with your group.

REND LAKE/ WAYNE FITZGERRELL STATE PARK

Whittington - *11094 Ranger Road and Fitzgerrell Drive, 62897. www.dnr.state.il.us/lands/landmgt/parks/r5/wayne.htm. Phone: (618) 629-2320 Admission to Illinois State Parks is free. Camping fees range from $6.00-11.00 per night, depending on amenities; a $5.00 fee is charged for camping reservations.* Make a splash in this huge lake, the second largest manmade lake in the state. Build a sand castle, play beach volleyball, take a swim or just kick back and relax at one of two public beaches. Rend Lake offers many recreation opportunities. Begin your adventure by exploring nature on foot, bicycle or horseback. A 4-mile bike trail runs the length of the park and connects Rend Lake Resort and Rend Lake College. Trails and hiking areas are outlined in a free watchable Wildlife Guide, available at the Rend Lake Visitor Center and the Rend Lake Visitor Center and the Rend Lake Project Office. Enjoy fishing, bird watching (blue herons and bald eagles), and power boating. Overnight visitors can stay at the Wayne Fitzgerrell State Park which has primitive and developed camp sites, or at the Corps of Engineers campgrounds on Rend Lake. For those who prefer not to camp, the Rend Lake Resort has waterside rooms, sport courts, playground, stables, horse and carriage rides, bicycle rentals, indoor (Rend Lake College) & outdoor swimming pool, & marina facilities.

SOUTHERN ILLINOIS ARTISANS SHOP & VISITORS CENTER

Whittington - *14967 Gun Creek Trail (6 miles north of town on I-57, just west of exit 77, Rend Lake), 62897. Phone: (618) 629-2220. Web: www.museum.state.il.us/ismsites/so-il. Hours: Daily 9:00am-5:00pm except major winter holidays. Admission: FREE.* Fine artwork is displayed here but families gravitate towards traditional craft products made by Illinois artists and sold at their marketplace. Ask for the daily schedule of crafters on-site, demonstrating their art. See work in metals, wearables, jewelry, painting, ceramics, glass and textiles - all made in Illinois.

RIVER FERRIES OF THE MIDDLE MISSISSIPPI RIVER VALLEY

❑   Phone: (800) 373-7007
      Web: www.greatriverroad.com/SecondaryPages/ferries.htm
❑   Hours: See website for schedule for each ferry.
❑   Admission: Some are FREE. Some have a small fee.

Early American ferries consisted of rafts, rowboats and horseboats that could cross rivers where demand for transportation existed but there weren't any easy crossings. The advent of railroads and bridges put most ferries out of business and motorized vessels replaced the earlier forms of transportation of those that survived. For modern travelers, the remaining ferries in operation can save time as well as providing scenic river views. The Middle Mississippi River Valley offers six ferries, two of which travelers can cross free of charge. Five of these ferries are located in the Meeting of the Great Rivers Scenic Byway area and the other crosses the Mississippi River at Ste. Genevieve, Missouri (Modoc).

Chapter 6
South West Area (SW)

Our Favorites...

* National Great Rivers Museum - Alton

* Cahokia Mounds - Collinsville

* Camp River Dubois, Lewis & Clark - Hartford

* Giant City State Park Resort - Makanda

* Mississippi Riverfront Events

*"New Members" of the
Lewis & Clark Expedition...*

ALTON MUSEUM OF HISTORY AND ART

2809 College Avenue/ Loomis Hall, **Alton** 62002

❑ Phone: (618) 462-2763 or (800) 258-6645
   Web: www.altonmuseum.com
❑ Hours: Monday-Friday 10:00am-4:00pm, Saturday-Sunday 1:00-
   4:00pm.
❑ Admission: $1.00-$2.50 per person.
❑ Miscellaneous: Around downtown squares visit the
   Lincoln/Douglas Debate spot where Abraham Lincoln and
   Stephen A. Douglas held their last debate while campaigning for
   U.S. Senate in 1858. At Monument & Fifth Streets, The Lovejoy
   Monument honors Elijah P. Lovejoy, an abolitionist editor who
   was murdered because of his support for freedom of the press.

The museum does pay particular tribute to one of it's cherished
citizens... Robert Pershing Wadlow. Robert is world renowned as
the tallest man on record (who grew to 8-foot-11½ inches). His
gentle demeanor and cheerful disposition lead to his being called
Alton's Gentleman Giant. A life-size cardboard cutout serves as an
interactive "measure" up to show proportions of a visitor to this tall
man. There is also a video that gives a glimpse of Roberts' life and
times. The Transportation room looks back to Alton's legacy as a
hub of commerce and travel. The Pioneer Room describes the
exploits of Lewis & Clark, The Wood River Massacre, The
Lincoln & Shields Duel, the Confederate Prison at Alton, and the
Black Pioneers.

NATIONAL GREAT RIVERS MUSEUM

#1 Lock and Dam Way, Melvin Price Lock & Dam (Illinois Route 3
intersects I- 270 approximately two miles east of the Mississippi
River. Take IL Route 3 North to Hwy 143 west 2 miles), **Alton** 62024

❑ Phone: (877) 462-6979
   Web: www.mvs.usace.army.mil/Rivers/ngrm.htm
❑ Hours: Daily 9:00am-5:00pm. Closed Thanksgiving, Christmas
   and New Years.
❑ Admission: FREE

National Great Rivers Museum *(cont.)*

❑   Miscellaneous: Free tours of the Melvin Price Locks and Dam are conducted daily at 10:00am, 1:00pm, and 3:00pm. Also explained are what causes floods, with emphasis on the Great Flood of 1993, and how the Corps of Engineers fights these destructive acts of nature, and what future strategies are being developed to limit their impact.

The Museum features state of the art interactive displays and exhibits that help visitors understand the many aspects of the Mississippi River and how humans interact with it. A large model of the bluffs of the region is in the center of the museum and provides information on the various wildlife from prairie plants and trees to birds and other animals. An aquarium displays the various species of fish that inhabit the Mississippi River. Stir river sediment banks; make a stairway of water; or make your own map. One display explains how the Mississippi has been used as a highway, not only by humans but by migrating waterfowl, and chronicles the different types of vessels used from canoes, through keelboats and steamboats, to modern day barges. The Pilot House simulator allows visitors to see what it's like to guide a 1,000-foot tow of barges under a bridge or through a lock. Take on the challenge of steering your barge as a team of parent and child. This, and the dam tour, are the kids' favorites. It sure is eventful when a big barge comes through during the 45-minute tour!

ILLINOIS CAVERNS STATE NATURAL AREA

10981 Conservation Rd. (I-255 S to Rte. 3 thru Columbia & Waterloo. Right on Kaskaskia Rd. Left on KK Rd. Right on G Rd.), **Baldwin** 62217

❑   Phone: (618) 458-6699 or (618) 785-2555
    Web: www.dnr.state.il.us/lands/landmgt/parks/r4/ilc.htm

❑   Hours: Illinois Caverns is open to visitors with valid permits from Thursday through Saturday. The hours of operation are 8:30am-3:30pm. No one is allowed to enter the cave after 2:30pm. Group size: Minimum of 4 persons. A group of 25 or more must pre-register for permits prior to arrival. Youth groups require 1 adult leader for each 5 minors.

❑ Admission: There is no admission charge, but guests are required to complete an application permit at the site office before entering the cave.

❑ Miscellaneous: The Kaskaskia River Fish & Wildlife area is on Baldwin Lake. Above ground, nearby Fults Hill Prairie State Nature Preserve is almost 1,000 acres of both upland prairie and lowland wetland marshes. A variety of plants and animals can be found in the preserve, some common and some can't be found anywhere else in the state. Illinois Caverns State Natural Area offers a half-mile long prairie trail through fields and woodlands at the site. The trail is a fine example of the flora of an Illinois prairie in its natural state.

True spelunkers can explore the only commercially operated cave in the state. The first paying customers came in 1901 (St. Louis World's Fair). The cave has the usual stalactites, stalagmites, and soda straw formations plus an underground stream. The cave is home to gammerus acherondytes, the Illinois Cave Amphipod, listed as a federal endangered species. A variety of other animals may be seen, including bats, salamanders, blind cave fish, cave crickets and other insects. Don a hard hat and travel through the cave chambers with only your handheld flashlight or lantern. It contains nearly three miles of walking-height passage, some of it through a knee-deep stream. Visitors must have proper caving equipment and be prepared for a physically-demanding experience. This caving is not for the hesitant - it is real exploration.

CAHOKIA COURTHOUSE STATE HISTORIC SITE

First and Elm Streets (I-55/70, exit State Route 3 South, 3 miles to State Route 157), **Cahokia** 62206

❑ Phone: (618) 332-1782
   Web: www.illinoishistory.gov/hs/Courthouse.htm
❑ Hours: Wednesday-Sunday 9:00am-5:00pm. Closed: Thanksgiving, Christmas, and New Year's Day. Open daily (summer).

Constructed as a dwelling about 1730, the building became a courthouse in 1793, and for twenty years it served as a center of political activity in the Old Northwest Territory. The Cahokia

Courthouse is an excellent example of early French log construction known as poteaux-sur-solle (post-on-sill foundation). Inside are four rooms that originally functioned as a courtroom, a schoolroom, and offices for attorneys and clerks. Nearby (east First & Church Streets) is the Holy Family Log Church. It is the oldest church structure west of the Allegheny Mountains and one of the oldest continuously operating parishes in the U.S. (since 1699). Both buildings originate from the Lewis and Clark era.

GREATER ST. LOUIS AIR AND SPACE MUSEUM

Cahokia - *2300 Vector Drive (Hanger 2, St.Louis Downtown Airport, 5 miles from the Arch), 62206. Phone: (618) 332-3664 or (877) 332-3664.* **Web: www.airandspacemuseum.org.** *Hours: Tuesday-Saturday 10:00am-4:00pm. Admission.* Devoted to accomplishments throughout the St. Louis region in all facets of aerospace, including lighter-than-air vehicles, airplanes, and spacecraft. Indoors and out, check out war planes, cutaways of engines, space suits and bi-planes. Stop in at Oliver's Restaurant for lunch or dinner and watch the planes through a bank of windows or look at the photos on the wall and see which celebrities have landed at this airport. Air traffic includes private planes, helicopters & St. Louis TV station weather copters.

CAIRO CUSTOM HOUSE

Cairo - 1400 Washington (Washington & 14th Streets), 62914. Phone: (618) 734-1019. Hours: Monday-Friday 10:00-Noon and 1:00-3:00pm. Admission: Donation requested. Tours: by appointment. In 1872, Cairo was named a port of delivery. A Surveyor of Customs inspected and collected fees after goods had passed the point of entry at New Orleans. The Custom House held a post office on the first floor and federal court on the third floor. Artifacts include a desk used by Ulysses S. Grant when he was a general in 1864. Former offices display an old pharmacy, dentist's office and general store. Also, look for a fire pumper of 1865, replica of the U.S.S. Cairo gunboat, Lewis & Clark, and many other displays preserved by locals.

FORT DEFIANCE

Cairo - *(off Rt. 51 -- 2 miles south of town), 62914. Phone: (618) 734-4127.* Located at the confluence of the Mississippi and the Ohio River, enjoy the view from the Boatmen's Memorial located in the park. Fort Defiance was an important Civil War camp for Union troops (a strategic position). This was a post commanded by General Ulysses S. Grant. A war hospital, a national cemetery and a gunboat factory were nearby. Today, you can enjoy picnicking and camping.

CARLYLE LAKE/ ELDON HAZLET STATE PARK/ SOUTH SHORE STATE PARK

Carlyle - *20100 Hazlet Park Road, 62231. Phone: (618) 594-2484. **Web:** www.carlylelake.com. Admission to Illinois State Parks is free. Camping fees range from $6.00-11.00 per night, depending on amenities; a $5.00 fee is charged for camping reservations. Miscellaneous: In town, the original suspension bridge crossing the Kaskaskia River now serves as a pedestrian bridge and historical attraction. www.carlyle.il.us/bridge.htm.* Carlyle Lake is the largest man-made lake in Illinois and a great source of outdoor recreation. A challenge for sailboats, many less-avid sailors choose jet skis, houseboats, and pontoon boats rented from the marina. Over 200 species of migratory birds, including eagles and blue heron, stop here in the fall and winter. Visitors can also fish, swim and beach, camp or cabin. The Lakefront Cottages at Eldon Hazlet State Park offer a great view of the Lake shoreline. The rustic-style cottages have a living room, kitchenette, wet bar, bath, bedroom and upstairs loft.

POPEYE STATUE AND PARK

Chester - *(off IL 3, Great River Road), 62233. Phone: (618) 826-2326.* The towering Popeye Statue in the Elzie C. Segar Memorial Park is found by crossing the Mississippi River, the Chester Bridge. The monument honors Elzie Segar, creator of Popeye who was born in Chester. There's more Popeye than spinach at Spinach Can Collectibles inside Chester's historic 1875 Opera House building. Popeye merchandise and a mini Popeye museum fill the space and headquarters the Popeye Fan Club.

RANDOLPH COUNTY CONSERVATION AREA

4301 S. Lake Drive (northeast of town a few miles, off Palestine Road), **Chester** 62233

❑   Phone: (618) 826-2706
     Web: www.dnr.state.il.us/lands/landmgt/parks/r4/rand.htm
❑   Admission: Admission to Illinois State Parks is free. Camping fees range from $6.00-11.00 per night, depending on amenities; a $5.00 fee is charged for camping reservations.
❑   Miscellaneous: Hiking, horseback riding trails, camping.

Randolph County Conservation Area *(cont.)*

<u>PINEY CREEK RAVINE STATE NATURAL AREA</u>: This scenic spot has steep rock formations and views of Native-American pictographs high on a rock wall. Pecked designs (petroglyphs) that can be seen within Piney Creek Ravine include human figures, deer, serpents and crosses. Painted designs (pictographs) within the ravine include human figures, deer, birds, human hands and a canoe. A hiking trail that winds along the top of a bluff overlooking the creek crosses scenic Piney Creek. The trail is especially beautiful in the autumn when fall colors abound, and also in the winter, when the leafless trees allow unrestricted viewing into the ravine below.

<u>FULTS HILL PRAIRIE</u> is located a few miles north of Prairie du Rocher and offers a spectacular view from the bluff overlooking the Mississippi flood plain. Prairie flowers, soaring eagles and hawks provide a breathtaking experience.

BROOKS CATSUP BOTTLE

Collinsville - *800 South Morrison Avenue (Hwy 159, just south of downtown), 62234. Web: www.catsupbottle.com Phone: (618) 345-5598. Miscellaneous: Their website even has an international fan club!* The "World's Largest Catsup Bottle" is the now empty, steel water tank and tower measuring 170 feet. This unique water tower was built by the W.E. Caldwell Company for the G.S. Suppiger catsup bottling plant - bottlers of Brooks old original rich & tangy catsup. The landmark, representing "Roadside Architecture at its Best," was constructed in 1949 and was restored in the Spring of 1995.

CAHOKIA MOUNDS STATE HISTORIC SITE

30 Ramey St (I-255 to the Collinsville Road exit 24. Go 2 miles west on Collinsville Rd, Hwy. 40 & Ramey St), **Collinsville** 62234

- ❑   Phone: (618) 346-5160. **Web: www.state.il.us/hpa/hs/Mounds.htm**
- ❑   Hours: Wednesday-Sunday 9:00am-5:00pm (Center). Open daily (summer). Grounds open 8:00am until dusk. Closed On The Following Days: New Year's Day, Martin Luther King Jr.'s Birthday, Presidents' Day, General Election Day (on even-numbered years), Veterans' Day, Thanksgiving Day, Christmas Day.

❏ Admission: FREE

❏ Miscellaneous: Today Cahokia is within sight of the famed
Gateway Arch in St. Louis, MO.

On this site are the remains of an ancient city where a
Mississippian culture flourished from 700-1400 AD and then
mysteriously vanished. Mississippians developed an agricultural
system with corn, squash, and several seed bearing plants as the
principal crops. The stable food base, combined with hunting,
fishing, and gathering of wild food plants, enabled them to develop
a very complex community with a highly specialized social,
political, and religious organization. Cahokia became a regional
center for the Mississippian culture after A.D. 900. It features 65
manmade earthen mounds, including 100 ft. Monks Mound, a
wooden calendar and a 33,000 foot modern interpretive center near
the Mound. After the short (15 minute) video, the screen glides up
and one of the best indoor diorama museums is revealed. Feeling
sick? - go to the "Sweat House". The Monks Mound is the largest
prehistoric earthen mound in the New World. Are you ready to go
outside and climb it?

SPLASH CITY FAMILY WATERPARK

10 Gateway Drive (I-55/70 to Hwy 157 exit north)

Collinsville 62234

❏ Phone: (618) 346-4571, **Web: www.splashcity.org**

❏ Hours: Daily 11:00am-8:00pm (late May-Labor Day week).
Closed Monday-Wednesday, mid-August to Labor Day weekend.

❏ Admission: $10.00 adult, $8.50 senior, $8.00 child (2-16). $3.00
discount for residents. Half price admission after 5:00pm.

❏ Miscellaneous: Every Tuesday night is Family Night. Food
specials, games & events with half price admission until 9:00pm.

Southern Illinois' newest water entertainment park features: water
slides, a "lazy river", sand volleyball courts, a zero depth-entry pool,
a child spray area, grass tanning areas and a wet sand play area. The
best part, the new Monsoon Mountain is a fifty-foot fortress of
multi-slides and climbing and a bucket dump every few minutes.

GATEWAY GEYSER

East St. Louis - *Front Street and Trendley Avenue, 62201. Phone: (800) 853-0017.* Currently the tallest fountain in the world, the Gateway Geyser rises as a testimonial to the engineering expertise and 16-year effort of Hydro Dramatics. Soaring to nearly 630-feet, the geyser's height mirrors that of St. Louis' famed Gateway Arch, located directly across the Mississippi River. The center fountain is complemented by four auxiliary fountains, which represent the four rivers that converge in the St. Louis area. The "park" setting around the geyser is FREE of charge to wander through.

GATEWAY GRIZZLIES

East St. Louis (Sauget) - *(just off I-255, exit 15), 62206. Phone: (618) 337-3000. Web: www.gatewaygrizzlies.com.* The Gateway Grizzlies minor league baseball team plays in the outdoor GMC Stadium. The 6,000-seat stadium includes reserved box seats, lawn seats, party suites and even a hot tub. This stadium is the area's own "field of dreams." It's minor league baseball at its finest in a small venue. There's a kids zone area where children can climb and play ball on their "turf." They get the kids involved on the field and every week there are theme nights (ex. Hat night, bobbleheads). Game tickets run $5.00-8.00.

BILBREY FARMS BED & BREAKFAST & ANIMAL ZOO

Edwardsville - *8724 Pin Oak Road (I-55 south to Rte. 143 east), 62025. Phone: (618) 692-1950. Web: www.bilbreyfarms.com. Hours: Animal Farm only open by appointment. Check in after 3:00pm, Checkout by 11:00am. Admission: By reservation only. Rooms range $106.00 to $122.00 per night (based on double occupancy). Discount for weekdays.* Bed and Breakfast accommodations include a country breakfast and rooms with themes from rainforest to castle to garden. Guests have access to the hot tub and on-site movie theatre. The Animal Farm hosts more than 40 animals including a zebra, an emu, a llama, pygmy goats, miniature horses and donkeys, and colorful macaws.

CHILDREN'S MUSEUM OF EDWARDSVILLE

Edwardsville - *722 Holyoake Road (Hwy 159 and Park Place. Next to Leclaire baseball field), 62025. Phone: (618) 692-2094. Web: www.childrens-museum.net. Hours: Tuesday, Friday, Saturday 10:00am-3:30pm. Admission: $3.00 per person (age 1+).* The Museum has several rooms with innovative exhibits and programs that stimulate curiosity and learning for children up to age 12. The kids favorite place is the Fix It Station where kids can take apart small appliances to see how they work. From magnets & Legos to Art & Science Kitchen and Puppets or Dress-up.

WATERSHED NATURE CENTER

Edwardsville - *1591 Tower Road, 62025. Phone: (618) 692-7578.* The Watershed Nature Center features two large lakes and wetland areas, tallgrass prairies and an upland forest. Visitors may walk on the 3,000 ft. wheelchair-accessible pathway at lake level or hike wood-chipped trails through the forested areas. An elevated walkway spans the wetlands and two observation towers, a wildlife viewing blind, & an outdoor amphitheater.

FORT KASKASKIA & KASKASKIA BELL STATE HISTORIC SITE

4372 Park Rd (6 miles N of Chester, Illinois, via Route 3. Turn West on Fort Kaskaskia Rd and go approx. 2 miles), **Ellis Grove** 62241

- ❑ Phone: (618) 859-3741
  Web: www.illinoishistory.gov/hs/Kaskaskia.htm
- ❑ Hours: Wednesday-Sunday 8:00am-4:00pm. Open daily (summer)
- ❑ Admission: FREE
- ❑ Miscellaneous: Garrison Hill Cemetery is also part of the historic site. The remains of some 3,000 gravesites were re-interred here. They were removed from several cemeteries on Kaskaskia Island as a result of the flood of 1881, which eventually destroyed the town of Kaskaskia, Illinois, the first state capital.

Fort Kaskaskia State Historic Site preserves what's left of the old fort—one of the first built on the Mississippi River. The fort was built to protect Kaskaskia from British attack during the American Revolution. Lewis and Clark's boats landed here, establishing a recruitment base and post office. All that remains today are the earth works around the perimeter. A scenic overlook offers views of the Mississippi and Kaskaskia Rivers and of Old Kaskaskia.

KASKASKIA BELL STATE HISTORIC SITE - King Louis XV of France presented this bell to settlers in 1743. The bell rang on July 4, 1778 to celebrate the village's freedom from the British. Now silent (from wear and tear), the bell sits next to the Church of the Immaculate Conception and is the focal point every July 4th celebration.

PIERRE MENARD HOME STATE HISTORIC SITE

4230 Kaskaskia Street, R.R.1 Box 58 (off Illinois Rte 3, located
near Fort Kaskaskia), **Ellis Grove** 62241

❑   Phone: (618) 859-3031

   Web: www.illinoishistory.gov/hs/Menard.htm

❑   Hours: Wednesday-Sunday 8:00am-4:00pm. Open daily in summer.
   Closed New Year's, Martin Luther King, Jr., Presidents, Veterans,
   General Election, Thanksgiving, & Christmas days.

❑   Admission: Suggested donation: $2.00 adult, $1.00 child.

The Pierre Menard Home is the finest example of French Colonial
architecture in the Central Mississippi River Valley. Built in the
early 1800's for Illinois' first lieutenant governor, this elegant
residence depicts the upper class French-American lifestyle of the
early 19th century. The home is furnished with many of the
Menard family's personal possessions and other period pieces. The
surrounding grounds and outbuildings include an herb garden,
smokehouse, springhouse, and adjoining kitchen.

HORSESHOE LAKE STATE FISH & WILDLIFE AREA 78

Granite City - *3321 Highway 111 (nearby Cahokia Mounds), 62040.
www.dnr.state.il.us/lands/landmgt/parks/r4/horsesp.htm. Phone: (618)
931-0270.* This state park has the ancient oxbow lake, wetlands and low
floodplain environments. The Walker Island bird walk is popular.
Evidence shows Native-American tribes were here around 800 BC.
Fishing, boating, picnicking and camping are available. Four miles of
hiking trails wander through the natural area on the island.

CAMP RIVER DUBOIS, LEWIS & CLARK ST. HISTORIC SITE

Illinois Rte. 3 & New Poag Road (Take 1-270 West to IL-3 North to
Poag Road just south of Hartford), **Hartford** 62048

❑   Phone: (618) 251-5811 or (800) 258-6645

   www.greatriverroad.com/lewclark/campriverdubois.htm

❑   Hours: Wednesday-Sunday 9:00am-5:00pm. (November –
   mid-April). Open daily (summer).

❑   Admission: FREE, donations accepted.

❑   Miscellaneous: Lewis & Clark National Historic Trail Site #1 is nearby at the confluence of the Mississippi and Missouri Rivers. Due to riverbank erosion, no one is permitted on the site, currently. On May 14, 1804, Captain Meriwether Lewis wrote "The mouth of the River Dubois is to be considered the point of departure." Visit the Lewis and Clark Interpretive Center, a replica of the 1803-04 winter encampment, and the Lewis and Clark Monument. The facility tells the story of how the Corps of Discovery assembled equipment, supplies and men at Camp River Dubois. At the Convergence Theater an original 15 minute, high definition film, "At Journey's Edge." is shown every 20 minutes. Highlighting the tour is the "Cutaway Keelboat," a 55 foot long replica of the keelboat Lewis had built in Ohio. The boat has been cut in half revealing how it was filled with "Tools of every Description." This is the room where kids can really explore! Be sure to ask the front desk for the scavenger/stamp hunt sheet. As you explore and log your provisions and usefulness, try to determine whether you would be able to pack and organize as well as these folks. Try it. Finished packing? Now, venture outside towards the reconstruction of Camp River Dubois. The volunteers act as guides to the fort where visitors can view the sleeping quarters of the men and the main building that served as guardhouse, storehouse, and the Captain's quarters. Be sure to behave so you don't get 100 lashings. The Camp often had visitors, many who provided information about the west. Today, you are invited to visit and share as many may have done before.

TRAIL OF TEARS STATE FOREST

3240 State Forest Rd (access from SR 127 or SR3 from the west

Jonesboro 62952

❑   Phone: (618) 833-4910

www.dnr.state.il.us/lands/landmgt/parks/r5/trltears.htm#nature

❑   Miscellaneous: Hiking trails, picnicking, horseback riding & camping (fee).

TRAIL OF TEARS STATE FOREST is a multiple-use site managed for timber, wildlife, ecosystem preservation, watershed protection and recreation. The forest lies within the southern section of the Ozark Hills, one of the most rugged landscapes in Illinois. The hills are composed of chert (a weathered limestone residue). Chert was mined (for making tools) at Iron Mountain, east of the Forest.

TRAIL OF TEARS: The disposed Cherokee along with Creek, Choctaw and other tribes were forced from their homes in the east and south and forced to migrate to Oklahoma in 1839. The trail of Tears as it came to be known entered Illinois at Golconda and then divided near Anna-Jonesboro before entering Missouri. The worst winter was at the encampment near Vienna in which almost 5000 people died. Many Southern Illinois families proudly trace ancestry to Cherokee people who left the trail during that time and became absorbed into the pioneer culture.

GATEWAY INTERNATIONAL RACEWAY

Madison - *700 Raceway Blvd (Illinois Route 203 and I-70/55), 62060. Phone: (618) 482-2400 or (888) 827-7333. www.gatewayraceway.com. Hours: Races typically on Fridays and Saturdays (March-October). Admission: Race tickets run from $20.00-50.00 average/person.* This motor sports facility offers a variety of weekly & special races each season.

GIANT CITY STATE PARK

235 Giant City Road (off IL 13 east of Carbondale, head south on Giant City; I-57 exit 45, SR 148 NW, follow signs), **Makanda** 62958

❑   Phone: (618) 457-4836 or (618) 457-4921 lodge
     Web: www.dnr.state.il.us/lands/landmgt/parks/r5/gc.htm
❑   Hours: Visitor Center open 8:00am-4:00pm.
❑   Admission: Admission to Illinois State Parks is free. Camping fees range from $6.00-11.00 per night, depending on amenities; a $5.00 fee is charged for camping reservations.
❑   Miscellaneous: Boating, fishing & camping are also in the park.

From camping and horseback riding to fishing and rappelling, it's an outdoor lover's paradise. The park was named for the massive rock structures nature formed that resembles a primitive city.

Visitors will love walking the many wilderness trails, especially hiking the Giant City Nature Trail, home of the "Giant City Streets" formed 12,000 years ago by huge bluffs of sandstone. The trail actually takes you through the "city" streets vs. just hiking overlooks. It's spectacular to stand against the tall rock "buildings". Trails range from 1/3 mile to 12 miles, so take your pick! Be sure to get an interpretive trail guide at the Visitors Center. The park features a 50-foot observation deck that provides panoramic views of large expanses of the area. The Visitor Center facility houses exhibits on the natural and cultural history of the park, as well as a gift shop, audio-visual room, and a discovery corner for children.

LITTLE GRASSY FISH HATCHERY

Makanda - *1258 Hatchery Lane (seven miles south of Carbondale), 62958. www.dnr.state.il.us/lands/education/interprt/litgras.htm. Phone: (618) 529-4100 Hours: Daily 8:00am-3:30pm. Tours: Offered year-round during both production and non-production season. Walk-ins and Scheduled are welcome.* Little Grassy is known primarily for production of warm-water species such as channel catfish, largemouth bass, redear sunfish, and bluegill. However, cool-water species (walleye, muskellunge) may be produced depending upon water temperature and egg availability. Little Grassy currently produces 15 million fish annually. During the non-production season, visitors may view the state-of-the-art facility. Various mechanical operations and fish production techniques and procedures are explained with aid of photo storyboards. During production season, visitors may view broodfish in spawning cubicles, eggs incubating in artificial hatching jars, and various sizes of fish in indoor rearing tanks. Young catfish in outdoor raceways may be fed by visitors. Can you believe how much pampering goes into these fish? With this many fish "growing up" here, there are plenty to look at.

LAKE MURPHYSBORO STATE PARK AND KINKAID LAKE STATE FISH & WILDLIFE AREA

Murphysboro - *52 Cinder Hill Dr (about one mile west of Murphysboro off Rt 149), 62966. Phone: (618) 684-2867 or (618) 687-4914 marina. www.dnr.state.il.us/lands/landmgt/parks/r5/murphysb.htm. Admission to Illinois State Parks is free. Camping fees range from $6.00-11.00 per night, depending on amenities; a $5.00 fee is charged for camping reservations.* Kinkaid Lake has hiking trails around the lake, camping facilities, and a 300-slip marina on the east end. The spillway is a beautiful natural rock waterfall, quite popular for sunning & swimming, and the pool formed by the runoff from the spillway has produced some record size bass & catfish. Lake Murphysboro State Park sits adjacent to the east end of Kinkaid Lake and offers hiking, fishing, and camping.

LITTLE GRAND CANYON

Murphysboro - *(seven miles south of town on IL 127, turn right on Etherton, take the 3rd turnoff to trailhead), 62966. Phone: (618) 529-4451 or (800) 526-1500.* This is Southern Illinois' version of a smaller Grand Canyon. A three-mile long trail descends into the forest then ascends to the bluff where the Mississippi River is visible on clear days. Pass woods, prairies and waterfalls plus hundreds of flowering plants and fern. Hiking shoes are recommended.

SHAWNEE SALTPETRE CAVE

Murphysboro - *(6 miles south of town, on IL 127), 62966. Phone: (618) 687-9663.* Nature's own amphitheater, Illinois' largest bluff shelter features strange rock formations, a roaring waterfall, picnic tables, nature trails, travel trailer parking and the use of paddle boats and canoes.

RAINBOW RANCH PETTING ZOO

Nashville - *9906 State Route 15, 62263. Phone: (618) 424-7979. Web: www.rainbowranchpettingzoo.com. Hours: Open Wednesday-Saturday 9:00am-5:00pm, Sunday Noon-5:00pm (April - October). By appointment, rest of year.* Wear old shoes to Rainbow Ranch Petting Farm near Nashville. On this farm you get to know donkeys, sheep, goats, cows, horses, fallow deer, pigs, chickens, ducks, geese, rabbits, llamas and even a camel by name. As you tramp through the paddocks, deer, sheep and even a yak come up to be petted.

HERITAGE HOUSE MUSEUM (DR. POOS HOME, SCHLOSSER HOMES)

Okawville - *114 West Walnut Street (I-64 exit 41. SR 177 west and south to town), 62271. Phone: (618) 243-5694. Admission: Donations. Suggested $2.00. Tours: By appointment and weekends from noon-4:00pm. Monday, Wednesday, Fridays often. Check in at the Schlosser Home first to arrange guided tour.* The Heritage House Museum in Okawville includes three different properties - Dr. Poos Home & Medical Museum, the Frank Schlosser Home which includes a turn-of-the-century house, barn, harness shop and commercial laundry and the Joseph Schlosser Home. Dr. Poos Home has an unusual outbuilding, which was intended to be a bathhouse that never opened, containing displays of medical paraphernalia used by Dr. Poos and others and also contains displays of other local historical artifacts. The home also features a working windmill that replaces one that stood over the backyard well until after the doctor's death. There are also several Poos family heirlooms on display, such as the 1893 Chicago World's Fair piano in the Victorian parlor.

PERRY COUNTY JAIL MUSEUM

Pinckneyville - *108 West Jackson Street, 62274. Phone: (618) 357-2228. Hours: Monday 9:00am - 4:00pm, Saturday 10:00am-3:00pm, Sunday 1:30pm-5:00pm.* This museum, operated by the County Historical Society, features rotating exhibits along with permanent rooms. At the Museum: Former Sheriff's Residence; Cellblock with Prisoner Artwork; displays on mining, agriculture and education; One-Room Schoolhouse; a Women's Cell; and Living History Shows.

PYRAMID STATE PARK

Pinckneyville - *1562 Pyramid Park Rd. 62274. Phone: (618) 357-2574. www.dnr.state.il.us/lands/landmgt/parks/r5/pyramid.htm. Admission to Illinois State Parks is free. Camping fees range from $6.00-11.00 per night, depending on amenities; a $5.00 fee is charged for camping reservations.* Pyramid State Park is the largest State Recreation Area in Illinois and gets its name from a coal mine that once existed here. There are 16.5 miles of foot and horse trails and this includes Mountain bike riding. Since many of the lakes can be reached only by foot, Pyramid affords an opportunity for the angler to get away from crowds. The park offers picnic sites and campgrounds, as well.

POMONA NATURAL BRIDGE

Pomona - *(c/o Murphysboro Ranger District. Off IL 127, north of town), 62975. Web: www.murphysboro.com/pomonanaturalbridge. Phone: (618) 529-4451 or (800) 526-1500.* This stone arch or "natural bridge", was formed by the forces of erosion over thousands of years. This natural bridge and other rock outcrops in the area consist of sandstone, which is a fairly soft, erodible bedrock. Water erosion had a powerful effect here, as it gradually washed away softer, less resistant sandstone leaving a natural rock bridge, spanning 90 feet. Located 25 feet above a trickling stream, this bridge spans 90 feet and is one of a few natural stone bridges in the country (see "Kids Love Kentucky" or "Kids Love Virginia" for others). Short loop trails lead through a mature forest. As the trail descends to the creek bottom an overlook reveals a view of the natural bridge from above.

There is a great photo spot at the base of the rock bridge where a semicircle of trees and rock outcroppings serve as a beautiful backdrop for this natural wonder. Picnic areas are available.

FORT DE CHARTRES'

1350 State Route 155, RR 2 (four miles west of town on SR 155)

Prairie Du Rocher 62277

❑   Phone: (618) 284-7230, www.illinoishistory.gov/hs/dechartres.htm
❑   Hours: Wednesday-Sunday 9:00am-5:00pm. Open daily (summer). Closed: Thanksgiving, Christmas, & New Year's Day.
❑   Admission: FREE. Donations accepted.

This great stone fort, formerly one of the strongest forts in North America, was built in 1753 as the seat of government for the French colony in America. Fort de Chartres' limestone gateway, guardhouse, and some of the outer walls have been rebuilt atop original stone foundations. The chapel, priest's room, commander's office and ammunition storage room (complete with cannon balls and weaponry) have been restored. The storehouse is home to the Piethman Museum, which uses discovered artifacts to interpret life in Illinois during the colonial period.

GATEWAY ARCH & MUSEUM OF WESTWARD EXPANSION

(St. Louis Riverfront), **St. Louis (MISSOURI)** 63102

❑   Phone: (877) 982-1410, **Web: www.gatewayarch.com**
❑   Hours: Generally 8:00am-9:00pm. Shorter hours in winter season.
❑   Admission: $10.00 adult, $7.00 youth (13-16), $3.00 child (3-12). Museum of Westward Expansion is FREE. Movie fees apply for showings.

The imposing Gateway Arch, America's tallest monument, is a must-see. The Arch and Old Courthouse sit on riverfront land where the original Route 66 passed by – forging a trail to the American West. Take a ride to the top of the Arch – 630-feet high over the Mississippi – which was built as a monument to President Thomas Jefferson's dream of a continental United States. The ride feels like a somewhat slower version of a carnival ferris wheel.

Although the "pods" you ride on are painted soothing robin egg blue, the "ride" is like a futuristic adventure in the dark (except for your lighted pod). You'll catch the frontiersmen's sense of adventure, for sure! *(Note: Visitors with claustrophobia or "fear of heights" may have trouble with this ride. If in doubt, ask an attendant to let you try a pod first.)* From the top of the monument, you'll get a 30-mile panoramic view of the river and St. Louis far below. Underneath the Arch, history comes to life with a museum and movies. In the Museum of Westward Expansion, you'll step back in time to see buffalo, covered wagons, Native American tepees, Lewis & Clark expedition dioramas and many other artifacts from America's western beginnings in St. Louis. "The Great American West" IMAX movie is shown daily and the documentary "Monument to the Dream" shows how the great Arch was built. The sight is one of those "must sees" for any family travelers.

At the nearby Old Courthouse, you can tour St. Louis history galleries and take part in a recreation of the Dred Scott slavery trial that led America to the Civil War.

VANDALIA STATEHOUSE STATE HISTORIC SITE

315 West Gallatin Street, Vandalia 62471

- ❑ Phone: (618) 283-1161
  Web: www.illinoishistory.gov/hs/Vandalia.htm
- ❑ Hours: Wednesday-Sunday 9:00am-4:00pm. Open until 5:00pm, daily (summer). Closed on major holidays.

Vandalia, the second capitol of Illinois, is steeped in history. The 1836 Statehouse Historic Site is the oldest Illinois State Capitol building. The Federal-style white building is impressive with its high ceilings, tall windows and vintage furnishings. At the top of the broad, curving staircase are the Senate and House of Representatives chambers, where Abraham Lincoln began his political career for the grand sum of $4.00 a day. The Courtroom is an imposing room - full of rich woods that make it very dark and serious. Visitors walk on the same floorboards where the future President made his early arguments against slavery.

SUGGESTED LODGING AND DINING

DRURY HOTEL, 602 N. Bluff, **Collinsville/St. Louis** (I-55/70 exit 11, IL157). (618) 345-7700 or **www.druryhotels.com**. Enjoy free long distance - one hour, every room, every night. Free high-speed internet. Evenings they serve complimentary snacks and beverages, mornings they offer free hot Quikstart breakfast. Also a nice indoor pool and spacious lobby/ food sit-down area. Just minutes from Illinois attractions, 10 miles from the Gateway Arch, Lewis & Clark or Great Rivers Museums.

GIANT CITY STATE PARK, **Makanda**. (618) 457-4921 or **www.giantcitylodge.com**. The multi-hued sandstone and the white oak timber Giant City Lodge (closed winters) has rustic beauty and holds many restored original furnishings. Three types of cabins offering forest views are available to accommodate overnight guests. Twelve historic cabins are one-room units; 18 prairie cabins are two-room units; and four bluff cabins, the largest and most scenic, can conveniently house a family of six. Each cabin has full baths, TV's, telephones and mini-fridge (no cooking appliances or cooking is allowed in the cabins). The Lodge also features an outdoor pool and a kiddie pool. The Bald Knob dining room serves breakfast, lunch and dinner daily and has a reputation for good food at a reasonable price. It is especially well known for its family-style, home-fried chicken (closed from mid-December thru January).

Chapter 7
West Area (W)

Our Favorites...

* Bishop Hill Historic Site - Bishop Hill

* Carl Sandburg Birthplace - Galesburg

* Woodland Palace - Kewanee

* John Deere Pavilion - Moline

* Rock Island & Mississippi River Visitor Centers

* Lakeview Museum - Peoria

* Wildlife Prairie State Park - Peoria

* Avanti Foods - Walnut

Learning the past and future of farming - John Deere Pavillion

WEINBERG-KING STATE PARK

Augusta - *Rural Route 101 (three miles east of town), 62311.* *www.dnr.state.il.us/lands/landmgt/parks/r4/weinberg.htm.* *Phone: (217) 392-2345.* Set on 770 rolling acres, the park is especially popular in winter for its cross-country skiing and snowmobiling. William Creek meanders through the park, providing habitat for an abundance of wildlife.

BISHOP HILL STATE HISTORIC SITE

P O Box 104 (17 miles east of I-74, SR 17/US 34 east, follow signs)

Bishop Hill 61419

- ☐ Phone: (309) 927-3345, **www.illinoishistory.gov/hs/Bishop.htm**
- ☐ Hours: Wednesday-Sunday 9:00am-5:00pm. Closes at 4:00pm winters. Daily in summer. Closed most major government holidays.
- ☐ Admission: FREE. Donations accepted.
- ☐ Miscellaneous: Because Janson would be considered somewhat of a cult leader in contemporary times, it is best to focus on the villagers and their craft and food, rather than the focus be on Janson, his leadership, and death.

It has been called "the most valuable Swedish monument outside Scandinavia...". In 1846, a Swedish religious leader named Eric Janson brought his followers to a new land where they could practice religious freedom in a settlement they named Bishop Hill. Many of the original colony buildings remain today and descendants of the original colonists have restored the area. Take a tour of historic buildings (Church, Hotel - modern by mid-1800 standards), eat at their wonderful Swedish eateries, do some shopping, and see full-time demonstrators in the shops. A new hobby might be spawned watching the craftspeople so closely. Our kids got easy beginner weaving kits (and started weaving as soon as we got back in the van!) The Heritage Museum has some exhibits, a video and internationally recognized folk art paintings of Olof Krans. The Henry County Museum has a scavenger hunt plus a working windmill outside. As you wander the village, be sure to stop by the Colony Store for treats and Swedish sodas (plus, a lot of cute gifts). We really liked P.L. Johnson (try Swedish meatballs, fresh breads, soups, salad dressings or pies) for lunch. Everything Miss Ann and company prepared was fresh and so yummy!

JUBILEE COLLEGE STATE HISTORIC SITE & PARK

13921 West Hwy 150 (I-74 exit 82 north to Kickapoo. Turn west on US 150), **Brimfield** 61517

- ❑ Phone: (309) 446-3758
  www.dnr.state.il.us/lands/landmgt/parks/r1/jubilee.htm
- ❑ Hours: Wednesday-Sunday 9:00am-4:00pm (or 5:00). Daily in summer.
- ❑ Admission: Fee for some activities.

JUBILEE COLLEGE STATE PARK is a facility situated in the Illinoisan drift-plan, complete with rolling hills and a meandering Jubilee Creek. Along the creek, you may see glimpses of mink, muskrat and beaver or one of over 160 species of birds. The park has campgrounds, horseback riding and bike trails (25 miles long). In winter the park also offers cross-country skiing and snowmobiling.

JUBILEE COLLEGE HISTORIC SITE was founded as a seminary in 1840 by the first Episcopal Bishop of Illinois. Jubilee College was the first American boarding college established in Illinois.

SILOAM SPRINGS STATE PARK

Clayton - *938 East 3003rd Lane (nine miles north of Route 104, off Route 24), 62324. www.dnr.state.il.us/lands/landmgt/parks/r4/siloamsp.htm. Phone: (217) 894-6205* Its forested terrain, dotted with wildflowers and accented with a sparkling lake, make this park an ideal setting for outdoor visits, whether your interest is hunting, fishing, camping, boating, picnicking, hiking or bird watching.

NIABI ZOO

Coal Valley - *13010 Niabi Zoo Road (off US 6), 61240. Phone: (309) 799-5107. Web: www.niabizoo.com. Hours: Generally 9:30am-5:00pm (spring & summer). Weekends only 11:00am-4:30pm (winter). Weekday reduced hours (fall). Open April-mid-December. Admission: $3.25-$4.50 per person (age 3+). Miscellaneous: Playgrounds, picnic areas and free stroller and wheelchair rentals.* Niabi Zoo is home to more than 900 animals on 40 acres. Large cats, monkeys, Asian elephants, birds, a petting zoo, Koi pond, and reptiles are some of the favorites. Ride the Express replica train and Endangered Species Carrousel.

ARGYLE LAKE STATE PARK

Colchester - *640 Argyle Park Road (Interstate 74 South to Route 34. Take Route 34 West to Route 67. Take Route 67 South to Route 136. Take Route 136 West), 62326.* **www.dnr.state.il.us/lands/landmgt/parks/r1/argyle.htm.** *Phone: (309) 776-3422. Admission to Illinois State Parks is free. Camping fees range from $6.00-11.00 per night, depending on amenities; a $5.00 fee is charged for camping reservations.* Located along an old stagecoach route between Galena and Beardstown, Argyle is home to rough terrain, beaver dams and more than 200 bird species. The heavily wooded park has a 93-acre lake for boating and fishing, 5 miles of rugged foot trails through luxuriant virgin forests, and full-service campgrounds. There are 12 trails and most are classified as difficult to very difficult, but Blackberry and Pitch Pine trails are rated as moderate. Be sure to look for the beaver dams along Shore Trail.

SAND RIDGE STATE FOREST

Forest City - *25799 East County Road 2300 N (Follow IL Rt 136 to Mason County Road 2800E), 61532. Phone: (309) 597-2212 or (309) 968-7531 Hatchery.* **www.dnr.state.il.us/lands/landmgt/parks/r4/sand.htm.** For those who think central Illinois is one big corn field, Sand Ridge State Forest will come as a very pleasant surprise. The forest is an island in a sea of agriculture. Just minutes southwest of Peoria, this 7,200-acre, the largest of Illinois' State Forests, boasts sweeping expanses of native oak-hickory, extensive plantations of pine, sprawling open fields, grasslands, and completely unique sand prairies. Forty-four miles of marked trails, ranging from 1.6 to 17 miles each, and 120 miles of fire lanes offer unequaled opportunities to the hiker, back packer, horseback rider or snowmobiler. While visiting the park, be sure to stop by the contemporary Jake Wolf Memorial Fish Hatchery, which has an excellent visitor center explaining how to manage a fishery.

CARL SANDBURG BIRTHPLACE

313 East Third Street (E. Main St., right on Seminary St., follow signs), **Galesburg** 61401

❑   Phone: (309) 342-2361, **Web: www.sandburg.org**

❑   Hours: Wednesday-Sunday 9:00am-5:00pm, closing one hour earlier during winters. Closed major holidays. Open daily (summer)

❑   Admission: Donations accepted.

In this small frame cottage, Pulitzer Prize-winning poet and Lincoln biographer Carl Sandburg was born in 1878. Carl

Sandburg worked from the time he was a young boy. He quit school following his graduation from eighth grade in 1891 and spent a decade working a variety of jobs. He delivered milk, harvested ice, laid bricks, and shined shoes in Galesburg's Union Hotel before traveling as a hobo in 1897. The home reflects the living conditions of a typical late-19th century working-class family and is furnished with many Sandburg family belongings. Located behind the home is Remembrance Rock, where Sandburg's ashes have been placed. A Visitor's Center is located next to the house which offers videos and museum exhibits. Great to start here to orient. What word did he detest most?..." "Exclusive" - to know him is to understand why. Children enjoy hearing Sandburg's folk tales, songs and poems composed in between major works about Lincoln. See one of his guitars and the typewriter he used to write part of the Lincoln volumes. Inspiring...

DISCOVERY DEPOT CHILDREN'S MUSEUM

Galesburg - 128 South Chambers Street, 61401. Phone: (309) 344-8876. **Web:** *www.discoverydepot.org. Hours: Monday-Saturday 10:00am-5:00pm, Sunday 1:00-5:00pm. Closed Mondays during school year. Admission: $3.50 per person. Last Thursday of each month – "Thrifty Thursday" $1.00 admission.* Explore a kid sized 2-story home, police car, and ambulance, and climb across a fire truck ladder in Safety City. Maybe play in a real caboose or a real combine. Shop at the Grocery and then prepare a meal at the Diner or sort, stamp and deliver mail at the Depot Post Office. Build with over 15,000 Legos in Legoland or visit the dentist at the Land of Ah-h-hs (which one sounds better?) Climb into and slide out of the Depot Tree House and identify leaf shapes or play with water or puppets. All interactive exhibits promote families to stimulate their curiosity.

PERE MARQUETTE STATE PARK AND VISITORS CENTER

Illinois Route 100 (five miles west of town), **Grafton** 62037

❑   Phone: (618) 786-3323 or (618) 786-2331 lodge

   www.dnr.state.il.us/lands/landmgt/parks/r4/peremarq.htm

❑   Admission: Admission to Illinois State Parks is free. Camping fees range from $6.00-11.00 per night, depending on amenities; a $5.00 fee is charged for camping reservations.

❑ Tours: The Sam Vadalabene Bike Trail runs from Pere Marquette State Park to the City of Alton, approximately 20 miles. The entire trail is paved, and a map is available showing the location of historic sites, restaurants, and other local attractions.

❑ Miscellaneous: The Lodge consists of both new facilities as well as those constructed by the CCC. Native stone and rustic timbers of the original Lodge blend with the new to provide first class accommodations in an historical setting. The mammoth stone fireplace in the lobby soars to a roof height of 50 feet, and is said to weigh 700 tons. There are 50 spacious guest rooms and 22 stone guest cabin rooms. Among the facilities available are a restaurant, gift shop, indoor swimming pool, whirlpool, saunas, game room and tennis court.

Pere Marquette State Park comprises 8,050 acres making it Illinois' largest state park. Named for Jacques Marquette, a French missionary who was a member of a European expedition led by Louis Joliet. They were the first Europeans to reach the confluence of the Mississippi and Illinois rivers. A large stone cross located east of the main Park entrance along Route 100 commemorates their historic landing. The Park is famous for the beauty of its fall colors and as a home for bald eagles in the winter. In addition to the spectacular views of the Illinois and Mississippi rivers from several scenic overlooks (can you find the Piasa Bird?), visitors can take advantage of a variety of year-round recreational activities, including hiking, biking, horseback riding, camping, fishing, boating, and taking part in interpretative programs. The Visitor Center welcomes you with a three-dimensional map of the park, a 300-gallon aquarium, and wealth of other displays and exhibits concerning the Illinois River, wildlife habitat, local history, and geology. Many comment that this is a nice haven to escape to quiet nature.

RAGING RIVERS WATERPARK

Grafton - *100 Palisades Parkway (along Great River Road), 62037. Phone: (618) 786-2345.* **Web: *www.ragingrivers.com.*** *Hours: Daily 10:30am-6:00pm (Memorial Day weekend thru Labor Day weekend). Open one hour later mid-summer. Admission: $14.95-$17.95 (age 3+). Save $4.00 after 3:00pm. Parking $5.00. Tubes Free except for Wave Pool* *which is $5.00-$7.00 per tube. Miscellaneous: Locker rooms, Showers, concessions. No coolers.* Raging Rivers WaterPark is cool when it's hot! From the zoomin' Cascade Body Flumes, to the tube (or tubeless) wave pool, to a lazy Endless River, there's something for everyone. SwirlPool: It's a two-bowl attraction that's really three rides in one. Slide quickly down the tunnel flume, spin swiftly in the giant vortex, then drop into a deep pool of water. If you think that was fun in the daylight, try going down the enclosed Swirlpool in the dark for a double dare! The milder Runaway Rafts Ride: Take this 600-foot long journey down the hillside and experience the real-life adventures of swift water and wild rapids. Or, ride the tubed Shark Slide: This ride floats you right down 45 feet of flume, into a catch pool. Fountain Mountain and TreeHouse Harbor are for the younger set.

CENTER FOR AMERICAN ARCHEOLOGY MUSEUM

Kampsville - *(IL 100, at Marquette and Broadway Streets), 62053. Web: www.caa-archeology.org/index.htm. Phone: (618) 653-4316. Hours: Tuesday-Saturday 10:00am-5:00pm, Sunday Noon-5:00pm (mid-May thru October). Admission: FREE, donations accepted. Tours: Guided tours of our facility, conducted by the CAA's staff of professional archeologists, are available by appointment and are available only to groups of 10 people or larger. A fee is charged for guided tours. Miscellaneous: Family Dig-It Weekends and Archeology Days are held throughout the summer.* With more than 10,000 years of human occupation and thousands of recorded archeological sites in a 4,000 square mile area, the region surrounding the confluence of the Mississippi River and the Illinois River has often been referred to as the "Nile of North America". Ancient towns like Koster and South Koster opened the door for the average person to visit an archeological site, learn about the past, and participate in the ongoing research. With at least 26 separate living horizons defined, major villages were present at Koster ca. 3300, 5000, and 6600 BC. Burials and trade routes have been uncovered. The visitors center contains artifacts, exhibits and displays that explain the history of the lower Illinois River Valley and how archeologists learn about the past. The Gift Shop has many items of interest to children.

BIG RIVER STATE FOREST

Keithsburg - *Rural Route 1, Keithsburg Road (off Hwy 17 or Hwy 164, look for signs), 61442. www.dnr.state.il.us/lands/landmgt/parks/r1/bigriver.htm. Phone: (309) 374-2496.* Big River State Forest is a remnant of a vast prairie woodland border area that once covered much of Illinois. Among its vegetation are two endangered plants - penstemon, commonly known as bearded tongue, and Patterson's bindweed, which N.H. Patterson documented in the forest in 1873 for the first time anywhere. Camp along the Mississippi waterfront or on the upper-level grounds. Launch your boat, walk on the sandy beach, cross-country ski or go snowmobiling on miles of trails. You can also hike the Lincoln Trail or the Pioneer Trail.

JOHNSON-SAUK TRAIL STATE PARK

Kewanee - *27500 North 1200 Avenue, 28616 Sauk Trail Road (off IL 78, 6 miles south of I-80 and 5 miles north of town), 61443. www.dnr.state.il.us/lands/landmgt/parks/r1/johnson.htm. Phone: (309) 853-5589 or (309) 852-4262 barn tour. Admission to Illinois State Parks is free. Camping fees range from $6.00-11.00 per night, depending on amenities; a $5.00 fee is charged for camping reservations.* One of the largest round barns in the country can be seen here. Situated on a glacial moraine, the park is along a trail Sauk Indians used in their treks between Lake Michigan and the confluence of the Mississippi and Rock rivers. The park's centerpiece is a 58-acre lake that offers both fishing and boating, as well as nearly two and a half miles of shoreline to explore. Johnson-Sauk Trail has 10 to 15 miles of trails, ranging from ¼ mile to 1½ miles in length, from easy to moderate and taking hikers along the lake or through land ranging from rolling prairie to pine plantations and bottomland hardwood forests. The grounds are ideal for fishing, winter sports, and camping. RYAN'S HISTORIC ROUND BARN: Take a guided tour of the round barn and visit the farm museum on the first floor. Tours are held May-October only.

WOODLAND PALACE

Francis Park (Route 34, 3 miles east of town), **Kewanee** 61443

❑   Phone: (309) 852-0511
❑   Hours: Monday-Friday 1:00-5:00pm; Weekends 10:00am-
      5:00pm (mid-April-mid-October).
❑   Admission: $1.00-$2.00.
❑   Tours: They'll give guided tours, last about 45 min.
❑   Miscellaneous: The park also sports camping sites, shelter
      houses, picnic areas, playgrounds and a baseball diamond.

The unique home of Frederick Francis was built in 1890 out of brick, stone and native wood. The house features disappearing doors and windows (can you find them - even the hidden drawers?), an air cooling system (using tunnels!), radiant heat deflectors in the fireplace chimney and running water, all without the benefit of electricity. Other inventions were interesting including a rear view mirror for bicycles and multi-functional furniture. This place is so unusual and a little creepy - as you can guess, Fred was a bit eccentric. Don't ask too many questions about his odd ways or his death to keep it from being scary. If you're in the area, it's a quirky must-see.

DICKSON MOUNDS MUSEUM

10956 N. Dickson Mounds Road (between Lewistown and Havana, off IL 97 and 78), **Lewistown** 61542

❑ Phone: (309) 547-3721

Web: www.museum.state.il.us/ismsites/dickson

❑ Hours: Daily 8:30am-5:00pm. Closed major winter holidays & Easter.

❑ Admission: FREE

❑ Miscellaneous: The front desk can give you maps to locate and see nearby Rockwell Mound (one of the largest burial mounds in the midwest).

Explore the world of the American Indian in a journey through 12,000 years of time in the Illinois River Valley - from the wild to the changes after the arrival of Europeans. Legacy, a large-screen video production, captures the past in a panoramic view of the valley. From the ice-age hunters to the tribal groups that left Illinois in the 19th century, Reflections of Three Worlds reveals the world of Mississippian people whose 800-year old sites surround the museum today. The end of the exhibit leads to a multimedia event of sights, sounds, symbols, music and voices of three worlds of Mississippian belief. Kids can apply what they've learned in the Discovery Center - a learning place with hands-on activities for visitors of all ages; discovery drawers, books, tapes, videos and a unique play scape area.

CELEBRATION BELLE PADDLEWHEEL BOAT CRUISES

2501 River Drive, **Moline** 61265

- ❏ Phone: (309) 764-1952 or (800) 297-0034, **www.celebrationbelle.com**
- ❏ Admission: Sightseeing $8.00-$12.00. Lunch $18.00-$27.00. Dinner $25.00-$35.00. All day cruises run $94.00-$123.00. The child's rate is for 3-10 year olds.
- ❏ Tours: Running mostly Thursday-Saturdays, lunch, afternoon and dinner tours. 100 mile all day cruise runs Tuesdays & Wednesdays.

Explore the majestic Mississippi River aboard a riverboat. Experience the power and mystique of the river that captivated the likes of Tom Sawyer and Huck Finn as it sweeps around the riverbend and flows east to west through the Quad cities for the only time in its great length. Cruise or dine aboard the huge 850 person capacity boat - the largest non-gaming luxury excursion vessel on the upper Mississippi River. Guests aboard can go topside and sit with the Captain of the Belle as he maneuvers the paddlewheel along the mighty river. Or, find a comfortable lounge chair and relax while a captain tells you about the history of the river, the Rock Island Arsenal, Lock & Dam 15, and other historic sites along the shore.

CHANNEL CAT WATER TAXI

2501 River Drive (Celebration Belle dock, riverfront), **Moline** 61265

- ❏ Phone: (309) 788-3360, **Web: www.qcmetrolink.com**
- ❏ Hours: Weekdays 11:00am-8:00pm, Weekends 9:00am-8:00pm (Memorial Day-Labor Day). Weekends only in September and on East Moline Quarter route.
- ❏ Admission: $5.00 adult, $2.00 child (2-10). Tickets are for all-day unlimited use on day of purchase. Buy your tickets on board or at Centre Station Gifts.

Take a trip on the Water Taxi open-air boat stopping at different boat landings on both the Iowa and Illinois banks of the Mississippi River. The Channel Cat returns every hour to take passengers back and forth across the river. Bicyclists use the Cat to go to bike trails on both sides of the river. You even go through an old lock and see the unusual system they used to pour concrete.

JOHN DEERE PAVILION & COLLECTORS CENTER

1400 River Dr. (riverfront @ John Deere Commons), **Moline** 61265

- ❑ Phone: (309) 765-1000, **Web: www.johndeerepavilion.com**
- ❑ Hours: Monday-Friday 9:00am-5:00pm, Saturday 10:00am-5:00pm, Sunday Noon-4:00pm. Closed on Easter, Thanksgiving, Christmas and New Years.
- ❑ Admission: FREE
- ❑ Miscellaneous: A couple of blocks away, the Collectors Center is the place for enthusiasts interested in the nostalgia and legacy of John Deere and the collection of early tractors, equipment and memorabilia…all in a replica 1950s John Deere dealership. THE GREAT RIVER TRAIL bike path follows the river along the Commons. It makes a great place to start or end your bike ride.

Celebrate the American heartland from the first horse-drawn plow to the latest modern-day combines and tractors. In the early 1900s, Moline was the undisputed agricultural center of the Midwest (taking advantage of the water power and transportation offered by the Mississippi River). The whole family can enjoy interactive, hands-on computer displays that include virtual tours of the company's combine factory and a fun and educational journey through the generations of a family farm. Watch the very inspiring video that is an Anthem to farming families. Games and a Kids Corner have fun trivia games. Children and adults can climb on or sit in the driver's seat of Deere's agricultural and construction equipment. This is the best part - you'll feel like a giant! Some cabs are equipped with CD players and AC - why? (think about it as the farmer's office). Other exhibits show the challenges of farming in the future. Can you figure out how to feed the nations better? This is a really fun center for the whole family.

RIVERWAY PARKS AND TRAILS

Moline - *Start at CVB Welcome Centers, 61265. Phone: (800) 747-7800. Web: www.riveraction.org. Admission: You can rent bikes by the hour or day. Riverway - the Quad Cities' scenic stretch of the Mississippi River with 65 miles of riverside parks, trails and overlooks between the river bluffs. Enjoy America's most famous river by walking or biking along its* riverfront trails. Even follow old train bridges over to small islands or along the river. Bike, roller blade, walk, or run with maps available online or at the Welcome Centers.

BACKWATER GAMBLERS WATER SKI SHOWS

5000 44th Street (I-74, take the John Deere Road West Exit. Ben Williamson Park on the Rock River), Travel approximately 2 miles. Turn left at 44th Street), **Moline (Rock Island) 61201**

- ❑ Phone: (309) 788-7312, **Web: www.backwatergamblers.com**
- ❑ Shows: Two shows each week at 6:30pm on Sunday and Wednesday (Memorial Day-Labor Day)
- ❑ Admission: FREE. A donation collection is taken at half-time. Bleacher Seating with Concessions.
- ❑ Miscellaneous: Before or after the show, stop by Happy Joe's Pizza for a bite to eat, (try veggie pizza with sauerkraut – it's really good), followed by yummy, thick Special Shakes (forget about using a straw) at Whitey's Ice Cream. Both are on 16th Street.

The Backwater Gamblers Water Ski Show Club was founded as a non profit organization: To provide free, quality water ski entertainment to the Quad City area; and, to become one of the top rated ski clubs in show competition. The free, one hour, fun-filled family show is a themed performance combining skits, music, dance, and water-skiing. Dare-devil maneuvers occur with flips and spins over the jump ramp; boat speeds up to 40 miles per hour pull skiers on their bare feet; and costumed girls slalom ski in a ballet line and gracefully turn and twist. The highlight: 18+ skiers pull together to build a huge pyramid formation in the air while continuing to water-ski.

BLACK HAWK STATE HISTORIC SITE

1510 46th Avenue (I-280, take the Milan Exit (U.S. 67), continue north through Milan to Rock Island's Black Hawk Road (State Route 5), **Moline (Rock Island) 61201**

- ❑ Phone: (309) 788-0177, **www.state.il.us/hpa/Blackhawk.htm**
- ❑ Hours: Black Hawk State Historic Site is open year-round from sunrise to 10:00pm. The Hauberg Museum is open Wednesday-Sunday 9:00am-5:00pm except for major holidays. Closes at 4:00pm winters. Open daily (mid-April – Labor Day)

Black Hawk State Historic Site (*cont.*)

- ❏   Admission: FREE. Donations accepted.
- ❏· Miscellaneous: The area is a nature preserve with picnic sites and hiking trails.

This site is a wooded, steeply rolling 208-acre tract that borders the Rock River. Prehistoric Indians and 19th century settlers made their homes in the area. It was even once an amusement park. It is most closely identified with the Sauk nation and the warrior whose name it bears - Black Hawk. Visit one of the largest Native-American centers in North America. The Hauburg Indian Museum interprets the Indian cultures with full-size replicas of Sauk winter and summer houses, dioramas with life-size figures depict activities of the Sauk and Mesquakie people typical of the period 1750-1830. There's also many artifacts, including authentic trade goods, jewelry, and domestic items.

CIRCA 21 DINNER PLAYHOUSE

Moline (Rock Island) - *1828 Third Avenue, 61201. Phone: (309) 786-7733. Web: www.circa21.com. Shows: Wednesday Matinee @ Noon; Wednesday- Saturday Evenings @ 6:00pm; Sunday Evenings @ 4:00pm. Admission: $32.00-$39.00 adult, $23.00 student. Prices include a professional production, a six entree buffet and tax. For the matinee performances there is a plated lunch served at your table with your choice of three entrees. No cancellations or refunds.* Experience the excitement of live theater with such shows as Fiddler on the Roof, Footloose or Winnie the Pooh, all directed, designed and performed by artists from New York and other top theatrical centers. Every seat is a box seat. Not only does it offer an intimate and unobstructed view of the stage, but it also surrounds you with the beauty of a refurbished 1921 décor. Before the performance, you'll enjoy a dinner buffet of snappy salads, sizzling beef, ham or seafood served by Roaring Twenties era wait staff. Friendly Bootleggers tend to your every need - even as they perform the rollicking pre-show musical review.

QUAD CITY BOTANICAL GARDEN

2525 4th Avenue (I-74 Moline River Drive, 7th Ave exit - head west.
In Rock Island, cross the tracks and take the first right on 5th. It
becomes 4th Ave.), **Moline (Rock Island)** 61201

❑   Phone: (309) 794-0991, **Web: www.qcgardens.com**
❑   Hours: Monday-Saturday 10:00am-5:00pm, Sunday Noon-
     5:00pm. Closed major winter holidays.
❑   Admission: $1.00-$3.50 (age 7+).

Impressive with its 70-feet tall skylight peak, the Botanical
Center's Sun Garden conservatory offers an indoor tropical
paradise. Visitors enter the foggy hidden garden at the back
spillway of a 14-foot waterfall. Spanish moss and orchids cling to
rocks as curving brick pathways lead visitors to the islands and
reflective pools that hold tropical plants and flowers changing each
season. Kids will admire tropical trees holding bananas, coconuts
and coffee beans. Special signs were made for all of the plants that
show the importance of tropical forests, whether for food,
medicine, beauty or fresh air. Japanese Koi fish swim in the
reflective pools that hold a variety of unusual water plants. Doors
lead outside to the Conifer and Perennial Garden. The Physically
challenged Garden features garden beds, a gazebo and water
fountain maintained by physically challenged gardeners. Youngsters
will enjoy the ABC Greenhouse Garden, which features plants and
flowers from every letter in the alphabet. The unusual variety of
flowers, whimsical art, a playhouse, garden tools, sand and soil
boxes, and a fish-filled water garden encourage children to interact.

ROCK ISLAND ARSENAL / MISSISSIPPI RIVER VISITOR CENTER

1 Rock Island Arsenal (I-74 exit 2, 7th Avenue (west). Right on
14th, across ramp to Rodman Ave. Right on Gillespie to Bldg. 60)

Moline (Rock Island) 61299

❑   Phone: (309) 782-5021, **http://riamwr.com/museum.htm** or
     http://www.mvr.usace.army.mil/missriver/
❑   Hours: Museum: Daily 10:00am-4:00pm. Closed only winter
     major holidays. Mississippi River Visitor Ctr: Daily 9:00am-5:00pm.

Rock Island Arsenal/ Mississippi River Visitor Center *(cont.)*

- ❑   Admission: FREE
- ❑   Tours: Lock and Dam tours on summer weekends at 11:00am and 2:00pm by appointment. Want to watch at home? Log on to the website web cam.
- ❑   Miscellaneous: Biking trails around the Island. Food Court open weekdays 6:00am-1:30pm. For security reasons all persons over age 16 must carry a photo ID to enter the island. Vehicles are subject to search.

ARSENAL MUSEUM: Arsenal Island was originally purchased by the government in 1804 as a part of a treaty with Sauk and Fox Indians. In 1817, a fort was built on the western end of the island. During the Civil War, over 12,000 prisoners were housed on the island. Factory buildings were built in the 1900s to supply military equipment. No longer used to build equipment, the original limestone buildings are now used for office space and defense warehousing. The Museum features the whole history of the island in exhibits and photos, a model of the first fort built, Fort Armstrong, and the world's largest collection of small firearms. In the Discovery Room, kids can try on all sorts of military costumes. Work puzzles or start a scavenger hunt here, too.

MISSISSIPPI RIVER VISITOR CENTER: From early April through mid December, visitors from around the world come to the visitor's center to watch boats pass through the lock. The main lock can hold nine barges at a time. The barges may be carrying coal, grain or scrap metal. It takes about one and one half hours to lock through here at #15 (with a double lockage). No turbines are used in locks, just water released or drained using a unique tunneled water system. The locks form a "stairway of water" and one barge carries more cargo than 15 jumbo railcars or 58 semi-trailers - thus, the reason cargo is still transported this way. The roller dam at Locks and Dam 15 is the largest in the world. Watch a working model of the Lock or flood a reservoir (using a bathtub). Observation deck, movie and exhibits are also at the Mississippi River Center (309-794-5338)

WYATT EARP BIRTHPLACE

406 South 3rd Street (Routes 34 & 67, southeast of city square, fifteen minutes west of I-74), **Monmouth** 61462

❑ Phone: (309) 734-3181 or (309) 723-6419 (curator)
    www.earpmorgan.com/wyattearpbirthplacewebsite.html
❑ Hours: Open from 1:00-4:00pm, by appointment.
❑ Admission: Donations.

Deputy U.S. Marshal Wyatt Earp, an American hero who helped tame the Old West, was born in Monmouth over 150 years ago. Wyatt attended the first free public school here. Wyatt's father, a constable, helped organize the Republican party in town. Wyatt became a lawman in 1869 and is world famous for the OK Corral gunfight in Tombstone, Arizona Territory in 1881. Relive the Old West at the OK Corral (replica next door). Earp's Birthplace Home and Museum is listed on the National Register of Historic Places. It contains 1848-1881 period rooms with many Earp displays and a gift shop area. TIP: rent some old Western movies to get the kids familiar with this time period. Bring your cowboy garb to play pretend in the OK Corral next door (they sell Wyatt Earp sheriff badges in the house).

NAUVOO STATE PARK

Nauvoo - *Durphy Street (IL 96, south edge of town), 62354. www.dnr.state.il.us/lands/landmgt/parks/r4/nauvoo.htm. Phone: (217) 453-2512 Admission to Illinois State Parks is free. Camping fees range from $6.00-11.00 per night, depending on amenities; a $5.00 fee is charged for camping reservations.* Its first name was Quashquema, a Fox Indian word meaning "peaceful place." Its current name is Nauvoo, a Hebrew word for "beautiful place" or "pleasant land." This historic town is the backdrop for Nauvoo State Park, on the banks of the Mississippi River. The 148-acre park includes a 13-acre lake with a mile-long shoreline. In addition to fishing, boating, camping and hiking, they offer a timbered nature trail and small prairie plot. The Rheinberger Museum within the park focuses on the grape industry started here...plus Nauvoo Blue Cheese and Nauvoo wine.

DELABAR STATE PARK

Oquawka - *RR 2, Box 27 (on the Mississippi River, one mile north of town, near Hwy 164), 61469. Phone: (309) 374-2496* **Web:** *www.dnr.state.il.us/lands/landmgt/parks/r1/delabar.htm.* Forested areas serve as natural habitat for a variety of wildlife species, including squirrel, rabbit, raccoon, deer, groundhog and quail. More than 50 species of birds have been identified in the park, making Delabar State Park a natural haven for birders from throughout the state. Enjoy camping under shady oak trees, boating access, and a children's play area. Many visitors take advantage of the backwaters of the Mississippi River for ice fishing and, when the ice is thick enough, ice skating.

PEORIA HISTORY TROLLEY

Peoria - *(depart from various eateries downtown), 61602, Phone: (309) 674-1921. Admission: $8.00-$12.00 per seat. Tours: Wednesday-Saturday Memorial Day weekend thru late October. 2 hour tours.* From the grand history of this River City to the grand homes. Visit Peoria's scenic drive that winds its way above the valley passing homes of today's and yesterday's prosperous merchants, landowners and professionals. Enjoy a trip back in time down Peoria streets with narration provided by trained guides from the Historical Society.

SPIRIT OF PEORIA RIVERBOAT

Peoria - *100 Northeast Water Street (Riverfront Park), 61602. Phone: (309) 636-6166,* **Web:** *www.spiritofpeoria.com. Admission: $7.00-$12.00 sightseeing; $12.00-$24.00 lunch cruise; $16.00-$32.00 dinner cruise. Miscellaneous: The Riverfront District is graced with cultural, entertainment, dining, shopping, historical and recreational activities. Home to many popular festivals, outdoor concerts, professional theater, parks, marinas, biking trails, and sport courts.* This authentic replica of a turn-of-the 20th-century paddle wheeler embarks on regularly scheduled cruises to various Illinois River destinations including Starved Rock State Park and Pere Marquette State Park. One-hour public sightseeing cruises are also scheduled on a regular basis, as are various theme cruises.

GLEN OAK PARK, ZOO & GARDEN

Peoria - *2218 North Prospect Road (Glendale Ave exit off I-74. Turn right on Hamilton Blvd, then right onto Knoxville Ave.. Which turns into Glen Oak. Stay left onto Prospect), 61603. Phone: (309) 681-2902 park or (309) 686-3365 zoo.* **Web:** *www.peoriaparks.org or www.glenoakzoo.org. Admission is zoo admission.* Glen Oak Park hosts daily visitors to the Zoo and Garden and various special events. Visitors can take advantage of the hiking/biking trail, fishing lagoon, fitness trail, picnic shelters, amphitheatre, lighted tennis and shuffleboard courts and several playgrounds. The Zoo has a reptile and primate house, aquatic animals, numerous exhibits and offers daily sea lion programs and critter chats, tours and behind-the-scenes tours. The Botanical Garden contains theme gardens including a children's garden and wildlife garden, and a conservatory.

PEORIA CHIEFS BASEBALL

Peoria - *730 SW Jefferson Street (O'Brien Field, I-74 exit 92, Glendale to Jefferson), 61605. Phone: (309) 680-4000. Web: www.peoriachiefs.com. Admission: $6.00-$9.00 per seat.* The Chicago Cubs Class A Affiliate Chiefs play a regular season April-September. The Chiefs play at O'Brien Field, which is the largest outdoor sports and entertainment facility in Central Illinois. The field features amenities such as luxury suites, closed-circuit televisions, an outfield video board and a play area for kids. In addition to their fireworks, each season brings special appearances by folks like Myron Noodleman, Zooperstars, BirdZerk and many concerts. Fans can also bring along a blanket & enjoy the game with an inexpensive lawn ticket.

WHEELS O' TIME MUSEUM

Peoria - *11923 N. Knoxville Avenue (Rte 40) (2 miles north of Rte. 6 on Rte 40), 61612. Phone: (309) 243-9020. Web: www.wheelsotime.org. Hours: Wednesday-Sunday Noon-5:00pm (May-October). Admission: $5.00 adult, $2.50 child (3-11).* With too many antique autos to store, a couple of guys erected a building to house the cars and display them as a museum. 55 collectors own the museum and share their collections with the public. Three buildings house displays of autos, farm equipment, trains, bicycles, toys, clothing, fire apparatus, tools, clocks, and music machines. Many displays are interactive. Listen to a Presidential barbershop quartet, toot a whistle, run a Lionel train and see a 1940s radio station.

LAKEVIEW MUSEUM OF ARTS & SCIENCES

1125 West Lake Avenue (I-74 exit 91/University Street north to Lake Avenue, east to Lakeview Park), **Peoria** 61614

- ❑   Phone: (309) 686-7000, **Web: www.lakeview-museum.org**
- ❑   Hours: Tuesday-Saturday 10:00am-5:00pm; Sunday Noon-5:00pm. Open until 8:00pm on Wednesdays.

Lakeview Museum Of Arts & Sciences *(cont.)*

❑ Admission: Gallery only $3.50-$5.00, Planetarium only $3.00-$4.00, Combo $5.00-$7.00.

❑ Miscellaneous: Gift shop is full of unusual, new educational toys.

Lakeview's large museum features a renowned planetarium and the world's largest solar system model, according to the Guinness Book of World Records. The driving 50 mile system begins at the Museum - the Sun. Every few months, the museum offers a constant stream of exhibits and programming. An affiliate of the Smithsonian Institute, this facility features both temporary and permanent art and science exhibits plus an Illinois Folk Art Gallery. They have a permanent outdoor sculpture exhibit with a self-guided tour brochure that allows visitors to leisurely stroll the artistic grounds. The Discovery Center is all hands-on and contains many original, easy areas of learning play. "Make an impression" on the Pin Screen - hilarious!; look at Fluorescent minerals; create lightning; make a kidquake or even a magnetic bridge. Simple, easy to understand physics! Good job.

WILDLIFE PRAIRIE STATE PARK

3826 N. Taylor Road (I-74 exit 82 or I-474 exit 3, follow signs to SR8), **Peoria** 61615

❑ Phone: (309) 676-0998
   Web: www.wildlifeprairiestatepark.org

❑ Hours: Daily 8:00am-8:00pm (May-Labor Day); 9:00am-6:30pm (September); 9:00am-4:30pm (rest of year). Closed mid-December through mid-March.

❑ Admission: $5.50 adult, $3.50 child (4-12). Free parking.

❑ Miscellaneous: Playgrounds and picnic areas. Craving BBQ? Head north to the Shops of Grand Prairie for some Famous Dave's BBQ (309-683-2663) or **www.famousdaves.com**.

West of the Illinois River bluffs, the land levels off into rolling grasslands, occasionally dissected by small rivers and streams. This park features native state animals such as bison, elk, wolves, black bear, cougar, river otter, waterfowl and raptors, as well as various songbirds, butterflies and other native birds. Stop by the

Park's Visitor Center and see their Animal Nursery and Museum. Join the excellent Naturalists at various interpretive programs. Ride the Park's train through restored Prairie Habitat, visit the Pioneer Farmstead Area, or hike 10 miles of trail and wildlife habitats. At 1:00pm each day, you'll want to watch the elk and bison being fed at a special platform where they come real close!

SPLASHDOWN WATERPARK AT EASTSIDE CENTRE

Peoria (East Peoria) - *One Eastside Drive (I-74 to the Camp Street Exit (95C). At the 2 stoplight take a right onto Meadow Avenue (Route 150). Follow that road for about 2 miles), 61611. Phone: (309) 694-1867.* **Web: www.fondulacpark.com/splashdown.** *Hours: Daily 11:00am-6:30pm (Memorial Day weekend through mid-August). Open one-half hour later on weekends. Admission: $7.00 adult (13-61), $5.00 senior and child (age 4-12). Spectators $3.00. Toddlers 3 & under Free. After 3:30 admission prices are reduced $1.00. Prices include use of all Attractions, Lifejackets, and Inner tubes.* Splashdown is a 3-acre water entertainment complex jam-packed with wet 'n wild activities. It's very affordable for families. Plus, it's 100% accessible to persons with disabilities. Use your imagination to discover the wacky, hands-on water effects found on Splashtower Island. Here, "drenching the unsuspecting", even Mom and Dad, won't get you in trouble. Plunge into summer head, or feet first on an inner tube that careens the crazy and unpredictable curves of the Wild Ride tube slide. Take a breather floating along the Lazy River. Or, sit back and watch as little tikes waddle through the Splash n' Play pool.

DRAGONLAND WATER PARK

Peoria (Pekin) - *1701 Court Street (just off Rt. 9 (Court St.) next to the high school stadium, Memorial Springs Park), 61554.* **Web: www.pekin.net/pekinparkdistrict/dragonland.htm.** *Phone: (309) 347-4000. Hours: Daily 11:30am-6:00pm (Memorial Day weekend thru mid-August). Admission: $4.00 per person (age 4+). Family nights (Tuesday and Thursday) - whole family =$7.50. Miscellaneous: Changing, shower and locker facilities. Lighting for night activities.* The water is heated and features a zero depth play/entry area with three exciting water slides. Children's sand beach play area has water equipment, sand volleyball and concessions.

TOWER PARK

Peoria Heights - *1222 E. Kingman (off 4900 N. Prospect & Grandview Drive), 61616. Phone: (309) 682-8732. Hours: Tuesday-Friday Noon-7:00pm, Weekends 11:00am-7:00pm. Summer Friday & Saturday evening open until 10:00pm. Closed Mondays except holidays. (April-October, weather permitting). Admission: $1.25-$1.75 (ages 5+).* The tower is the only structure of its kind in the United States, and features a glass elevator that glides up to the top of the 170 foot tower. View the many miles of the Illinois River Valley. On top of 500,000 gallons of clear, pure well water, there are three separate observation decks designed to provide a spectacular panorama in all directions. There are three telescopes available for even closer viewing.

HISTORIC OWEN LOVEJOY HOMESTEAD AND COLTON SCHOOLHOUSE

East Peru Street (Rtes. 26 & 6, east of Main St), **Princeton** 61356

❑   Phone: (815) 879-9151, **Web: www.lovejoyhomestead.com**
❑   Hours: Friday, Saturday and Sunday 1:00-4:00pm (May-September). April and October by appointment only.
❑   Admission: Small admission is charged.
❑   Miscellaneous: The Colton Schoolhouse is located on the Owen Lovejoy Homestead property. This one-room schoolhouse was moved from its original location 2.5 miles east of the homestead. The school was built in 1849, with sessions of school held in the building from 1850 until the school's official closing in 1945.

Owen Lovejoy came to Princeton in 1838 to assume the ministry of a local church. He was a fiery abolitionist who preached his views from the pulpit, causing dissension in a community already divided by the slavery issue. An acquaintance of Abraham Lincoln, Lovejoy was elected to the State Legislature in 1854 and to the House of Representatives in 1856, where he served 5 terms. His home was one of the most important stations on the Underground Railroad in Illinois. Runaway slaves were harbored by the Lovejoy family until arrangements could be made for them to travel to the next station on their way to Canada and freedom. Furnishings in the Lovejoy home reflect the Civil war era and include pieces that are original to the family. There is also a document room with photos and copies of Lovejoy's speeches and letters. Once an important stop on the Underground Railroad, the restored Lovejoy Homestead is now on the National Register of Historic Places & open for tours.

HENNEPIN CANAL PARKWAY STATE PARK

Sheffield - *16006-875 East Street (I-80 & IL 40), 61361. Phone: (815) 454-2328. www.dnr.state.il.us/lands/landmgt/parks/r1/hennpin.htm. Admission to Illinois State Parks is free. Camping fees range from $6.00-$11.00 per night, depending on amenities; a $5.00 fee is charged for camping reservations.* Originally a canal waterway, the parkway was closed in the 1950s and re-opened as a recreation park. In the Visitors Center there are several displays that help illustrate the canal's past -- including tools used to build and operate it. At the time the canal was built workers often made their own tools by hand. There's also a model of a lock with a boat going through it and a model of an aqueduct. Get a peek at the plant and animal life at the park through other displays at the center. Now, go outside and explore the 104-mile waterway and 5,000 acres for canoeing, fishing, hiking, horseback riding, biking, cross-country skiing, snowmobiling & camping.

SKI SNOWSTAR

Taylor Ridge (Andalusia) - *9500 128th Street West (just off IL Rt. 92 in Andalusia), 61284. Phone: (309) 798-2666. www.skisnowstar.com. Hours: Daily 9:00am-9:00pm (Thanksgiving - mid March). Admission: $15.00-$30.00 lift passes.* When the snow flies, it's time for winter fun with downhill ski runs of all levels, a tube hill and plenty of lifts. Snow tubing allows all ages to slide down one of the groomed chutes on giant inner-tubes and then a specially designed tow takes them and the tube back to the top. (tubers must be 4 years old). The Ski School teaches beginners from age 4 and up. The lounge area has fireplaces and an outside patio with firepot.

AVANTI FOODS

109 Depot Street (I80 to SR 40N to SR 92E about 5 miles. Right on Main, left on Depot), **Walnut** 61376

❑   Phone: (815) 379-2155 or (800) 243-3739
    Web: www.avantifoods.com

❑   Hours: Monday-Friday, 8:00am-5:00pm and Saturday, 8:00am-1:00pm. Viewing area open each day the shop is open.

❑   Tours: Offered only in April and May. Self-guided tours anytime open - best weekday mornings.

Avanti Foods (*cont.*)

In 1932, Walnut Cheese was founded as a market for the milk produced by surrounding dairy farmers. In 1964 Avanti Foods was formed to produce frozen pizzas under the "Gino's" and "Swiss Party" labels (they produce several thousand pizzas per day). Their own Mozzarella cheese is used for the topping. Using time-tested methods and modern equipment, Bruno, the master cheesemaker, oversees daily production of 50,000 lbs. of milk into cheese. Watch through the observation windows as milk is turned into curds and whey, drained, flavored and cut. Next, venture across the street to watch 10 or more ladies hover over the conveyor table layering pizzas that are then quickly led to the freezer and wrapped and shipped. Need pizza making supplies? This is the place. New facilities make it possible for visitors to view the pizza and cheese production or browse in the Cheese and Gourmet Shop. Try their blue-ribbon State Fair Longhorn cheese - yum.

ROCK ISLAND TRAIL STATE PARK

Wyoming - *311 East Williams Street (I-74 west to SR 6 west exit. Turn north on Allen Road & follow curve), 61491. Phone: (309) 695-2228. Web: www.dnr.state.il.us. Admission: FREE.* Rock Island Railroad busily carried freight and passengers between Peoria and Rock Island for over 40 years. By 1915, however, rail volume declined and ceased altogether by the mid-twentieth century. One of the premier rails-to-trails facilities in Illinois, this trail has 27 miles for hiking, biking and cross-country skiing between the communities of Alta and Toulon. Running through regenerated forest and tallgrass prairie habitats, the trail offers improved access at its southern terminus in Alta, at the Kickapoo Creek Recreation Area, at the Williams Street Depot Museum in Wyoming, and at the trail head in Toulon.

SUGGESTED LODGING AND DINING

MONMOUTH SODA WORKS, 112 South First Street, **Monmouth**. (309) 734-3221. An 1800's building restored to a turn of the century ice cream parlor and mercantile. The 1874 building once served as a meat packing plant, grocery store, sewing machine factory and auto dealership. Exposed brick walls, tin ceiling, amber-hued pine floors, huge street-side windows and an old Dodge automobile tell a bit of history. The upstairs, which once was a billiard hall, now contains one-room school-house memorabilia. Today it serves old-fashioned ice cream sodas and soups and sandwiches. Like new flavors, try an old-fashioned Green River soda ($1.29, plus 30 cents for one refill), which is a sweet, lime-flavored soda.

COCONUTS RESTAURANT & MAPLE CITY CANDY, 109 E. Broadway/69 Public Square, **Monmouth**. (309) 734-8999. Multi-floors of candy, ice cream and themed gifts at every turn and nook makes this place adorable. A Caribbean-style motif and food plus a fun Kids Menu.

WILDLIFE PRAIRIE STATE PARK LODGING & DINING, 3826 N. Taylor Road, **Peoria**. **www.wildlifeprairiestatepark.org** or (309) 676-0998. Spend the night on the Prairie! Several unique lodging facilities, including the Cabin on the Hill (with an adorable mini-cabin "next door" for the kiddies - the cabin is fashioned just like the Little House on the Prairie), Cottages by the Lake, Prairie Stables and Santa Fe Train Cabooses (most cabins are $60 - under $100 per night). Accommodations overlook the bison range or lake. All Facilities Include: Two days Park admission, Charcoal grills and picnic tables, Televisions, Linens, Bathroom with showers, Bank fishing, and use of the Recreation Room located near the Prairie Stables. The Prairie View Café awaits you with good food and a breathtaking view of the bison range. Lunch and Sunday brunch.

RADISSON ON JOHN DEERE COMMONS, 1415 River Drive, **Moline**. (309) 764-1000 or **www.radisson.com/molineil**. The scenic river front property, located right next door to the John Deere commons is within a walk or short drive of most attractions. Relax in this spotless, friendly hotel along the banks of the mighty Mississippi River with spacious rooms featuring wi-fi, Sleep Number beds (dial-your-own comfort). Try the indoor pool and jacuzzi after you eat a casual, fun-food meal or snack at the attached T.G.I. Fridays.

LAGOMARCINO'S, 1422 Fifth Avenue, **Moline**. Downtown, just blocks from the John Deere Pavilion. **www.lagomarcinos.com**. (309) 764-1814. In 1908, Angelo Lagomarcino, an immigrant from Northern Italy, founded this Confectionary and Ice Cream Parlor. Homemade candy remains a big part of the business. At Easter and Christmas, Lagomarino's continues the old European art of casting chocolate eggs or ornaments filled with individually wrapped chocolates or children's candies. Now also serving lunch, try ham salad or a tuna melt with a signature soda - a Green River (tastes like liquid lime Jell-O) or a fruity Lago. Top it off with a famous Hot Fudge Sundae. On your way out, purchase a box of some unique chocolate bark - peppermint, lemon, pretzel or almond.

Chapter 8

Seasonal &
Special Events

JANUARY

N – ILLINOIS SNOW SCULPTING COMPETITION - Rockford, Sinnissippi Park. (815) 987-8800. Watch snow-sculpting teams form stunning figures from giant blocks of snow. Giant dragons, abstract shapes and whimsical figures take shape under the skilled hands of 30 top competitors. FREE. (third full week of January)

W – EAGLES ON THE RIVER - Meredosia, River Museum. (217) 584-1356. Come experience eagle watching along the Illinois River, attend "Watchable Wildlife" workshops and children's activities. Raptor Show (small fee). FREE. (second full weekend in January)

W – BALD EAGLE DAYS - Moline (Rock Island), QCCA Expo Center. (309) 788-5912. Environmental fair celebrating the annual southern migration from Canada. Includes live wolves, birds of prey and river otters, exhibits, live eagle presentations and outdoor eagle watching. (weekend after New Years)

FEBRUARY

C – ABRAHAM LINCOLN'S BIRTHDAY BASH - Lincoln, Postville Courthouse State Historic site. (217) 732-8930. Take a tour through the historic courthouse. Historians will be present and will speak in Abe's historic courtroom. Enjoy period music and exhibits while eating birthday cake. Admission. (second Saturday in February)

C – MAPLE SYRUP TIME - Springfield, Lincoln Memorial Garden. (217) 529-1111 or www.lmgnc.com. Visitors can experience the entire maple syrup process from tapping trees to collecting sap to actually cooking the sap into syrup. Demonstrations are held each Saturday and Sunday. FREE. (weekends mid-February thru early March)

EC – LINCOLN'S BIRTHDAY OPEN HOUSE - Danville, Vermilion County Museum, 116 N. Gilbert. www.vermilioncountymuseum.org. (800) 383-4386. This event, which has taken place for well over 35 years, acquaints visitors with the time of Illinois history when Lincoln was traveling the Judicial Circuit. Admission. (first Sunday in February)

N – PALEOFEST - Rockford, Burpee Museum of Natural History. (815) 965-3433. The annual celebration of fossils and dinosaurs bringing world-famous dino experts together for workshops, children's activities, fossil ID and Jane. FREE. (third weekend in February)

**N – PRESIDENT RONALD REAGAN BIRTHDAY CELEBRATION
- Tampico**, 111 Main Street. (815) 438-2130. Celebrate the 40th President's birthday in the town where he was born. Enjoy cake, punch, Reagan videos, movies and tours. FREE. (February 6th)

MARCH

C – ILLINOIS AUTHORS BOOK FAIR - Springfield, Illinois State Library. 300 S. Second Street. (217) 588-2065. Showcasing Illinois authors or works about the State of Illinois, this event features more than 30 authors who will autograph their books, present writing workshops and panel discussions. Also features children's area and bookstore. FREE. (first Saturday in March)

CL – SUGAR BUSH FAIR - Schaumburg, Spring Valley Nature Sanctuary. 1111 East Schaumburg Road. (847) 985-2100. A celebration of nature's sweet gift of maple syrup featuring historical demonstrations, activities and a pancake breakfast. (mid-March)

EC – FUNKS MAPLE SIRUP - Shirley. Funks Grove, 5257 Old Route 66, RR #1 (off I-55, fifteen minutes south of Bloomington). **www.route66.com/funksgrove/**. (309) 874-3360 or There's more than maple syrup at Funk's Grove. Since 1824, the Funk family has been producing its special brand of pure maple sirup (yes, it's spelled that way on purpose) from more than 6,000 taps in this grove of maple trees. Leave time for a timber walk and visit to the mineral museum on the property. FREE (early spring, daily except Sunday/Monday daytime)

MARCH / APRIL

CL – BUNNY BRUNCH - Libertyville. Country Inn Restaurant of Lambs Farm. Please call the Country Inn Restaurant for reservations. (847) 362-5050. Hop over to Lambs Farm for a delicious buffet and some fun with the Easter Bunny. Kids will enjoy a magic show, face painting, a wagon ride, a photo with the Bunny, and planting seeds in a flower pot they'll decorate themselves. Seatings at 10:00am & Noon. Admission includes meal. (Friday and Saturday of Easter weekend)

EC – ORIGINAL AMERICAN PASSION PLAY, THE - Bloomington, Center for Performing Arts, 110 E. Mulberry Street. A historically accurate and emotionally touching performance detailing the ministry of Christ with over 50 amazing set changes, live animals and a choir. Admission. (all performances are Saturday (and some Sunday) matinees, starting one month before, leading to, Easter weekend)

March / April *(cont.)*

SW- EASTER SUNRISE SERVICE - Alto Pass, Bald Knob Cross (IL 127). (618) 893-2344. One of the most visible and most famous of Southern Illinois' attractions, the 111-foot cross tops Bald Knob Mountain. When illuminated at night, it can be seen for miles. The road winding up to the cross is an adventure in itself, and the view from the top of Bald Knob is spectacular year-round. Thousands attend the Easter sunrise services that have been conducted annually since 1937. In 1951, the Bald Knob Christian Foundation Inc. began efforts to place a permanent shrine on Bald Knob Mountain, the highest point in Southern Illinois. Ground was broken in 1959 and the cross finished in 1963. FREE. (Easter morning)

SW – EASTER EGG-CITEMENT & BREAKFAST WITH THE BUNNY - Belleville, Eckert's Country Store & Farms. 901 South Green Mount Road. (618) 233-0513 or **www.eckerts.com**. Did you know the Easter Bunny's favorite meal is scrambled Easter eggs with a side of pancakes? Join the Bunny for breakfast at the Restaurant from 8:00am until 9:30am for a hearty country meal to start this fun-filled day! No registration required. Hop on down the bunny trail and fill your basket with fun! Eckert's Annual Egg Hunt, baby chicks & bunnies, face painting, a photo with the Easter Bunny, plant a seed and savor a yummy Easter treat. This is the largest Egg Hunt in Southwestern Illinois. Fee for breakfast, separate fee (~$12.00) for Egg Hunt. (weekend before and of Easter)

APRIL

C – NINE FINGERS RENDEZVOUS - Litchfield, Lake Lou Yaeger, 4313 Beach House Trail. (217) 324-3416. Reenactment of life in pre-1840. Watch traditional contests all weekend. (first weekend in April)

C – LINCOLN PILGRIMAGE - Springfield, New Salem, Lincoln's Tomb, Parade to the New State Capitol. (217) 546-5570 or **www.alincolnbsa.org**. Walk in Lincoln's footsteps as you follow where he walked through New Salem village as a young man, traveled from courthouse to courthouse in central Illinois as a circuit-riding attorney, climbed the steps of the Old State Capitol as a state legislator, and was carried to his final resting place at Lincoln Tomb. FREE. (last full weekend in April)

N – TRADING POST REENACTMENT - Rockton, Stephen Mack Home and Whitman Trading Post. I-90 to Rockton Road to IL 75 south and old IL 2 southwest. (815) 877-6100. More than 100 re-enactors demonstrate early American frontier life and Native American cultures of the 1650's – 1850's. Old-time crafts, historic foods, period music plus a skirmish re-enactment, voyageur landing, tomahawk throwing, archery and black powder shooting demonstrations. Admission. (third week of April, weekdays are school days, too)

MAY

C – HIGHLAND GAMES & CELTIC FESTIVAL - Springfield, Illinois State Fairgrounds. (217) 546-9800. Join the fun of this traditional Scottish & Irish country fair, complete with bag piping, ancient athletic competitions, Scottish Highland dancing, Irish Step Dancing, and a variety of Celtic foods and gifts. Admission. (third Saturday in May)

CL – SUE'S BIRTHDAY CELEBRATION - Chicago. The Field Museum, Stanley Field Hall. (312) 922-9410. Help celebrate the birthday of Sue, the world's most famous T-Rex. What birthday would be complete without cake? Visitors cast votes for the most imaginative of six cakes on display prepared by pastry chefs from well-known restaurants. The winners received blue ribbons and then, at 11:00am, it is free cake for all! May 17 is a day of free admission to the Field Museum. FREE. (May 17th)

CL – AURORA UNIVERSITY POW WOW - Aurora. Aurora University Quad, 347 S. Gladstone Avenue. (630) 844-5402 or **www.aurora.edu/museum/powwow.htm**. A celebration of native cultures for all people featuring authentic Native American dance contests, food, authentic arts & crafts. Admission. (Memorial Day weekend)

CL – GAELIC PARK IRISH FEST - Oak Forest. (708) 687-9323. Irish eyes can't help but smile at this annual four-day celebration. Irish dancing, foods and crafts, plus five stages full of Emerald Isle music and merriment. Children can enter freckle contests, see a magic show and ride ponies. Admission. (days before Memorial Day)

EC – RAGGEDY ANN FESTIVAL, ORIGINAL - Arcola. Arcola Center and Museum. Main Street. (800) 336-5456 Celebrate Raggedy Ann's Birthday with kids sing-alongs, Adventureland, Children's crafts, pony rides, carnival, Toyland parade, Look-a-Like Contest, and displays and sale of collectibles. FREE, some activities require fee. (third weekend in May)

N – DUTCH DAYS - Fulton, 4th Street and Heritage Canyon. (815) 589-4545. Come celebrate Fulton's Dutch heritage in a quarrytown setting. Dutch dancing, a parade, Dutch costumes, food vendors and crafts. An authentic Dutch dinner and tours of the 90 foot high authentic Netherlands windmill. FREE. (first long weekend in May)

May (*cont.*)

SW – STRAWBERRY FESTIVAL - **Belleville**, Eckert's Country Store and Farm, Route 15 & Green Mount Rd. (618) 233-0513 or **www.eckerts.com**. Enjoy outdoor festival foods, kettle corn, roasted sweet corn and country music at this old-fashioned all-American festival. Free wagon rides out to the strawberry patch to pick sweet, juicy berries. Live music from Noon–4:00pm each day. Kid's activities include pony rides, children's play area, petting farm, and carnival rides. Strawberry treats in the bakery, custard shop and restaurant. Fee charged for some activities. (Memorial Day weekend)

SW – CAMP DUBOIS RENDEZVOUS & DEPARTURE DAY - **Hartford (Wood River)**. Historic Site area (Route 143 and Route 3). (618) 288-3860 or **www.greatriverroad.com/Cities/Wood/duBois.htm**. Celebrate the fur trapping era that lasted from 1700 to 1840 at the historic Camp DuBois site. Come and commemorate the departure of the Lewis and Clark Expedition. This encampment of living history is held every spring with re-enactors portraying pre-1840 historical characters including French & Indian War soldiers, Colonial militia, fur trappers, and Native Americans. This event also includes historical crafts and skills demonstrations, along with children's activities. FREE, donations encouraged. (first & second full weekends in May)

SW – LOGAN DAYS - **Murphysboro**, General John Logan Museum. 1613 Edith Street. (800) 526-1500. The museum devoted to an important general of the Civil War, John Logan (born here in 1826) is the base for a history festival for students and the public. Learn about the turn of the century, pioneer days and Civil War re-enactments. Vintage baseball and eating contests, too. (third weekend in May)

JUNE

C – NATIONAL ROAD FESTIVAL - **www.nationalroad.org**. (888) 268-0042. Begin in Marshall on the East, E. St. Louis on the West or some point in between. The National Road – mostly US Rte 40, today parallels I-70 across most of the state. There will be bluegrass music, car & motorcycle shows, museum tours, bocce ball tournaments, historic reenactments, and food. (Father's Day weekend)

C – INTERNATIONAL CARILLON FESTIVAL - **Springfield**, Washington Park. (217) 753-6219 or **www.carillon-rees.org**. Carilloneurs from around the world take part in this weeklong festival of bells, music, and entertainment, including spectacular fireworks. FREE. (first full week in June)

C - POTAWATOMI TRAIL POW WOW - Taylorville, Christian County fairgrounds. (217) 824-4919. Annual American Indian Pow-Wow with authentic artifacts and wares, dancers in full regalia, authentic food, gourd dance to honor Veterans. (first weekend in June)

CL - TASTE OF CHICAGO - Chicago. Grant Park, Monroe Street to Balbo Street on Columbus Drive. (312) 744-3315. What began as a one-day event on Michigan Avenue that featured a few dozen restaurants has grown to a multi-faceted, multi-day event highlighting more than 65 restaurants every year. Festival fans can watch food prep by Chefs from around the world and around Chicago – then, receive a copy of the recipes to take home to try out new cooking ideas. Local bands of every musical genre can be heard. Family Village located at the south end of Taste right next to the Water Flume and the Ferris Wheel. Here, kids have their own entertainment stage and crafts to do. FREE (ten days beginning late June thru July 4th)

CL - BALLOON FESTIVAL - Lisle. Lisle Community Park. (630) 733-9811. Twenty-plus hot air balloons float above the Community Park. Fireworks, food vendors, arts-and-crafts booths, a petting zoo and carnival complete with fun. Admission. (late June thru July 4th)

EC - ILLINOIS HIGH SCHOOL RODEO - Altamont. Effingham County Fairgrounds. (217) 342-4147. Illinois high school rodeo athletes compete for the glory, fun and the opportunity to advance to the Nationals. Rodeo sports are action packed including bull and bronco riding, barrel racing and calf roping. Little buckaroos can compete in mutton bustin' and the littlest cowpokes can saddle up for the stick horse events. Admission. (second weekend in June)

EC - VW FUNFEST - Effingham. MidAmerica Motorworks, North Rte. 45. (800) LUV-BUGG. Want to hug a bug…how about a Jetta…the Thing…or maybe a vintage VW Bus? Gather the family and head to see hundreds of VWs from cute Beetles to sleek new driving machines. Family activities include a craft area where kids paint a VW matchbox craft. The Corvette Museum is transformed into a VW showcase with memorabilia on display and for sale. FREE (second weekend in June)

EC - GRAND VILLAGE OF THE KICKAPOO POW WOW - LeRoy, Grand Village of the Kickapoo Park. (309) 962-2700. Experience the Kickapoo Pow Wow in the Grand Village where the buffalo, native crops, native plants and grasses are being restored. Admission. (first weekend in June)

June (*cont.*)

EC – MUSKET AND DRUMS MUSTER - Shelbyville, Lake Shelbyville, Dam East Recreation Area. (800) 8-SHELBY. Revolutionary War reenactment complete with battle demonstrations, a period style show, children's games, British & Continental camps and 18th century crafters. FREE. (third weekend in June)

N – GREAT GALENA BALLOON RACE - Galena, Eagle Ridge Resort. (800) 892-2269. Friday night balloon glow. Weekend hot air balloon launch for Hare and Hound races, bicycle race, kite flying and a skydiving show. (third weekend in June)

N – RAILROAD CROSSINGS DAYS - Mendota, Mendota Museums and Union Depot Railroad (Main & Washington Sts). (815) 538-3800 or **www.mendotamuseums.org**. Memorabilia and discussion on Wild Bill Hickok, Prairie farming bldg., model railroad, locomotives on display, food, face painting and live entertainment. (third weekend in June)

N – FIELDS PROJECT AND ARTS FESTIVAL - Oregon, banks of Rock River and Ogle County airport. (815) 732-2100. The Fields Project and Arts Festival is a unique art venue, which showcases field sculpture and also an outdoor art show. These events attract artists, photographers and sculptors to the area and provide them an opportunity to "paint the land." Airplane rides providing aerial viewing of the field sculptures, art in the park, live music, games, and good food round out the weekend fun. Admission. (last weekend in June)

N – AMERICAN AIR SHOWS PERFORMANCE - Peru, Illinois Valley Regional Airport. **www.illinoisair.com**. Enjoy 8 aerobatic acts including a parachute team and military drop. Airplane and Helicopter rides. Refreshments available. Admission (12+) for show, additional for rides. (third Saturday in June)

SE – SUPERMAN CELEBRATION - Metropolis. Downtown. (800) 949-5740. The Man of Steel gets a hero's welcome in his hometown with a museum and statue to visit, a DC Comics costume contest, carnival rides and games. Superboy and Supergirl contests. Man of Steel timberjack contest. Often, celebrities from Superman films make appearances. FREE (second long weekend in June)

SW – GREAT RIVERS TOWBOAT FESTIVAL - Grafton. 500 Front Street. (618) 786-7000 or (800) 745-0513. Any visitor to the Grafton area will almost certainly see the giant towboats that travel up and down America's Great Rivers. Conditions permitting, there will be a tow boat docked on the riverfront that will be available for guided tours. Music and storytelling, food, exhibits, and deckhand and tow-rope throwing contests. Demonstrations of radio-controlled riverboat replicas. FREE. (last weekend in June)

SW – RENDEZVOUS AT FORT DE CHARTRES - Prairie du Rocher. (618) 284-7230. The Midwest's largest gathering of 1700s era soldiers, settlers, traders and campers. Period craft demos like pottery, blacksmithing, silversmithing, coopering, pewter casting, bow making, weaving and woodworking. Military competitions. Period music & dance. FREE (parking fee). (first weekend in June)

SW – GRAND LEVEE & NATIONAL ROAD FESTIVAL - Vandalia. Statehouse Historic Site. (618) 283-1161. The Grand Levee, held each June, recalls the social life that was part of Vandalia during its days as capital. The event includes music, craft demonstrations, and a candlelight tour of the statehouse. FREE. (third weekend in June)

W – RAILROAD DAYS - Galesburg, Railroad Museum, 423 Mulberry Street. (309) 342-9400. Street fair, food, carnival, railroad exhibits, city and rail yard tours, concerts, mud volleyball, car show and much more. See 1900s memorabilia housed in a former Pullman parlor car, climb up into a caboose or postal car. Model Train show at nearby Sandburg College. (last weekend in June)

W – GENERAL GRIERSON DAYS CIVIL WAR REENACTMENT - Jacksonville, Community Park. (800) 593-5678. The Midwest's largest Civil War reenactment gets better each year in the hometown of General Benjamin Grierson, a famous Civil War leader. Authentic battle reenactments, period vendors, lots of food and fun. FREE. (third weekend in June)

W – GREEK CULTURAL FESTIVAL - Moline. John Deere Commons, downtown. (309) 757-9700. Assumption Greek Orthodox Church hosts this annual event with live Greek music and dance performances, Greek specialties such as shish kebabs, gyros on pita bread, baklava, and spinach pie. Check out the gift shop and cultural tent to learn about the country. Admission. (first weekend in June)

W – GUMBO YA YA - Moline (Rock Island), River Plaza, 18th & 2nd Avenue. (309) 788-6311. Come enjoy Cajun & zydeco music, New Orleans style food, Barkus dog parade, crawfish eating contest, children's activities and street performers at this all-ages event. (second weekend in June)

JULY

C - 4TH OF JULY CELEBRATION - Litchfield, Lake Lou Yaeger. (217) 324-5253. Gigantic fireworks display over the lake. Camping, swimming and boating. (fourth of July)

C - INDEPENDENCE DAY CELEBRATION - Springfield, Knight's Action Park/ Caribbean Water Adventure/Route 66 Twin Drive In. **www.knightsactionpark.com**. (217) 546-8881. After a great family outing in the park and before the double feature at the drive-in, enjoy the largest free fireworks display in the area. Admission for park and drive-in, Fireworks. Admission. (July 4th)

CL - CITY OF AURORA 4TH OF JULY - Aurora, downtown and Westfield Shoppingtown Fox Valley. (630) 844-4FUN. Enjoy the parade with patriotic floats, marching bands, clowns, horse units and more (morning). Later, the Summer Concert Band performs patriotic selections before the fireworks.

CL - TASTE OF CHICAGO - INDEPENDENCE EVE - Chicago. Grant Park, Monroe Street to Columbus Drive. (312) 744-3315. Experience July fourth with food, music and fireworks in Chicago's historic Grant Park and the new Millennium Park. Cap off the evening with the annual Independence Eve Fireworks Celebration. Accompanied by Chicago's own Grant Park Orchestra, the 20-minute fireworks spectacular features more than 5,000 fireworks from around the globe. FREE. (July 4th)

CL - CIVIL WAR WEEKEND - Glenview, The Grove. (847) 299-6096. See authentic Union and Confederate encampments with Blue vs. Gray skirmish each afternoon. View field artillery demonstrations, musket shooting and military drills. General store merchandise on sale. Admission. (fourth weekend in July)

CL - EYES TO THE SKIES HOT AIR BALLOON FESTIVAL - Lisle, Community Park, **www.eyestotheskiesfestival.com**. Rte 53 and Short Street. One of ABA's top 100 events in North America, it features twice daily hot air balloon launches, entertainment, fireworks. Admission. (first four days of July)

CL - DODGEBALL DAYS - Schaumburg, 1675 Old Schaumburg Road. (847) 490-7020. National Amateur Dodgeball Associations Championship tournament is a day-long celebration of one of America's oldest and most well-known games. FREE admission to spectators. (fourth weekend in July)

EC – MILLROAD STEAM THRESHERMAN'S FESTIVAL & ANTIQUE TRACTOR SHOW - **Altamont**, Effingham County Fairgrounds. (618) 483-5201 or (217) 536-6400. Horse Pull, Antique Tractor Pull, Train Show, Free rides on Little Obie, Civil War living history reenactment. Lawn mower pull and steam engine display. (last weekend in July)

EC – FIREWORKS AT DUSK - **Arthur**. Jurgens Park and Fairgrounds south of Rte. 133. Arthur Fireworks at dusk. Parade downtown. One of the largest fireworks displays downstate. Huge ground displays, skydivers, mock WW1 bi-plane aerial battles. Arrive early for best location and plan for traffic delays when leaving after the show. Donations accepted. (July 4th weekend)

EC – PATRIOTIC SERVICE - **Bement**, Bryant Cottage. (217) 678-2881 or **www.bement.com**. Parade, tours and fireworks. (July 4th)

EC – FREEDOM CELEBRATION - **Champaign**. First Street, Virginia Theatre & Memorial Stadium. (217) 366-3777 or **www.july4th.net**. Parade, Patriotic concert, ice cream and fireworks coordinated and simulcast w/ music. FREE. (4th of July)

EC – RED, WHITE AND BLUE DAYS - **Charleston**. Morton Park (IL 16/Lincoln Ave @ Division Street). (217) 348-0430. Two days of family fun and top name concerts. Parades, Fireworks (Coles County Memorial Airport) simulcast on local radio. MTO Air Show will host military and civilian fly-bys and static displays, professional air show performances airport firefighting and snow removal equipment on display. Central Illinois Air will be selling airplane and helicopter rides. A variety of food and beverages will be available. Bring your chairs and enjoy great music entertainment. FREE (Fourth of July weekend)

EC – 1845 INDEPENDENCE DAY - **Lerna**, Lincoln Log Cabin State Historic Site. (217) 345-1845. Celebration of 1845 July 4th with militia activities, patriotic speeches, games and more. (Saturday after July 4th)

EC – FREEDOM FEST - **Mahomet**. Lake of the Woods Forest Preserve. (217) 586-3360 or **www.ccfpd.org**. Family activities followed by fireworks set to music. (4th of July)

EC – BAGELFEST - **Mattoon**, Peterson Park. (800) 500-6286. Family event with food vendors, major entertainment, World's Biggest Bagels, World's Biggest Bagel Breakfast, baby bagel and doggie bagel contests. FREE. (third long weekend in July)

July *(cont.)*

EC – FIREWORKS TRAIN - Monticello, Railway Museum. (800) 952-3396. Ride the train from downtown Monticello to the museum site – view the fireworks – ride back to town. Food vendors, reservations for train ride required. Admission. (night before July 4th)

EC – FIREWORKS OVER THE LAKE - Shelbyville, Lake Shelbyville beach. (217) 774-2221. Food, band, fireworks over the lake. (July 4th)

N – INDEPENDENCE DAY CELEBRATION - Elizabeth, Apple River Fort State Historic Site. (815) 858-2028 or **www.appleriverfort.org**. Costumed interpreters portray the Apple River Fort settlers as they bravely celebrate Independence Day in the year 1832. Despite the ongoing war, neighbors gather to commemorate the day. Military speeches, demonstrations, a reading of the Declaration of Independence, and 1830s version of baseball, games and more. FREE. (July 4th)

N – OLD TIME THRESHING AND ANTIQUE SHOW - Freeport, Stephenson County Fairgrounds. (800) 369-2955. Antique steam and horse powered engines and equipment, featuring John Deere Tractors and equipment. Demonstrations, blacksmith, sawmill, antique steam tractor and horse pulls. Ride the antique steam train. Admission. (last weekend in July)

N – INDEPENDENCE DAY CELEBRATION - Galena, Main Street and Grant Park. (815) 777-2111. Fourth of July parade and fireworks. FREE. (4th of July)

N – FREEDOM FEST - Rochelle, 20th Street & 10th Avenue. (815) 562-7031. Spectacular fireworks display at dusk following a concert at the Atwood Park performed by the local orchestra. FREE. (4th of July)

N – INDEPENDENCE DAY CELEBRATION - Stockton, High School and Memorial Park. (815) 947-3963. Food, music, live entertainment, classic Chevy car show, BBQ, and fireworks at dusk. Charge for car show. (4th of July)

N – 4TH OF JULY CELEBRATION - Streator, High School. **www.streator.org**. Streator is known for having the largest fireworks display in downstate Illinois. Launched with simultaneous live musical broadcast on local radio, the event includes several days of carnival, contests and parades. (June 30-July 4th)

N – FOURTH OF JULY WEEKEND - Union, 7000 Olson Road. (800) Big-Rail. A red, white and blue weekend at the Illinois Rail Museum. On July 4th, view the annual trolley pageant – the largest display of trolleys in the Midwest. Admission. (July 4th weekend)

N – **INTERTRIBAL POW WOW** - **Utica**, Starved Rock State Park. (800) 868-7625. The beat of native drums, the colorful rituals and clothing. Native American wares, dances and rituals with vendors selling food and crafts. Admission. (third weekend in July)

SE – **TASTE OF FREEDOM FESTIVAL** - **Benton**, Rend Lake Dam. (618) 439-3477. Two days of music, food and other activities. Centralia Philharmonic Orchestra performance choreographed to the area's largest fireworks display. Local bands and a Broadway show. Parking donation per car. (weekend before July 4th)

SW – **NATIONAL OUTBOARD HYDROPLANE BOAT RACES** - **Centralia**, Raccoon Lake. (888) 533-2600. Come see the National Championship Outboard Hydro Plane Boat Races competition heats on Friday and Finals over the weekend. Food available. Small admission for 12 years and older. (second weekend in July)

SW – **WORLD'S LARGEST CATSUP BOTTLE SUMMERFEST** - **Collinsville**, 216 E. Main Street. (618) 345-5598. Street festival complete with car show/cruise, games, food, music, entertainment and contests. The biggest one-day event around. FREE. (second Saturday in July)

SW – **FREEDOM FESTIVAL CELEBRATION** – **Du Quoin**, Keyes Park. (618) 542-9570. The event features live musical entertainment, a craft show, and games. The huge fireworks display will be held at the fairgrounds. (weekend before/of July 4th)

SW – **OLD FASHIONED 4TH OF JULY CELEBRATION** - **Mascoutah**, Scheve Park. (618) 566-2964. A family-centered festival that celebrates the best of America right down to mom's apple pie. Join for food, music, sports and a fireworks gala. FREE. (4th of July)

W – **SKY CONCERT** - **Peoria**. The Riverfront. (309) 837-3700. Best viewing at Liberty St & Hamilton for annual celebration and fireworks display set to music plus food, beverages, and music. (July 4th)

AUGUST

C – **LINCOLN ART AND BALLOON FESTIVAL** - **Lincoln**, Logan County Fair Grounds and downtown. (217) 735-2385 or www.lincolnillinois.com. Come and enjoy the hot air balloons during their launches and evening glows. Carnival, concessions, soap box down hillers, a children's Adventure Zone. Small admission. (last weekend in August)

August *(cont.)*

C – ILLINOIS STATE FAIR - **Springfield.** Fairgrounds along Sangamon Avenue and Peoria Road. (217) 782-6661 or (866) 807-7918 or **www.agr.state.il.us/isf.** Hundreds of thousands of people flock here for the rides – both mechanical and living – games, hands-on exhibits, and entertaining demonstrations such as high-divers, birds of prey, lumberjacking, and more. Music, food, car and horse races. Adventure Village is a small carnival next to the main entrance open all summer. Conservation World is a 22 acre setting that offers family activities, fishing with exhibits, large fish tank, and a lumberjack show. Step back in time inside the Old Firehouse Building #7 and see antique fire service memorabilia, art works, equipment, and sculptures. The museum houses an authentic 1857 horse drawn hand pumper, complete with water buckets. The antique pumper is parked next to a shiny brass fire pole once used by state fairgrounds firefighters. A fully restored 1939 Diamond T Pumper has also taken up residence at the museum along with a replica of the 1948 Ford used by the old state fairgrounds fire department. Admission. (mid-August for 10 days)

CL – AIR AND WATER SHOW - **Chicago.** Along the lakefront centered at North Avenue Beach. (312) 744-3370. The oldest and largest free admission air exhibition of its kind in the United States, featuring civilian and military aircraft and watercraft. FREE. (third weekend in August)

CL – VIVA! CHICAGO LATIN MUSIC FESTIVAL - **Chicago.** Grant Park. (312) 744-3370. Offering Latin music from around the world including merengue, salsa, tropical, cumbias, ballads, ranchero and mariachi. Traditional food, jewelry and clothing vendors will also be on site. (last weekend in August)

EC – PONTIAC SUMMERFEST - **Pontiac**, Museums and downtown. (800) 835-2055. Heritage Days focuses on tours of the Jones House & Yost Museum. Downtown hosts old time craft demos, food, riverside activities. Hot Air Balloon Festival lift off at dusk, with night glows. Christian music concert. Rte. 66 Antique Tractor Road show. Admission. (second weekend in August)

EC – WORLD FREE FALL CONVENTION - **Rantoul**, Octave Chanute Aerospace Center. (217) 222-5867 or **www.freefall.com**. The sky is filled with parachutes of every color. Airplanes, balloons, helicopters and jets gracing the sky, too. People watch or dare to jump for a fee. (ten days early August)

N – DEPOT DAYS - **Amboy**, East Main Street & South East Avenue, Depot Museum. (815) 857-3814. Built in 1876, this depot was headquarters for the Illinois Central Railroad. See artifacts from the area, tour the Depot and Schoolhouse, have a old-time soda at the Amboy Pharmacy, or glance at wood carvings (three presidents from IL) made from tree trunks at City Park. Also carnival, food, parade, entertainment and a vehicle show. (last few days of August)

N – BOONE COUNTY FAIR - **Belvidere**, 8791 Route 76, Fairgrounds. (815) 544-4066 or **www.boonecountyfair.com**. Come and see one of the best fairs in the region including harness racing, farm animals, demolition derby, carnival rides, booths and food. The one-room schoolhouse is open for tours. (six days early August)

N – SUMMER HARVEST FESTIVAL - **Franklin Grove**, Chaplin Creek Historic Village, Whitney Road. (815) 456-2382. Celebrate the harvest in this 19th-century Midwestern prairie village featuring buildings from the region. Scenes and demonstrations are set in the mid-to-late 1800s time period. (first weekend in August)

N – CIVIL WAR REENACTMENT - **Galena**, Eagle Ridge Inn. (800) 892-2269. A weekend of events with historically reenacted Civil War battles, participation opportunities with medics, a presentation of Mr. Lincoln's Gettysburg Address and an evening dance with the Virginia Reel. (mid-August weekend)

N – SWEET CORN FESTIVAL - **Mendota**. **www.sweetcornfestival.com**. Free, hot, buttered Del Monte sweet corn will be the highlight of this annual festival with over 60,000 visitors consuming nearly fifty tons of corn during the weekend. Downtown area provides entertainment, a parade and carnival. Enjoy one of the Midwest's oldest and largest festivals. FREE. (second weekend in August)

N – WILD WEST DAYS - **Rockford**, Midway Village & Museum Center. (815) 397-9112. Gunfights, bank robberies, stagecoach rides and cowboy music create an atmosphere of the wild west in this weekend festival in the streets of the village's country town. Admission. (mid-August weekend)

SW – BALLOON FEST - **Centralia**, Foundation Park. (888) 533-2600. Over 40 hot air balloons grace the summer sky during this three-day family festival. Balloon races, balloon glows, cardboard boat races, free children's activity area, car show, pop/rock performances, and parades. Small admission. (third weekend in August)

August *(cont.)*

SW – <u>OLDEN DAYS FESTIVAL</u> - **Grafton** and **Jerseyville**, Tri-County Antique Club Grounds, Rte 3 and IL 109. (618) 498-4192. Family oriented event features threshing, sawmilling, steam and gas engines, kids activities, antique tractors and farm equipment, car show, food and live entertainment. (last weekend in August)

W – <u>HERITAGE DAYS</u> - **Galesburg**, Lake Storey Park. (800) 916-3330. Pre-1840s rendezvous and Civil War reenactment, children's activities, period demonstrations, crafts, storyteller, petting zoo, music and food. (third weekend in August)

W – <u>YA MAKA MY WEEKEND</u> - **Moline (Rock Island)**, Great River Plaza. (309) 788-6311. Take a trip to the Caribbean islands at this all ages event – Caribbean fare, reggae music, Jamaican food, children's village, pirate costume contest and a sand volleyball tournament. (third weekend in August)

W – <u>WYATT EARP'S BIRTHDAY WESTERN WEEKEND</u> - **Monmouth**. Wyatt Earp Birthplace. (309) 734-3181. Deputy U.S. Marshal Wyatt Earp, an American hero who helped tame the Old West, will have his birthday celebrated at his birthplace. Wear your Western duds and relive the West. The public is invited to eat and meet Earp fans and columnists. The Birthplace home will be open, live "saw" music performed, and even an O.K. Corral reenactment. (second weekend in August)

W – <u>BROWN COUNTY FAIR</u> - **Mt. Sterling**, Brown County Fairgrounds (Mt. Sterling & Jefferson Sts). (217) 773-3268. Tucked inside the gate of the Fairgrounds is the Whistle Stop Depot Museum, home to many items. The fair has 4-H, animals, entertainment and rides. Admission. (first week in August)

W – <u>ERIN FEIS</u> - **Peoria**. Riverfront Park. (309) 689-3019 or **www.peoriaparks.org**. Experience the ambience of a grand Irish festival featuring music, dance, food, heritage displays and merchants in a fun, family environment. (last weekend in August)

W – <u>FARM HERITAGE DAYS AND THRESHING SHOW</u> - **Peoria**. Three Sisters Park. **www.threesisterspark.com**. (309) 274-8837. Two days of agricultural heritage fun including antique tractors, gas engines and autos. Threshing and craft demonstrations, live entertainment and children's activities.

W – <u>GRAND NATIONAL TT RACES</u> - **Peoria**. Riverfront Festival Park and PMC Race Track. (309) 697-4981 or **www.peoriatt.net**. Annual downtown festival rally to celebrate the TT races with food, live music, swap meet, motorcycle parade, antique and custom motorcycle show and finally, motorcycle racing on Sunday at the track. Admission. (third weekend in August)

W – PRAIRIE AIR SHOW - Peoria. Greater Peoria Airport. **www.prairieair.com.** (309) 697-6757. Army Aviation Demonstration Team and other headliners perform Aerobatics. Monster truck, go-cart and helicopter rides. Navy Rock Band. Air Show Vendors will have their children's entertainment area including a rock wall, a power jump trampoline, a 35' inflatable double slide, a 40' space shuttle slide, a bounce room, an obstacle course, and an M-4 simulator. U.S. Army will have interactive displays including Armored Personnel Carrier, Patriotic Humvee and Rock Climbing Wall. Admission (first weekend in August)

W – GREAT RIVER TUG FEST - Quad Cities. Mississippi River between Port Bryon, Illinois and LaClaire, Iowa. (800) 747-7800 or **www.tugfest.org.** This annual event is the only tug-of-war across the mighty Mississippi that puts teams from Iowa and Illinois against each other in a huge tug-of-war. Eleven teams from each side are formed from different organizations to compete. On this day, barge traffic, pleasure boats, and paddleboats yield the right of way to a 2,400 foot, 680 pound rope that stretches across the river. There are live bands, fireworks, and children's games including a children's tug. Admission. (second weekend in August)

SEPTEMBER

C – LONG NINE HERITAGE FEST - Athens, Menard County Cemetery and Long Nine Museum. (217) 636-7227. Parade, presentation by costumed living village re-enactors representing pioneer days with demos including blacksmithing and milling. Historical Vignettes depict the life of Abraham Lincoln as a student, postmaster, surveyor and a re-creation of banquet held in honor of the opening of the Museum. Cruise in the carriages and horse-drawn wagons. Voices from the Past tour of cemetery and town with 1st person demonstration. (fourth Saturday in September)

C – PRAIRIE CELEBRATION - Decatur, Rock Springs Center. (217) 423-7708. Music, food, wagon rides, historic tours, trappers and traders, star planetarium, reptiles and prairie hikes. (second weekend in September)

C – RAILSPLITTING FESTIVAL - Lincoln, Logan County fairgrounds. (217) 732-4795. Good Ole' National Railsplitting Contest. Admission. (third weekend in September)

September *(cont.)*

C - COAL CREEK RENDEZVOUS - Pana, Tri-County fairgrounds. (217) 562-4716. Rendezvous with craftspeople, demonstrations, traders, food, old-time music of the 1800s. Tours will be given of the four original log cabins, heritage gardens and even a cemetery showing the different ways graves were marked in the 19th century. (last weekend in September)

C - AIR RENDEZVOUS - Springfield, Abraham Lincoln Capital Airport. (217) 789-4400 or **www.spirngfield-il.com/airshow**. Current and vintage military and professional air-craft perform and are on display at this annual air show that also has sightseeing rides and an extensive Children's Village. Admission. (mid-September weekend)

CL - APPLEFEST - Chicago. Giddings Plaza, 4731 N. Lincoln Avenue (Lincoln Square). (773) 728-3890. A full day of activities including a farmers market, food vendors, games, Apple Recipe contest and Pie Eating contest. FREE. (third Saturday in September)

CL - CELTIC FEST CHICAGO - Chicago. Grant Park, Jackson & Columbus. (312) 744-3370. Celebrate the music, dance, art, products and cuisine of Celtic regions. Regions represented include Brittany, France, Ireland, Galicia, Spain, Scotland, Isle of Man, Cornwall, Wales, Nova Scotia and the U.S. (third weekend in September)

CL - CHEESECAKE FESTIVAL - Chicago. Eli's Cheesecake World, 6701 W. Forest Preserve Drive. (773) 308-7000. During this annual festival, enjoy an entire weekend of cheesecake samples, cooking demos, a cheesecake eating contest, live performances and games. FREE. (third weekend in September)

CL - CHICAGO INTERNATIONAL TOY AND GAME FAIR - Chicago. Navy Pier. (847) 677-8277 or **www.chitag.com**. One of the only shows in the Western Hemisphere to provide consumers with the opportunity to preview, play and purchase the widest selection of toys and games offered directly by manufacturers before the fourth quarter when the hot new products are introduced. (Labor Day Weekend)

CL - COUNTY FAIR - Chicago. Garfield Park Conservatory, 300 North Central Avenue. (312) 746-5100. Garden demos, pony rides, petting zoo, face painting alongside World Music Festival performances. (third Saturday in September)

CL - FALL HARVEST FESTIVAL - Aurora, Blackberry Farm's Pioneer Village. (630) 892-1550 or **www.foxvalleyparkdistrict.org**. Find out what harvest time was like on an 1800s farm. Costumed pioneers prepare food, shell corn & press cider. Admission. (third Saturday in September)

CL – MIDWEST LITERARY FESTIVAL - **Aurora**, 44 W. Downer Place, downtown. (630) 897-5581 or **www.midwestliteraryfestival.com**. A two-day event featuring the biggest and brightest literary talent from the Midwest, New York Times best-selling authors, book signings, kids area, teddy bear tea & vendor fair. Most events are FREE. (second weekend in September)

CL – BIG ROCK PLOUGH MATCH - **Big Rock**, Plowman's Park, Hinkley Road, south of Rte. 30. (630) 556-3310. The only event of its kind in the state. This plowing competition began in 1894. Steel-or rubber-wheeled tractors, pedal tractor pull, parade, food and miniature train rides. (September)

CL – FOX VALLEY FOLK MUSIC AND STORYTELLING FESTIVAL - **Geneva**, downtown. (630) 897-3655 or **www.foxvalleyfolk.com**. A barn dance, storytelling, hands-on music, a children's area, food and more than 30 acts. Admission (age 13+). (Labor Day weekend)

CL – DEPOT/SMILE DAYS - **Lisle**, Depot Museum and Main Street. (630) 968-0499 or **www. lisleparkdistrict.org**. Lisle Station Museum will feature historical demonstrations and activities, special attractions, games and contests, model railroad displays, food and beverages. Main Street, Lisle will have live entertainment, a carnival, sidewalk sales, craft fairs, interactive family activities, & food courts. (third weekend in September)

CL – STRAWBERRY FESTIVAL - **Long Grove**. Long Grove Historical Village. (847) 634-0888 or **www.longgroveonline.com**. Celebrate with strawberry treats, lots of great food, family entertainment and 101 ways to enjoy strawberries. (last weekend in June)

CL – ILLINOIS & MICHIGAN CANAL RENDEZVOUS - **Willow Springs**, Columbia Woods Forest Preserve (I294 exit 75th Street west). (773) 267-0948. Step into the 19th-century fur-trade era along the Des Plaines River at the Forest. Revelers can sip homemade root beer, as they cheer the canoe races and listen to Native American storytellers. Early American food, tomahawk exhibitions, music and games. Admission. (second weekend in September)

EC – SCHUETZENFEST - **Altamont**, Effingham County fairgrounds. (618) 483-5532. Authentic German food (2 tons of homemade brats are consumed), music, square dancing and entertainment. Trap shoot. Rock and polka bands play throughout the weekend. Admission. (third weekend in September)

September *(cont.)*

EC – BROOM CORN FESTIVAL - Arcola, Main Street. (800) 336-5456 or **www.arcola-il.org**. The fest celebrates Arcola's legacy as the one-time broom corn capital of the world. Stroll Main Street to watch broom-making demos, carnival rides, country music and catch the rousing Lawn Ranger's Broom Brigade Parade. (second weekend in September)

EC – AMISH COUNTRY CHEESE FESTIVAL - Arthur. Downtown. **www.arthurcheesefestival.com**. Free cheese sliced from huge wheels with crackers provides a free snack sandwich each day. National Cheese Curling Contest, Cheese Eating Contest, Kiddie Tractor Pull, merchants sidewalk sales, live entertainment, kids games, carnival rides, food and craft vendors. FREE. (Labor Day weekend)

EC – NATIONAL SWEETCORN FESTIVAL - Hoopeston, McFerron Park, Route 1 & W. Penn St. (800) 383-4386. The festival boasts 29 tons of free corn on the cob, parade, carnival, demo derbies, and the National Sweetcorn pageant. Admission. (extended Labor Day weekend)

EC – 1812 ENCAMPMENT - Hutsonville, Hutson Cabins. (618) 563-4719. Encampment, trader's camp, 1812 crafts, demos, children's games, talent show, candlelight tour and dinner. (third Saturday in September)

EC – PIONEER CITY RODEO & LABOR DAY FESTIVAL - Palestine. Main Street, Leaverton Park and Pioneer City Arena. Performances of the PRCA Rodeo, Lunch with the Rodeo Clowns, and Camping. Chuckwagon Breakfast – about 2000 other hungry people join you to share 800 pounds of whole hog sausage, 400 pounds of pancake batter, 1200 cartons of milk, and 200 gallons of coffee (free will donation only). Live bands, carnival, and parade. FREE for festival. Tickets required for rodeos. (Labor Day weekend)

EC – CENTRAL STATES THRESHERMEN'S REUNION - Pontiac, Thresherman Reunion Park, 2 miles north of town on Rte. 23. (800) 835-2055. Enjoy steam engines, 2 trains to ride, bailing hay, running sawmill, entertainment and tractor, horse & semi pulls. Admission. (extended Labor Day weekend)

EC – HEATH BAR HARVEST FESTIVAL - Robinson, County Square. (618) 546-1577. Home of the Heath Candy Bar, Olde Candy Shop, food parade, Heath Toffee Recipe contest, and live entertainment. (end of September, beginning of October weekend)

EC – ILLINOIS RENAISSANCE FAIRE - Urbana. Champaign County Fairgrounds, 902 N. Coler. **www.illinoisfaire.com**.

EC – BARNSTORMING DAYS - **Watson**, Percival Springs Airport, 6900 S. Rte. 45. (217) 536-9990 or (888) 536-5352. Annual celebration of Aviation Transportation. A broad group representing samples of general and sport aviation aircraft will be on display. Helicopter rides. Powered parachute introductory flights. Gospel music. (last weekend in September)

N – PIONEER FESTIVAL - **Belvidere**, Boone County Conservation District, 603 N. Appleton Road. (815) 547-7935. Relive the 1800s with blacksmithing demos, open-fire pottery making, Native American lore, a Civil War encampment and an 1830s log cabin. Watch as soap, apple butter and sauerkraut are made. Have a taste of buffalo stew and other traditional pioneer culinary fare. (last weekend in September)

N – MUSIC FESTIVAL - **Rockford**, Waterfront. (866) 8-rockin or **www.rockinsummer.com**. Illinois' largest music festival spans 30 blocks and features more than 240 hours of music on 9 stages. In addition to music, there are 30 special events including a Kids' Kastle with hands-on activities, a Marketplace, 40 food booths and fireworks every night. (Labor Day weekend)

N – WORLD WAR II DAYS - **Rockford**, Midway Village. **www.midwayvillage.com**. (815) 397-9112. Watch as more than 300 members of the Historical Re-enactment Society transform Midway Village into a European village with reenactments and pyrotechnics. Then, learn period dances and dance with soldiers. Admission. (September)

N - FALL FESTIVAL - **Yorkville**, Lyon Farm and Village. 7935 Route 71, south of Oswego. (630) 554-3064. Variety of exhibits on historic farming practices and performance demonstrations on threshing, plowing, and log cutting. Admission. (last weekend in September)

SW – APPLE FESTIVAL - **Murphysboro**. (800) 406-8774 or **www.murphysboro.com**. Apple pie and apple butter contests, an apple pie-eating contest, a pet parade, street entertainment, the Appletime Grand Parade, and lawnmower drag races. (third long weekend in September)

SW – APPLE FEST - **Belleville, Millstadt, Grafton**. Eckert's Country Store & Farm. (618) 233-0513 or **www.eckerts.com**. Wagon rides, music, live entertainment, great festival foods, children's activities. Ride a pony, feed the goats, and help your young 'uns get acquainted with common farm animals. Children's carnival and/or activities at all three farms. Funnel cakes, roasted sweet corn, caramel apples, and apples to pick. The last weekend of the month, hear the story of Johnny Appleseed, sing "Happy Birthday" and have birthday cake. Even meet ol' Johnny himself. School group educational tours offered. Fee for some activities. (weekends in September)

September *(cont.)*

SW - FESTIVAL OF FAITHS & CULTURES - Belleville, Shrine of our Lady of the Snows Center. (618) 397-6700 or **www.snows.org**. With the theme of Celebrate People, Celebrate Peace, this festival allows you to experience the lifestyles, languages and cultures of many ethnic backgrounds and faiths. Sample food and enjoy stage performances. International Children's Village and playground with crafts. FREE. (second Saturday in September)

SW - POPEYE PICNIC - Chester. Segar Memorial Park & Spinach Can Collectibles. (618) 826-4567 or **www.chesterill.com**. For over 75 years, Popeye has been a popular cartoon. One of his cartoons airs somewhere in the world nearly every minute of every day. Popeye's creator, Elzie C. Segal, was born in Chester and many of his comic strip characters were modeled after town residents. FREE. (weekend after Labor Day)

SW - ITALIAN FESTIVAL - Collinsville, Main Street, downtown. (800) 289-2388. Paisan pedal push, entertainment, Fest Olympics, cooking contest, Bocce Ball, Grape stomp, and Italian fare. FREE. (third weekend in September)

SW - HERITAGE DAYS ON THE GOSHEN TRAIL - Godfrey. Lewis & Clark Community College (5800 Godfrey Road, Rte. 67). **www.greatriverroad.com/RV/heritage.htm**. (618) 465-7338. The goal of Heritage Days is to educate the public in the customs, manners, clothing, food and early tools used by the fur traders, Native Americans, explorers, and early settlers in the years from 1700 to 1840. This annual event is a re-creation of period history, with black powder and other historical demonstrations, primitive encampments, music, crafts and food. Admission. (last weekend of September)

SW - HOMESTEAD HARVEST DAYS - Highland, 1464 Old Trenton Road. (618) 654-6781. A farming history show with threshing, plowing and grinding, plus tours of the Latzer 13-room Victorian home and mini-Pet Milk Factory, children's tractor pull, entertainment, food. Admission. (second long weekend in September)

SW - APPLE FESTIVAL - Jerseyville, Jersey County Historical Society, Rte. 67. (618) 498-3514. Celebrate the annual fall harvest of numerous orchards in the region. Historical tours, games, entertainment, parades, kids activities, great food, apple products, desserts, fresh apple cider. (last weekend in September)

SW – **VICTORIAN FESTIVAL** - **Jerseyville**. Hazel Dell Farm (1.5 miles north of town). **www.greatriverroad.com/vicfest.htm**. (618) 498-5590. This large Civil War Era re-enactment is centered around the 1866 Fulkerson Mansion, which is open for tours during the festival. The event promotes "History in Motion" through Civil War reenactments, encampments, agricultural demonstrations, and working crafts, taking a step back in time to view our history and to give visitors an opportunity to get closer to our past. Stagecoach and buggy rides. Tours of the Cheney Mansion, too. Admission. (Labor Day weekend)

W – **ANTIQUE ENGINE & TRACTOR SHOW** - **Atkinson**, 19030 E. 2120 Street. (309) 937-1255. Come visit the museum, sawmill cutting lumber, threshing, plowing, corn shelling, steam engines, gas engines, music and re-enactment of 1954 farm show. (third weekend in September)

W – **JORDBRUKSDAGARNA (AGRICULTURE DAYS)** - **Bishop Hill** State Historic Site, US Hwy 34. (309) 937-1255. Celebrate with 19th-century Swedish harvest activities and demonstrations, hands-on activities, children's games, farm produce and Colony stew and live music. (last weekend in September)

W – **ANTIQUE GAS ENGINE SHOW** - **Colchester**. Argyle Lake State Park. (309) 776-3422. A festive celebration of times past. You'll see demonstrations of wheat threshing, hay baling, sawmilling, sorghum making and blacksmithing. You can also watch crafts persons make quilts, whittle and make rugs. In addition, hundreds of antique tractors, cars and gas engines are on display. FREE. (Labor Day weekend)

W – **ANTIQUE STEAM ENGINE SHOW** - **Jacksonville**, Prairieland Heritage Museum, 105 W. Michigan Avenue.(800) 593-5678. Featuring antique steam engines and tractors, threshing demonstrations, hay bailing, a horse plow pull – all in the village with a vet's office, general store, blacksmith. (last weekend in September)

W – **HOG DAYS** - **Kewanee**, downtown. (309) 852-2175. Participate in the world's largest pork chop barbeque and the Hog Day Stampede, parade, carnival and market. (long Labor Day weekend)

W – **ERIN FEIS IRISH FAMILY FESTIVAL** - **Moline (Rock Island)** Arts & Entertainment District, Great River Plaza. (563) 359-8016 or **www.stpatqc.com**. St. Patrick's Day in September? It features food, drink, memorabilia, culture displays, events for children and an array of continuous Irish entertainment on two stages. (second Sunday in September)

September *(cont.)*

W – MORTON PUMPKIN FESTIVAL - Peoria (Morton), downtown. **www.pumpkincapital.com**. (888) 765-6588. Home of Nestle/Libby's pumpkin plant, Morton processes 85 percent of the world's canned pumpkin. The entire community celebrates the beginning of the canning season with a Pumpkin' chunkin' contest, pumpkin picking, hayrack rides, corn maze, live entertainment, parade and plenty of pumpkin products. (third long weekend of September)

W – WORLD'S LARGEST KART RACE - Rock Island District. **www.rockislandgrandprix.com**. (309) 788-6311. Go-karts will rule the streets. This race brings over 250 drivers from 32 states and countries. The world's best drivers come to compete for one of karting's largest cash purses. Festival week includes a race to raise money for charity, nightly outdoor concerts, driver's parade, fan autograph session, and car shows with food sold. (Labor Day Weekend)

SEPTEMBER / OCTOBER

CL – A-1 FARM FALL FESTIVAL - Aurora, A-1 Farm Stand, 2122 Jericho Road. (630) 859-2780. Country store, pumpkin patch, fall decorations, petting zoo, hayrides, large and small theme barns and straw maze. Free admission; charge per activity. (mid-September thru October)

CL – JOHANSEN FARMS - Bolingbrook, Johansen Farms, 710 W. Boughton Road. (630) 759-8711 or **www.johansenfarms.com**. Hayrides, two-story air slides, train rides (weekdays after 3:00pm), hold baby chicks, Amazing Corn Maze, Hay Tunnel, Goat Mountain, Rabbit hotel, pony rides (Oct. only), Jump in the Giant Castle, Toddlers Jumping Jail, Noah's Ark Challenge, and concessions. Admission. (daily, mid-September thru October)

CL – GOEBBERT'S PUMPKIN PATCH - Hampshire, Goebbert's Farm, 42 W 813 Reinking Rd. & Rte 47. **www.pumpkinfarms.com**. (847) 464-5952 or U-pick pumpkins, petting zoo, corn stalk maze, pig races, wagon ride, Goat Mountain, Bunny Town, pumpkin launch, fun maze and weekend magic show and pony rides. Café and group tours. Admission. (last weekend in September through October, daily)

CL – **BENGSTON PUMPKIN FARM** - **Lockport,** 13341 West 151 Street. **www.pumpkinfarm.com.** (708) 301-3276. You'll experience hours of enjoyment including a relaxing Hayrack ride, a giggling animated Fun Barn, the famous action-packed Pig Races, the adorable Petting Zoo, Mr. Scarecrow's Corn Maze, The Pumpkin Launcher, a Train Ride, Bluegrass playing Skeleton Band, Farm Animals, Straw Tunnel, Pony Rides, the all new Frog Hopper Ride, delicious refreshments, eats & treats. Admission. (late September through October)

CL – **DOLLINGER FAMILY FARM** - **Minooka,** 7420 East Hansel Road (I-80 to Minooka Exit #122 (Ridge Road) south past Route 6 until it ends at Hansel Road – turn right). (815) 467-6766 or **www.dollingerfarms.com.** Farm animals, petting zoo, corn maze, hayrides and train rides. Admission for some activities. (late September thru October)

CL – **FALL HARVEST DAYS** - **Mundelein,** Quig's Farm. 300 South IL 60/83. (847) 566-4520 or **www.quigs.com.** Quig's is a great place to come apple picking in the fall- but they also have orchard hay rides, a moon-walk, a children's pumpkin house, a daytime haunted barn, pony rides, and petting zoo. Restaurant on premises. Admission per activity. (every weekend in September & October)

CL – **GREAT PUMPKIN** - **Prairie View,** Didier Pumpkin Farm. 16678 W. Aptakisic Road. (847) 634-3291 or **www.didierfarms.com.** Pick your own pumpkin and explore the corn maze. At the Great Pumpkin Weigh Off, locals weigh in their product – some pumpkins weigh over 700 pounds. Then, take the kids for a pony ride before visiting the farm animal zoo and scarecrow alley. Admission. (last weekend in September through October)

CL – **GOEBBERT'S PUMPKIN FARM** - **South Barrington,** Goebbert's Farm, 40 W. Higgins Road. **www.pumpkinfarms.com.** (847) 428-6727. Pumpkins, animal land (barnyard and exotic), corn stalk maze, strawtown maze, wagon rides, camel rides, pony rides, and weekend pig racing. Café and group tours. Admission. (last weekend in September through October, daily)

EC – **THE GREAT PUMPKIN PATCH** - **Arthur,** 2 miles south and ½ west of town. (217) 543-2394 or **www.thegreatpumpkinpatch.biz.** Pumpkins, corn maze, straw maze, farm animals, concession, and historic One Room schoolhouse. Newer areas include: a unique Children's Garden, a history of The Great Pumpkin Patch and farm, and bird display. Admission. (daily, early September thru October)

September / October (*cont.*)

EC – CURTIS ORCHARD - Champaign. 3902 S. Duncan Road. **www.curtisorchard.com**. (217) 359-5565. Curtis Orchard is an 80-acre apple orchard, pumpkin patch and entertainment farm. The bakery offers pies and donuts plus apple cider. Seasonal apple and pumpkin picking, kids play structures, a giant slide, several mazes including the Giant Jungle Maze, petting zoo, pony and horseback trail rides, and an orchard wagon tour. Admission. (daily, August thru October)

EC – PUMPKIN WORKS - Paris, 21788 E. Terre Haute Road (11 miles SE of town). (217) 275-3327 or **www.pumpkinworks.com**. 9 mazes (some are wheelchair accessible), bon fires, hayrack rides, 50 varieties of pumpkins, gourds, and corn, and offering school tours. Admission. (Labor Day weekend through end of October)

EC – HARDY'S REINDEER RANCH - Rantoul. (217) 893-3407 or **www.reindeerranch.com**. Besides the curious reindeers, Hardy's features the 10-acre Cornfusion Corn Maze (daytime and nighttime), PYO pumpkin patch, hayrides, a realistic Indian tepee and a pedal cart racetrack. Enjoy a chuck wagon meal on the ranch or pick up a sweet treat at the country barn. Admission. (August thru October)

N – PUMPKIN PATCH, THE - Caledonia, Fiorello's Farm, 3178 Hwy 173. (815) 765-258 or **www.thegreatpumpkinpatch.com**. Two miles of trails and turns in the corn maze, pick your own pumpkins, pony/wagon rides, cornstalk maze. Pumpkin Launching and Artists House for Free Personalization of Your Painted Pumpkin, face painting; Expanded Free Petting Zoo. Free to the grounds, petting zoo and barn; Admission to attractions & activities by tickets or wristbands. (daily, September & October)

N – SYCAMORE PUMPKIN PATCH - Dekalb (Sycamore), 15326 Quigley Road (one mile south of IL 64). (815) 895-3276 or **www.sycamorepumpkinpatch.com**. Pumpkins, apples and cider and such at the market. Hayride, maze of corn, Giant Pumpkin Patch, Charlotte's Web, barnyard animals and refreshments. Pumpkin Festival display of 1000s of decorated pumpkins, downtown, last week in October. Admission. (daily, late September thru October)

N – SANDY PINES ELK FARM - Deer Grove. (9 miles south of Rock Falls, just off Hwy 40 west on Habnaman Road). (815) 438-2463 or **www.sandypineelkfarm.biz**. Join the Henrekin family at their unique farm which offers wagon rides up into the elk area to see some of the largest bulls in the world. One of the family will share with you the essentials of raising and breeding elk (pre-arranged tours). The gift store offers many elk products including meat, lamps and cookbooks. Chuck Wagon Concession (try elk meat sandwiches), pumpkin patch and seven-acre corn maize. During October, an evening meal and campfire is offered, where you can listen to the calls of the elk as you eat. Admission. (daily September thru October)

N – **PUMPKIN JUNCTION** - **Freeport**, 1583 South Adams Avenue, I-65, take exit 95 (TN 386) to exit 7. (815) 232-6103. Pick your own pumpkin, wagon rides, corn maze, pony rides, petting zoo and haunted barn. Some weekends offer face and pumpkin painting. (last weekend in September thru October)

N – **ROYAL OAK FARM** - **Harvard**, 15908 Hebron Road. www.royaloakfarmorchard.com. (815) 648-4141. Petting zoo, u-pick-um and play area. Each guest can purchase Entertainment tokens good for any one of our Train, Carousel or Orchard Tour rides. Pony rides and orchard tours only on Saturdays (fee). Entertainment tokens are available at $2.50 per token. (daily, except Sundays in September and October)

N – **JONAMAC ORCHARD** - **Malta**, 19412 Shabbona Road. www.jonamacorchard.com. (815) 825-2158. Fresh apples, pumpkins and other fall produce at the market daily. Kids activity area, wagon rides, 10 acre corn maze, hayrides, apples train & apple launcher. Admission. (weekends in September and October)

SE – **BANDY'S PUMPKIN PATCH** - **Johnston City**, (half mile west of Johnston City on Pumpkin Patch Road just off the Herrin/Johnston City Road). (618) 983-8676. Explore a large maze – different shape each year, petting zoo, little kids straw maze, barn activities, hayrides and pumpkin carving contests. Admission. (September and October)

SE – **FALL FESTIVAL AT INGRAMS' PIONEER VILLAGE** - **Kinmundy**. Ingrams' Pioneer Log Cabin Village. (618) 547-7123 or www.iplcv.com. Leisurely walk the streets of the Log Cabin Village and be transported back in time to a pre-Civil War era. Visit log cabin homes, a general store, doctor and apothecary, preacher's cabin, cobbler shop, cooper, and carpenter shop. Visit Jacob's Well, which was frequented by Abraham Lincoln. The festival brings the village to life with demonstrators. Admission. (last two weekends in September and first weekend in October)

September / October (*cont.*)

SE – LIVING LEGACY HOMESTEAD MAZE - Mt. Carmel. 3759 N. 900 Blvd. (Located between Keensburg & Bellmont). (877) 538-3276. Individuals can navigate a 5-acre maze of sorghum and Sudan grass, 6-8 feet high, in some unique shape. Other activities include wiener roasts, farm produce, tour of the farm, and hay rides. Small Admission. (beginning in September & lasting thru October)

SW – GREAT GODFREY MAZE - Godfrey, Glazebrook Community Park. (618) 466-1483 or **www.greatgodfreymaze.com**. This popular 2 ½ mile maze open extended weekends. (September and October long weekends)

SW – MILLS APPLE FARM - Marine, 11477 Pocahontas Road (north of I-70 and east of I-55, go north on Duncan Street and east on Pocahontas Rd). (618) 887-4732 or **www.millsapplefarm.com**. Primarily a family run pick-your-own apple and peach orchard with choose-and-cut Christmas trees. On-farm bakery produces made-from-scratch pies, cookies and other products. Apple and Pumpkin educational tours. Kids play area. Farm animals. Wagon rides in season. Apples to pick from august through October. PYO Pumpkins in October. Admission. (daily, September & October)

W – SHADY KNOLL FARM - East Moline, 3115 Dennhardt Road. (309) 496-9636. This generational family farm produces asparagus and pumpkins. Pumpkin Patch includes pick-your-own, corn maze, petting zoo and bunnyville. (third Saturday in September through October)

W – ADVENTURE QUEST - Moline (Rapid City). 3501 207th St – just off I80 and 88. (309) 764-3619 or **www.adventurequest.com**. They have it all for fall fun: entertainers, inflatable games, paint ball, train rides, zip lines, hay rack rides, hiking trails, summer sleds, corn maze, panning for gems, nature trails & food service. Admission. (select dates/times in September & October)

W – APPLE BLOSSOM FARM - Peoria, US 150 west to 9809 North Illinois Rte 91. (309) 243-5757 or **www.appleblossomfarm.com**. The farm is home to an orchard, bee apiary and a 10-acre walk-thru "corn maze" that changes each year. Visit the farm's gift shop/bakery/produce market or have lunch at the Applewood Grill, or top it off with the farm's famous apple cider doughnuts from the bakery. Happity Acres is a children's petting zoo featuring extra-well-fed rabbits, goats and pot-bellied pigs. The facility's Corn Crib Playground features the "Farmers Freeway" where kids of all ages can race pedal cars or zip down the giant 80-foot gunny sack slide. Admission. (beginning in August thru October)

W – **FURROW'S RED BARN VILLAGE** - **Peoria**, US 24 east to SR 251 in El Paso, turn north. (309) 527-8200 or **www.furrowwinery.com**. Pumpkins, squash, and other produce are sold to retail visitors along with a corn maze and petting zoo for families to play in. (September/October)

W – **TANNERS ORCHARD** - **Speer**, 740 IL 40, Junction 17. **www.tannersorchard.com**. (309) 793-5442. The Apple Express Barrel Train is happily chugging along in this orchard. It's just one of the great entertainment options for families visiting the orchard. And with fun things like Climb and Clamber fun, Billy Goat Bridge and Tree House, Pony Rides, Wagon rides, farm animal zoo, and a family corn maze, be sure to save room for apples, pumpkins and cider. Admission. (daily 8:00am-8:00pm September/October)

W – **LAZY U FARM** - **Tiskilwa**, 8939 - 2040 East Street. (815) 646-4551. Hayrides - Petting Zoo - Craft Store - Corn Maze - Museum - U-pick Pumpkin Patch. (daily until dusk from mid-September thru October)

OCTOBER

C – **COUNTRY BUMPKIN PUMPKIN PATCH** - **Grandview**, 5556 E. 150th Road (south of Illinois Route 16 between Paris and Kansas). (217) 273-4099 or **www.countrybumpkin.net**. Chow down at the Yak-n-snack, Country Fair, Hillbilly Golf, Tractor-drawn wagon and pumpkins. Admission. (weekends in October)

C – **INTERNATIONAL RTE 66 MOTHER ROAD FESTIVAL** - **Springfield**, downtown. (866) RTE-66IL or **www.route66fest.com**. Hundreds of vintage cars, entertainment, and celebrity guests from the U.S. and Canada fill the streets of historic downtown Springfield for a three-day celebration of cars, food, music, and friends of the heyday of US Route 66. Rte 66 Authors & Artists, and the World's Largest Sock Hop. FREE. (first weekend in October)

CL – **PUMPKIN TROLLEY** - **Elgin**, Fox River Trolley Museum. **www.foxtrolley.org**. (847) 697-4676. Enjoy hay rides, trolley rides, pumpkins, food and some evening movies. The trolley rides mid-month on to take you out to the pumpkin patch. Pick a pumpkin and then enjoy a small treat. Admission. (month-long in October)

CL – **PUMPKIN TRAIL AT THE GROVE** - **Glenview**, the Grove. (847) 299-6096. Enjoy the fall colors while you search for and buy the right pumpkin for carving. Hayrides on Grove trails, festive games and snacks of taffy apples and cider. FREE (third weekend in October)

October *(cont.)*

CL – HARVEST DAY - Joliet, Garfield Farm Museum. (630) 584-8485. **www.garfieldfarm.org**. A major event in the Fall at Garfield Farm is Harvest Days which feature demonstration of pioneer farming skills like the candle making shown here as well as a sheep dog demonstration, black smithing, and displays of farm and home items. Also a story teller & guided walk through the farm prairie areas. Admission. (first weekend in October)

CL – FALL COLOR FESTIVAL - Lisle, Morton Arboretum. (630) 719-2465. 1700 acres of trees ablaze in color. Hand-dipped taffy apples, pumpkin decorating and a corn maze. (month-long in October)

CL – APPLE FESTIVAL - Long Grove, Route 83 & 53. **www.longgroveonline.com**. (847) 634-0888. Apple treats abound at this autumn festival, including cider, doughnuts and muffins, plus caramel apples for decorating. Live music, square dancing and a car show. (first weekend in October)

CL – KUIPERS FAMILY FARM - Maple Park, Kuipers Family Farm. 1 N 318 Watson Road, 5 miles west of Rte. 47. (815) 827-5200 or **www.kuipersfamilyfarm.com**. Take a Pony Ride, Run Through a Cornfield Maze, Feed Baby Animals, Sample Home-grown Squash, Enjoy a Horse-drawn Haywagon Ride, Get Lost in a Maze, Pick Pumpkins Right from the Patch, Giggle in a Cornstalk Tunnel, Roll in the Straw, Peddle in a Tractor Derby, Chat with a Scarecrow, Satisfy your hunger at the Corncrib Café, Stroll through the Nature Walk or Ride in the Johnny Popper Grain Train. Admission. (daily, except Monday, in October)

CL – PUMPKIN PATCH - Palos Park, The Center Children's Farm, 12700 Southwest Hwy. **www.palospark.org/center.htm**. (708) 361-3650. Experience life down on the farm with guided family tours or hike on the peaceful nature trail. Hayrack rides out to the pumpkin patch allow groups to be lead through the farm by a guide who will teach the children about each of the animals and invite the children into the animal pens for a close look and feel. FREE. (October weekends)

CL – AUTUMN HARVEST FESTIVAL - Schaumburg, Spring Valley Nature Sanctuary & Farm. (847) 985-2100. An old-fashioned harvest festival featuring hayrides, 19th century farm life demonstrations, food, games, & music. (first Sunday of October)

CL – SCARECROW FESTIVAL - St. Charles, downtown. (800) 777-4373. More than 100 handmade scarecrows strut their stuff(ing) at this huge arts-and-crafts show. Children can make their own scarecrows to take home. Carnival, entertainment. FREE. (second weekend in October)

EC – **SCARECROW 'N PUMPKIN FEST** -**Farmer City**, Main Street. (217) 766-2979. Scarecrow and pumpkin creations, food, entertainment, carnival rides. (first long weekend in October)

EC – **HARVEST FROLIC & AGRICULTURAL FAIR** - **Lerna**, Lincoln Log Cabin State Historic Site. **www.lincolnlogcabin.org**. (217) 345-1845. The Fair includes period cooking, applesauce making, food drying and preservation, quilting, grist milling, period music, and numerous hands-on activities. Visitors may also stroll the trades area which features period trades and craftspeople demonstrating their wares. These will include blacksmithing, pottery, wood carving, paper cutting (Scherenschnitte), weaving, broom making, candle making, and wood turning on the "Great Wheel." Many of the trades and crafts people will be selling their wares. FREE. (first weekend in October)

EC – **SCARECROW DAZE** - **Shelbyville**, 308 E. North 9th Street. (800) 874-3529. Games for kids, pumpkin carving contest, make and take scarecrows, bingo, scavenger hunts and a parade. FREE. (second weekend in October)

N – **FALL FESTIVAL** - **Fulton**, downtown. (815) 589-4545. Enjoy pumpkin painting, a downtown scavenger hunt and tours of Fulton's Fiber Mill and Windmill. (mid-October Saturday)

N – **SCARECROW FESTIVAL** - **Rockford**, Midway Village & Museum Center. (815) 397-9112 or **www.midwayvillage.com**. Costumed interpreters help re-create the atmosphere of an old-fashioned harvest fest within the living history village. Fun fall activities include period games and crafts, live music and wagon rides around the village. Plus, you'll be able to make your own scarecrow to take home. Old time baseball on Saturday. Admission. (second weekend in October)

SE– **FORT MASSAC ENCAMPMENT** - **Metropolis**. Fort Massac. (618) 524-9321. Both days begin with posting of colours, continue with entertainment, river activities, and children's games. Military and civilian craft activities and demonstrations. FREE. (third weekend in October)

SE - **FALL FESTIVAL** - **Louisville**, Clay County Museum. (618) 665-3847. This building was originally the county jail and is listed on the National Registry of Historic Places. (Saturday before Halloween)

SW – **JUMPIN' PUMPKIN JAMBOREE** - **Belleville**, Millstadt, Grafton. Eckert's Country Store and Farms. (618) 233-0513 or **www.eckerts.com**. Ride the wagons out to the pumpkin patch to search for your great pumpkin. Their pumpkins range from a couple of pounds to more than 150 pounds. Wagon rides, country music, live entertainment, pony rides, make-a-scarecrow, funnel cakes and festival foods make this a fun-filled weekend for everyone. School group educational tours offered. Children's activities. Petting farm. Fee for some activities. (weekends in October)

SW – OKTOBERFEST - Maeystown. **www.maeystown.com**. (618) 458-6660. Nestled in the Mississippi bluffs, Maeystown is noted for its collection of elegant stone buildings that were constructed in the 1800s to form a German settlement. Enjoy crafts, entertainment and great food as you stroll through the restored village, with quaint attractions that include a general store, sweet shop, and museum. (second Sunday in October)

SW – AMERICAN THRESHERMEN'S FALL FESTIVAL - **Pinckneyville**, Perry County Fairgrounds. (618) 527-5456. Steam and gas engine demonstrations and displays, apple butter, cider and sorghum making, horse & tractor pulls. Admission. (third weekend in October)

W – GATHERING OF THE WATERS RENDEZVOUS - **Grafton**. A Historical Re-enactment of the 1700-1840's Frontier Era. **www.greatriverroad.com/RV/waters.htm**. Celebrates the French Fur Trading era which began after Louis Joliet and Jacques Marquette journeyed through the area in 1673 and ended around the time when Grafton was established in 1838. Teepees, tents, campfires, and costumed living history re-enactors adopt personas and carry on the day-to-day lifestyle as it would have been done 200 years ago. Hawk & Knife Throw, Primitive Bow Shoot, Canoe trip, Artisans/Traders, Authentic foods & music, & Children's Activities are also offered. FREE. (3rd weekend in October)

W – OLD SETTLERS DAYS - **Kampsville**. Riverside Park. (618) 465-2114 or **www.greatriverroad.com/RV/kSettle.htm**. Held on the banks of the Illinois River this event depicts the life and times of the early Calhoun settlers. Activities include: Mountain Man, Period demonstrations, fiddle contest, artisans/traders, Riverside encampment, food, children's activities, live entertainment & carriage rides. FREE. (second weekend in October)

W – GARDEN HARVEST FESTIVAL - **Rock Island**. Quad City Botanical Center. (309) 794-0991 or **www.qcgardens.com**. Carding wool, panning for gold, petting a goat, tasting fresh apple cider, watching a broom maker in action – these are some of the activities that await families at this festival. Kids can make a friendship bracelet; do laundry by hand like the pioneers did; shave like Pa; mill grain and roll dough into buns; or play with pioneer toys and puzzles. Food, entertainment & dance demonstrations. Scarecrow contest. Kettle Korn, petting zoo, hayrides, too. Admission (ages 13+). (October)

W - SPOON RIVER VALLEY FALL FESTIVAL - Fulton County-wide. Spoon River has been a lifeline of water for eons, with Indians harvesting fish and mussels from the waters. The mussel shells were used for utensils/spoons, hence came the name: Amaquonsippi, or Spoon River. Along the scenic drive, apple pies are freshly make and applebutter is cooked in black kettles over open fires at Riverside Park, London Mills. Butterfly porkchops and steaks are favorites at Mt. Pisgah Park, Smithfield, Cuba, and Avon. Farmington is known for its baked potatoes "ala everything," apple dumplings, and elephant ears. Red Brick School, Smithfield is known for its chicken and noodle dinners. Bernadotte, Fairview, and Lewistown have funnel cakes. Duncan Mills is known for its baked goods and beef and noodles. Along with the food, sounds of music, dancing, clogging, playgrounds, and tours of historic homes and museums. (first two full weekends in October)

NOVEMBER

C – FESTIVAL OF TREES - Litchfield, LLCC Southern Region Arts & Technology Building. (217) 324-5253. Beautifully decorated artificial Christmas trees are silent auctioned off for charity. Performances, vendor booths, children's activities. Admission. (third weekend in November)

C – FESTIVAL OF TREES - Springfield, Orr Building, Illinois State Fairgrounds. (217) 788-3293 or **www.memorialmedical.com**. Enjoy a winter wonderland of spectacular and unusual Christmas trees and wreaths and a showcase of incredible gingerbread houses...from log cabins to castles. Admission. (week before and including Thanksgiving weekend)

EC – FESTIVAL OF TREES - Bloomington, Interstate Center. (309) 452-1170. A family centered celebration with a walk through gingerbread village, sampling holiday cookies, hundreds of decorated trees, wreaths or get a photo with Santa. Admission. (mid-November weekday)

SW – AMERICAN LEGION AVENUE OF FLAGS - Vandalia, Gallatin Street Cemetery Visitors Center. (618) 283-2728. Veterans Day display of more than 1,000 flags with each flag having been donated by family of a deceased veteran. (Veterans Day)

NOVEMBER / DECEMBER

CL – CHRISTMAS AROUND THE WORLD & HOLIDAY OF LIGHT - **Chicago**. Museum of Science & Industry. (773) 684-1414 or **www.msichicago.org**. Showcases more than 50 trees in an enchanted forest, decorated by Chicago's ethnic communities with traditional ornaments. Holiday of Light explores holiday traditions that celebrate light in this season of the year. Workshops and performances including a reading of the classic holiday tale, The Polar Express. (weekend before Thanksgiving through the first full weekend in January)

CL – ZOOLIGHTS - **Chicago**. Lincoln Park Zoo. (312) 742-2000. Zoolights is a free event that features more than one million holiday lights, a spectacular water laser show, live ice carving, Santa's workshop and of course, zoo animals. FREE. (weekend after Thanksgiving - first week of January)

CL – COUNTRYSIDE CHRISTMAS IN HISTORIC LONG GROVE - **Long Grove**, Rtes. 53 & 83. (847) 634-0888. Victorian buildings trimmed in lights, covered bridge and luminary-lined cobblestone walkways. Costumed carolers, strolling musicians, live reindeer and Santa and Mrs. Claus. Free Holly Trolley on weekends. FREE. (mid-November through Christmas Eve)

CL – HOLIDAY MAGIC - **Brookfield** Zoo. (708) 485-0263. Twinkling lights create a winter wonderland, with fun for all ages, including carolers, ice-carving demonstrations, crafts and games (on weekends). Each night, stroll walkways illuminated by millions of twinkling lights. Enjoy magicians, music, storytellers and photo ops with Children's Zoo Animals. Restaurants and gift shops will be open. Admission. (Thanksgiving weekend thru days before, then after, Christmas)

EC – CHRISTMAS AT CLOVER LAWN - **Bloomington**, David Davis Mansion State Historic Site. (309) 828-1084 or **www.davismansion.org**. The house is lavishly decorated throughout the season for a traditional, late-Victorian Christmas. The tours include period costumes, Christmas foods, authentic ornaments and seasonal music of the era. (Wednesday-Sundays, day after Thanksgiving through weekend before Christmas)

EC – WONDERLAND IN LIGHTS - **Effingham**, Community Park. (800) 772-0750. The winding road reveals a surprise at every turn. Follow the colorfully lighted road into every colorful fantasy. Reindeer fly, elves are busy decorating their home, and around the next turn, a forest of giant candy canes and gingerbread. Giant toys parade thru the hollow. The Nativity is nestled against a hillside and an American flag, complete with fireworks caps off the display. Visit with Santa, take a buggy ride or sip hot cocoa on the Courthouse lawn. Admission, donations. (nightly, Thanksgiving weekend through New Year's Eve)

EC – **MATTOON LIGHTWORKS** - **Mattoon**, Peterson Park. (800) 500-6286. Drive through an awesome seasonal display conveying the Christmas Spirit to all. FREE. (mid-November - day after Christmas)

EC – **CHRISTMAS LIGHTING & FIREWORKS** - **Palestine**, Leaverton Park, South River Road. (618) 586-2222 or www.pioneercity.com. The park is filled with thousands of lights and displays. Bonfire, caroling, Santa, snacks and some fireworks. Free will donation. (day after Thanksgiving through New Years)

EC – **HOLIDAY IN THE PARK** - **Paris**, West Lake Park. (217) 465-4179. Drive through beautiful lighted displays of businesses, individuals and organizations. (nightly viewing starting the Saturday after Thanksgiving through New Years)

EC – **VICTORIAN SPLENDOR LIGHT FESTIVAL** - **Shelbyville**, Forest Park. (800) 874-3529. Share the music of the holiday season as you drive through light displays in town and then experience the Starflake Trail throughout the county. Donations. (daily mid-November thru New Years nights)

SE – **OLNEY CHRISTMAS LIGHT DISPLAY** - **Olney**, White Squirrel Drive. (618) 392-2241. Tens of thousands of lights decorate the Olney City Park, along with cartoon characters and Santa. FREE. (weekend after Thanksgiving through New Years)

SW – **CHRISTMAS WONDERLAND** - **Alton**, Rock Springs Park. (866) 465-7890. Drive through Rock Springs Park to see more than 2.5 million lights adorning trees and lighting displays throughout the park. Admission per car. (weekend after Thanksgiving through end of December)

SW – **WAY OF LIGHTS** - **Belleville**, Shrine of Our Lady of Snows. 442 S. DeMazenod Drive. (618) 397-6700 or www.snows.org. This 1.5 mile drive-through Christmas display is lined with more than a million lights and leads to a life-size straw-lined manger cradling the baby Jesus. Indoors you'll find seasonal displays, a restaurant and gift shop. FREE. (nightly, mid-November thru New Years week)

SW – **HOLIDAY LIGHTS FAIR** - **DuQuoin**, State Fairgrounds. (618) 542-1515. Holiday Lights Fair is a gigantic drive-through route traversing the fairgrounds. Visitors can see countless lights and displays. Indoor Old Tyme Christmas Village, entertainment, food and Santa. Admission per car. (weekend after Thanksgiving through end of December)

November / December (*cont.*)

W – JULMARKNAD - Bishop Hill, County Rte. 39. (309) 927-3345. Christmas market with special music, Swedish folk characters, Swedish food, handmade wares, Make and Take Holiday workshops, Cookie Walk and Chocolate Walk. (Thanksgiving weekend and first weekend in December)

W – FESTIVAL OF LIGHTS - East Peoria. (Folepi's, I-74 to exit 96). Maps and info available at Riverfront Visitors Center. (800) 365-3743. The festival begins with the Parade of Lights (Saturday after Thanksgiving) as 40 lighted floats glide through the heart of East Peoria ending with a display of fireworks. Now, drive in the warmth of your vehicle through an electric park featuring two miles of parade floats and lighted animated displays. Folepi's Fireworks Spectacular features 37 lighted displays towering 40 feet in the air, simulating a fireworks grand finale. Now, take in the sights and sounds of a realistic nativity scene as you view the five detailed near life-size structures and tune into your car radio for a 2-minute narration that makes the scene come alive. Santa is in the Enchanted Forest as are decorated Christmas trees, animated displays and decorated buildings in Fon du Lac Farm Park. Like theatre? Annually, Eastlight Theatre presents Joseph and the Amazing Technicolor Dreamcoat on select days in December. Admission for drive-thru, enchanted forest and theatre production. (Thanksgiving weekend thru December evenings)

W – SPIRIT OF PEORIA HOLIDAY SHOWS - Peoria. Spirit of Peoria, Peoria Riverfront, base of Main St . (800) 676-8988 or **www.spiritofpeoria.com**. Intimate and Merry Holiday Revue aboard the historic paddlewheeler. Matinee or dinner features homemade buffet, riverboat cruise and entertainment. Admission. (Saturday after Thanksgiving thru mid-December)

W – AVENUE OF LIGHTS - Quincy, Wavering/Moorman Park. (217) 222-7980. Two-mile long animated light festival that has over one million lights and 40 displays. Admission per car. (Thanksgiving - New Years)

CHRISTMAS PARADES

Marching bands, wonderful floats, & of course, Santa & his elves. FREE.

- ❏ **C – Lincoln**, downtown. (217) 735-2385. (first Thursday in Dec.)
- ❏ **C – Litchfield**, downtown. (217) 324-5253. (first Saturday in Dec)
- ❏ **C – Pana**, downtown. (217) 562-4240. free kids movie afterward. (Saturday after Thanksgiving)

❑ **C – Springfield**, downtown. (217) 528-8669 or www.springfieldjaycees.org.

❑ **CL – Aurora**, North Island Center. (630) 844-4FUN. Firework, tree lighting. (Saturday after Thanksgiving)

❑ **CL – Westmont**, Veterans Memorial Park. (630) 963-5252. Part of Holly Days.

❑ **EC – Charleston**, Courthouse Square. (217) 348-0430. Movie, carriage rides, entertainment. (first Saturday in December)

❑ **EC – Clinton**, downtown. (866) 4-DEWITT. (last day of Nov.)

❑ **EC – Fairbury**, downtown. (815) 692-3899. Carriage rides, Live Madrigal, holiday housewalk, festival of trees. (first Saturday in December)

❑ **EC – Marshall**, citywide. (217) 826-9023. Breakfast with Santa, live entertainment, soup supper. (first Saturday in December)

❑ **EC – Monticello**, downtown. (800) 952-3396. (first Saturday in Dec.)

❑ **EC – Pontiac**, downtown. (815) 844-6692. (second Friday in Dec)

❑ **EC – Rossville**, Christman Park, downtown. (217) 748-6888. Live Nativity. (first weekend in December)

❑ **EC – Sullivan**, American Legion & downtown. (217) 728-4223. children's workshop. (Saturday after Thanksgiving)

❑ **N – Ottawa**, downtown. (866) 7LASALLE. Donations put on the Toy & Book Float. (day after thanksgiving)

❑ **SW – Carbondale**, downtown. (618) 529-8040. (first weekend in Dec)

DECEMBER

NUTCRACKER

The holiday ballet where young Clara's encounters with twirling flutes, snow nymphs and battling mice burst to life with dazzling costumes, striking sets and imaginative choreography. Admission.

❑ **CL – Chicago**. Auditorium Theatre of Roosevelt University. (312) 922-2110. Joffrey dancers. (mid-December-late December)

❑ **CL – Schaumburg** Dance Ensemble. (10 days early December)

❑ **W – Peoria** Ballet. www.peoriaballet.com (second weekend in December)

December (*cont.*)

C – **CHRISTMAS SHOW** - **Carlinville**, Anderson Mansion. (217) 854-2850. Each room decorated with this year's theme. Take the trolley to or from the Christmas market. (first weekend in December)

C – **CHRISTMAS TIME AT THE ZOO** - **Decatur**. Scovill Zoo. (217) 421-7435. Children can visit Santa and his elves at his workshop, enjoy more than 100,000 lights and decorations and meet all the winter loving animals: the bobcat, Arctic fox, emu, wallabies, wild turkeys, pheasants, llamas, birds of prey, and domestic animals. The herpaquarium with reptiles, amphibians, invertebrates and fish will also be open. Be sure to meet the newest additions cheetahs, Runako and Jafari. Be sure to allow time to ride the new "Endangered Species" carousel. Admission. (month long in December)

C – **CHRISTMAS CAROLING AT THE CARILLON** - **Springfield**, Thomas Rees Memorial Carillon, Washington Park. (217) 753-6219. Community sing-along to the music of the bells. (third Sunday in Dec.)

C – **DANA-THOMAS HOUSE CHRISTMAS** - **Springfield**, Dana-Thomas State Historic Site. (217) 782-6776. Recall the splendor of a bygone era as you tour this spectacular Frank Lloyd Wright designed home completely bedecked in turn-of-the-century finery for the holiday season. Suggested donation. (month-long in December)

CL – **LEHNERTZ AVENUE CHRISTMAS DISPLAY** - **Aurora**. (630) 898-2615. Be one of the 10,000 cars that pass through this awesome five block Christmas lights display. The Charlie Brown fixtures are always a hit. (December 1st through January 2nd)

CL – **ZOO HOLIDAYZE** - **Aurora**, Phillips Park Zoo. (630) 898-7228. Stroll the illuminated path at Phillips Park Zoo and enjoy the sights of over 6,000 holiday lights and the sounds of carols. (month long December)

CL – **WINTER WONDERFEST** - **Chicago**. Navy Pier. (800) 595-PIER or **www.navypier.com**. Features sparkling lights, hundreds of decorated trees, and Santa Claus with his toy-making elves. Activities will include an indoor ice skating rink, a musical carousel, a unique model train display and entertainment. FREE. Admittance to activities require purchase of a wristband. (mid-December through day after New Years)

CL – **ELGIN HISTORICAL MUSEUM HOLIDAY OPEN HOUSE** - **Elgin**, 360 Park Street. (847) 742-4248 or **www.elginhistory.org**. In the permanent exhibit rooms, children can get behind the wheel of a reproduction road race car or have their picture taken with Ralph Mulford, winner of the first road race held in 1910. The Watch Factory room features a wall mural of the clock face that once graced the watch factory tower and the 13th watch produced on the famed assembly line. Visitors are invited to view a 6-minute introductory video. Admission. (first Sunday in December)

CL – CANDLELIGHT RECEPTION - **Joliet**, Garfield Farm Museum. **www.garfieldfarm.org.** (630) 584-8485. Experience the tradition of winter visiting as practiced by families like the Garfield's in their 1846 Brick Inn. Hospitality, food, music, and bake-sale. Donations Accepted. (first weekend in December)

CL – POLAR EXPRESS SANTA TRAIN - **Lisle**, Metra Station, Main St & Burlington Avenue. (630) 963-4280. All aboard for a ride re-created from the classic children's book. Two Metra trains travel from Lisle to the North Pole (Chicago). Along the way, Santa listens to Christmas wishes, and elves entertain. Admission. (weekend in mid-December)

CL – WINTER WONDERLAND - **Libertyville**. Country Inn Restaurant of Lambs Farm. (847) 362-5050. Enjoy a delicious brunch with all your favorite winter friends including the one and only Santa Claus! After brunch, kids will enjoy sleigh rides, crafts and a photo with Santa. To wind down after a day of excitement, gather around the fireplace and grab a soothing mug of hot chocolate for some of your favorite winter stories. Seatings at 10:00am & Noon, by reservation only. Admission includes meal. (second and third weekends in December)

CL – VICTORIAN CHRISTMAS TOURS - **Oak Park**, Frank Lloyd Wright Home and Studio. (708) 848-1976. Special tours led by junior interpreters featuring stories of how the Wright family celebrated the holidays at the turn of the last century. FREE. (second & third Sunday in December)

CL – POLAR EXPRESS - **South Elgin**, Fox River Trolley Museum. (847) 697-4676. Board the all reserved "Polar Express" at Blackhawk Forest Preserve for a ride north to meet Santa and experience the magic of the season. Reservations and admission only. (first Sunday in December)

EC – BEMENT CHRISTMAS - **Bement**, Library and Bryant College. (217) 678-8184. Parade &   holiday open house with luminaries ablaze. (second weekend in December)

EC – CANDLELIGHT TOURS - **Clinton**, C.H. Moore Homestead. (217) 935-6966 or **www.chmoorehomestead.org58**. Candlelight tours, entertainment, gift shop. Admission. (Friday evenings in December)

December *(cont.)*

EC – CHRISTMAS WITH THE FITHIANS - **Danville**, Vermilion County Museum. (217) 442-2922 or **www.vermilioncountymuseum.org**. Tour of two historic Fithian homes, house of Dr. William Fithian 1890s; house of grandson early 1900s. Admission. (first weekend in December)

EC – HOLIDAY LIGHTS - **Danville**, Kennekuk County Park. **www.vccd.org**. (800) 383-4386. Open house & old-time Christmas. Holiday lights nightly. (daily in December)

EC – CHRISTMAS ON THE PRAIRIE - **Lerna**, Lincoln Log Cabin State Historic Site. (217) 345-1845 or **www.lincolnlogcabin.org**. Christmas Candlelight Tours - Christmas as we know it today was not widely celebrated on the prairie in the early 1800s. At the Lincoln Cabin, the family will gather around the hearth while the women are busy with their spinning and knitting. Meanwhile, at the Sargent Farm, members of the Sargent family will celebrate the holiday with good food, simple decorations, and readings from the Bible. Period music and song. FREE. (second weekend evenings in December)

EC – LUNCH WITH SANTA ON THE TRAIN - **Monticello**, Old Wabash Depot. (800) 952-3396. Ride the train and enjoy lunch and a visit with Santa and elves. Reservations required. Admission. (first weekend in December)

EC – CHRISTMAS AT THE JONES & YOST HOUSE - **Pontiac**. (815) 844-7401. See how Christmas was celebrated during the early 1900s at the Yost Museum and the late 1800s at the Jones House. Admission. (Sundays in December)

N – CHRISTMAS AT ELLWOOD HOME - **DeKalb**, Ellwood House. (815) 756-4609. Tour this elegant 1879 Victorian mansion decorated for the holidays and featuring live music, a craft bazaar, a visit from Santa in his sleigh and refreshments. Call for prices. (first and second weekend in December)

N – KEEPING CHRISTMAS - **Elizabeth**. Apple River Fort. **www.appleriverfort.com**. Experience the sights, sounds and smells of an 1830s Christmas. Costumed interpreters demonstrate candle dipping, sausage making, target shooting, and customs of Christmas. Also discussed are sometimes controversial ideas regarding the celebration of Christmas as a holiday. Hot cider will be served around warming fires. FREE (second weekend in December)

N – **CHRISTMAS TEA** - **Freeport**, Silvercreek Museum and Stephenson County Historical Museum. (800) 369-2955. Tour these mansions decorated for the Christmas season with holiday lights and oil lamps. Tea and cookies served. Small admission or donation accepted. (first weekend in December)

N- **CHRISTMAS IN THE CANYON** - **Fulton**, Heritage Canyon, North Fourth Street. (815) 589-2838. At these events, the Early American Crafters, the Civil War re-enactors, and other historical groups take us back in time as they recreate history in the mid-1800's. The setting is a 12-acre quarry settlement. Paths through wooded hillsides lead you to a church, schoolhouse, covered bridge, swinging bridge and more. Donation. (first weekend in December)

N – **NIGHT OF THE LUMINARIA** - **Galena**, Riverfront & Trolley Depot. (815) 777-9050. More than 5,000 luminaria trace the riverfront levee, steps, hillsides and parks. Cookie Walk. Trolley rides viewing the luminaria, hot cider and caroling. FREE to walk around, Fee for trolley rides & Cookie Walk. (third Saturday in December)

N – **BETHLEHEM WALK** - **Manteno**, The Christian Church of Manteno. (815) 468-6468. As a patron of the Bethlehem Walk, you will enter the marketplace as a shopper and be alternately greeted, wooed and accosted by costumed Roman and Jewish characters in the streets & vendor's booths. (second weekend in December)

N - **LUCIA FEST** - **Rockford**, Haight Village Historic District (Erlander Home Museum & First Lutheran Church), South Third Street. (815) 963-5559 or **www.SwedishHistorical.org**. Guided tours of the Erlander Home, Kaffe Stuga (coffee house), Julmarknad (holiday market) of Swedish gifts and foods, Lucia Pageant, storyteller, candlelight ceremony and horse-drawn wagon rides between sites. Admission. (first Saturday in December)

N – **CHRISTMAS AT WEBER'S** - **Streator**, Weber House. (815) 672-8327. Enjoy the home and gardens of the Weber house. Candles illuminate the house and each room has a story to be told. (December)

SE – **CHRISTMAS HOME TOUR** - **Golconda**, Main Street. (618) 683-9702. Starting at the Pope County Museum, tour two log cabins, one historic church and four beautiful homes. Christmas in the Courtyard with a candlelight walk and caroling. Admission. (first Saturday in December)

December *(cont.)*

SE – <u>OLDE TYME CHRISTMAS</u> - Metropolis, Fort Massac. (618) 524-9321. Different rooms in the replica of the 1802 American Fort will represent the Christmas traditions form the 1750 to 1865. Re-enactors will welcome visitors to the fort and tell of the Christmas traditions from the historical period they represent. The Visitors center will be decorated and period music and refreshments will be served. FREE. (second Saturday in December)

SW – <u>BRUNCH WITH SANTA</u> - Belleville, Eckert's Country Store and Farm. (618) 233-0513 or **www.eckerts.com**. Join them for a meal with Santa on the farm. Children can show their holiday spirit by singing Christmas carols and telling Santa their Christmas wishes. Santa has a special gift for each child. They will capture the moment in a photo of your child with Santa. Reservations are suggested. Seating at 9:00am and 11:30am. While there, pick your own Christmas tree (either pre-cut or head out to the tree farm and cut one yourself). Admission for visit & brunch. (first three Saturdays in December)

SW – <u>LEWIS & CLARK'S ARRIVAL IN CAHOKIA</u> - Cahokia, Courthouse State Historical Site. (618) 332-1782. The anniversary celebration of the explorers' arrival in Cahokia will feature updates on the progress of the Corps of Discovery through exhibits. FREE. (December 7th)

SW – <u>ARRIVAL AT CAMP RIVER DUBOIS</u> - Hartford, Lewis & Clark State Historic Site. (618) 251-5811. Witness the arrival of the Lewis and Clark expedition as re-enactors arrive at the mouth of the River DuBois to establish their 1803-04 winter encampment. Join the members of the Corps in a military demonstration of the 1803 US Army Expedition and much more. FREE. (second weekend in December)

SW – <u>HOLIDAYS AT THE HOMESTEAD</u> - Highland, Louis Latzer Homestead. (618) 651-8271. Thirteen room 1901 home, decorated Victorian style with each room decorated by a different group. Admission. (first weekend in December)

SW – <u>HOLIDAY OPEN HOUSE</u> - Vandalia Statehouse State Historic Site. (618) 283-1161. Candlelight tour of Illinois' oldest existing capitol building and period music. FREE. (second Saturday in December)

W – <u>LUCIA NIGHTS</u> - Bishop Hill, Historic Village. (309) 927-3345. Bishop Hill will be illuminated by candlelight. "Lucias" serve coffee and sweets in museums and shops. Special music and singing at various locations. FREE. (second weekend in December)

W – CHRISTMAS AT HISTORIC DEERE-WIMAN HOUSE AND BUTTERWORTH CENTER - **Moline.** Deere-Wiman House and Butterworth Home. (309) 765-7971 or **www.butterworthcenter.com**. John Deere legacy homes feature Christmas decorations typical of the Victorian era. The dining room is set for a formal Victorian Christmas dinner. Mrs. Butterworth was the granddaughter of John Deere. Dried flowers from the garden add a special touch to the house's many evergreen wreaths, garlands and trees. FREE, donations accepted. (first Sunday in December)

W – HOLIDAY POPS CONCERT - **Moline.** The Mark on the Deere Commons. (563) 322-0931. The concert features the Quad City Symphony Orchestra; the Quad City Arts Visiting Artist performer; skaters from the Figure Skating Club; The Sanctuary Choir and the Holiday Pops Children's Chorus. Come early and enjoy the FREE "Lighting of the Commons". Take a horse-drawn wagon ride; meet Santa; listen to carolers; warm up with cider and cookies; and see the lights and fireworks brighten the sky. Admission for concert. (Saturday before Christmas)

W – THE SEASON OF LIGHT – STAR OF BETHLEHEM - **Moline (Rock Island).** Augustana College Planetarium. (309) 794-7327. Daily evening or matinee shows portray just what the Wise Men may have seen when they looked to the skies some 2,000 years ago. Reservations are required for this star-gazing show. FREE. (first Monday in December thru weekend before Christmas)

FIRST NIGHT CELEBRATIONS

A non-alcoholic, family-oriented, New Year's Eve celebration of the arts. Revelers ring in the new year with music, dancing, visual art, drama and fireworks. Admission.

- ❑   **C – Springfield**, downtown. (217) 753-3519 or www.springfieldartsco.org.
- ❑   **CL – Aurora**, downtown. (800) 477-4369.
- ❑   **CL – Evanston**, downtown. (847) 328-5864.
- ❑   **EC – Pontiac**, downtown. (815) 844-6692.
- ❑   **SE – Centralia**, Recreation Complex. (888) 533-2600.

Master Index

Activity Index

PROUDLY

MADE IN THE USA

Travel Journal & Notes:

Travel Journal & Notes:

Travel Journal & Notes: